The Financial Analyst's Guide To Fiscal Policy

Edited by
Victor A. Canto
Charles W. Kadlec
Arthur B. Laffer

PRAEGER

PRAEGER SPECIAL STUDIES • PRAEGER SCIENTIFIC

New York • Philadelphia • Eastbourne, UK
Toronto • Hong Kong • Tokyo • Sydney

Library of Congress Cataloging in Publication Data

Main entry under title:

The Financial analyst's guide to fiscal policy.

  Bibliography: p.
  Includes index.
  1. Fiscal policy—United States—Addresses, essays,
lectures. 2. Supply-side economics—United States—
Addresses, essays, lectures. I. Canto, Victor A.
II. Kadlec, Charles W. III. Laffer, Arthur B.
HJ257.2F49   1986   339.5   85-19339
ISBN 0-03-004139-2 (alk. paper)

Published and Distributed by the
Praeger Publishers Division
(ISBN Prefix 0-275)
of Greenwood Press, Inc.,
Westport, Connecticut

Published in 1986 by Praeger Publishers
CBS Educational and Professional Publishing, a Division of CBS Inc.
521 Fifth Avenue, New York, NY 10175 USA

© 1986 by Praeger Publishers

6789 052 987654321

Printed in the United States of America on acid-free paper

INTERNATIONAL OFFICES

Orders from outside the United States should be sent to the appropriate address listed
below. Orders from areas not listed below should be placed through CBS
International Publishing, 383 Madison Ave., New York, NY 10175 USA

Australia, New Zealand
Holt Saunders, Pty, Ltd., 9 Waltham St., Artarmon, N.S.W. 2064, Sydney,
Australia

Canada
Holt, Rinehart & Winston of Canada, 55 Horner Ave., Toronto, Ontario, Canada
M8Z 4X6

Europe, the Middle East, & Africa
Holt Saunders, Ltd., 1 St. Anne's Road, Eastbourne, East Sussex, England BN21
3UN

Japan
Holt Saunders, Ltd., Ichibancho Central Building, 22-1 Ichibancho, 3rd Floor,
Chiyodaku, Tokyo, Japan

Hong Kong, Southeast Asia
Holt Saunders Asia, Ltd., 10 Fl, Intercontinental Plaza, 94 Granville Road, Tsim
Sha Tsui East, Kowloon, Hong Kong

**Manuscript submissions should be sent to the Editorial Director, Praeger
Publishers, 521 Fifth Avenue, New York, NY 10175 USA**

To Ana, Joyce, and Traci

Preface

Most economics books that focus on policy implications of government actions analyze them in the context of whether those actions are the appropriate solution to the problem in question. Very seldom is policy analysis carried to the point where practical implications for businessmen and financial analysts are clearly and fully derived. In schools of business where economic courses are taught, this is an important issue. In general, students are unaware of how the knowledge of economics is translated into potential earnings.

A book such as this can, in some measure, fill that void. Our approach is straightforward. In each chapter, we identify a particular policy problem and present an economic analysis of the problem. The second step, the one most economic books fail to take, is to draw the reader beyond the usual type of analysis and into a consideration of the practical implications and strategies that are vital to business managers, financial analysts, and investors in general.

In the process, the book provides a lucid presentation of incentive economics. We attempt to illustrate how incentives and disincentives affect economic behavior and the performance of the economy. In addition, we present a top-down approach that shows the reader how to trace the impact of government policies through the economy and thereby derive investment implications that will be helpful for investors and policy makers alike, from portfolio managers and financial analysts to corporate strategists and government officials.

This book focuses on fiscal policy, and in particular on the disincentive effects of government exactions. This approach documents and emphasizes the importance of substitution effects created by economic policies and argues that they are much greater than traditional views suggest. This approach deemphasizes the income effect associated with aggregate demand models and stresses the substitution effects created by distortive taxes. Above all, this book provides a succinct exposition of what has become known as supply-side economics. It is a nontraditional perspective on the problems faced by U.S. economy, as well as the solutions to the great economic problems of our time: inflation, unemployment, and the federal budget deficit. In addition to presenting a guide to the better understanding of the effect of fiscal policy on the overall economy, we have attempted to provide in these chapters a policy prescription for sustained growth in the U.S. economy for the remainder of this decade and into the next.

Victor A. Canto
Charles W. Kadlec
Arthur B. Laffer

Rolling Hills Estates, California
March 15, 1985

Acknowledgments

This book is an outgrowth of ongoing research at A. B. Laffer Associates and at the University of Southern California into the interactions between government policy and economic growth, between opportunity and the financial markets. Over the years, we have benefited from the comments, suggestions, and contributions of many individuals and colleagues. Our special gratitude goes to Allen V. C. Davis who originated the concept of the Productive Employment Program and provided a research grant for the development of PEP; and Chris Petruzzi, who provided assistance in documenting the poverty trap created by government transfer programs.

We wish to thank our past and present colleagues at A.B. Laffer Associates, including Thomas J. Gillespie, Kevin Melich, Thomas Nugent, and Wayne Steele Sharp; and our colleagues at the University of Southern California, including Richard V. Eastin, who unselfishly read the manuscripts and contributed to the final product through their many comments and suggestions. We especially wish to thank Edward P. Mooney for his tremendous help in editing and assembling the final manuscript, and Margaret Hansen for her editorial assistance. We also wish to thank Susan Hanasab and Sin Poe Soh for their statistical suppport, and Norma Baker, Dorothy Cooper, Scott M.L. Cunningham, Holly Lindstrom, and Lauren Welsh, who aided in the production of the various stages of the manuscript.

Finally, we are grateful to the clients of A.B. Laffer Associates, without whose support this book would not have been possible.

Contents

List of Tables

List of Figures

1

The Ellipse: An Explication of the Laffer Curve in a Two-Factor Model

Arthur B. Laffer

SUMMARY

The economic policies of recent administrations, whose policies have focused only on the management of aggregate demand, reflect the aggregate supply. A more appropriate policy is one one that focuses also on the elements of supply, hence the term *supply-side economics*. The ellipse is a theoretical framework capable of illuminating the complex issues of taxing and spending policies. Tax rate changes on any single factor of production will affect its participation in market activity. This, in turn, affects output and the tax base. This is the essence of the Laffer Curve. It is also true, however, that the availability of any single factor of production will affect wage rates paid to other factors as well, influencing their market participation, output, and the tax base. Clearly, any analysis of tax rate changes must take into consideration the entire constellation of tax rates. A general solution, the ellipse, provides a framework that relates tax rates in a two-factor model, government spending and output.

July 28, 1980

With the Employment Act of 1946 and subsequent legislation, active management of the overall U.S. economy has fallen ever more into the purview of the federal government. Within the Congress alone, committees such as the Joint Economic Committee, the Senate and House Budget Committees, the Joint Committee on Taxation, as well as more narrowly defined committee structures, actively monitor the economy and examine legislation, the express purpose of which is to alter the economy in some prespecified manner. Within the Reagan Administration, an equally impressive expansion of activities has occurred. Here and abroad the explicit management of the overall economy is considered an increasingly important function of government. State and local governments are no exceptions to this pervasive trend.

Federal spending illustrates a growing tendency toward a government-controlled economy. State and local spending trends corroborate the general nature of the phenomenon as well (Fig. 1.1). To stop here would grossly understate the magnitude of the incursion of government into the economy. Regulations, restrictions, controls, and mandated expenditures all are reflections of the expanded role played by government. These latter incursions, however, are difficult to quantify but could well be as important in their effects on the economy as are explicit spending items. Therefore, total spending should be taken as indicative of the increasingly important role of government and not as comprehensive. Government spending unquestionably understates the level of government involvement while the bias in the trend itself could go either way.

VARIANTS ON A THEME OF AGGREGATE DEMAND MANAGEMENT

The publication of *The General Theory* by John Maynard Keynes (1936) began the major conversion of the academic profession from a general classical perspective to the perspective of aggregate demand management. By the early 1950s the conversion was nearly complete. Virtually every major academic institution in the United States was dominated by economists with a distinct orientation toward aggregate demand as the most appropriate form of economic analysis to explain, diagnose, and thus prescribe for the behavior of macroeconomic variables. Classical thought had all but disappeared and once eminent classical economists were held in disrepute. A striking example was the total reversal of opinion of Harvard professor Alvin Hansen. When *The General Theory* first appeared, Professor Hansen wrote a review that effectively dismissed the book as not being economics. Within a few years, however, he had become Keynes' most ardent advocate in the United States, and his book, *A Guide to Keynes* (Hansen 1953), was *de rigeur* in any classroom where macroeconomics was taught.

FIGURE 1.1. Federal, state, and local spending as a percentage of GNP

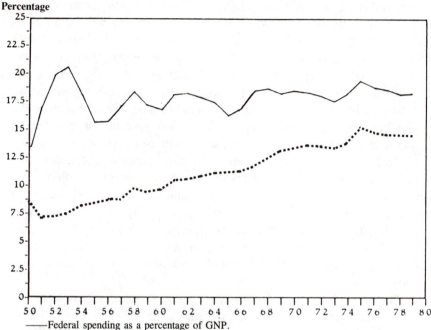

Federal spending as a percentage of GNP.
···· State and local spending as a percentage of GNP.
Source: Economic Report of The President, 1980. Government Printing Office, Washington, D.C.

While great diversity exists among alternate formulations, the Keynesian income-expenditure approach distinguishes two forms of aggregate demand. Demand can be either induced or autonomous. Induced expenditures are those that depend on income, whereas autonomous expenditures depend on other factors. In simple terms, investment, government spending, and exports are representative categories of autonomous expenditures. Imports and consumption, on the other hand, represent induced expenditures. Whether induced or autonomous, each of these categories represents demand. Supply demarcations are omitted in their entirety.

Within the framework of Keynesian economics the level of output, and thus total employment, hinges on the magnitude of autonomous expenditures, the amount of induced spending for consumption and imports per unit of income, and the increase in tax payments per unit of income. The higher autonomous expenditures are, the greater will be output and employment. Likewise, a high marginal propensity to consume will also result in high output and employment. For imports and tax payments, the reverse is true. High tax payments and imports result in low income and employment. As a result, government policies that have the effect of increasing investment, exports, or government spending will, at an equal rate, increase output and employment. Likewise, those government policies that increase consumption at the expense of savings, imports, or tax payments will also increase output and employment.

It follows directly, therefore, that the Keynesian prescription for alleviating either slow growth or a low level of output would include the following types of policy measures: increased government spending or lower taxes; lower interest rates via increases in the money supply to entice greater investment; currency depreciation to expand exports and discourage imports; and raised taxes on savings and imports to discourage those activities and thereby increase consumption. In the early stages of its development, the Keynesian framework basically dismissed the inflationary consequences of government policies as being of little consequence. As the post–World War II era unfolded, however, inflation rates increased, and inflation itself became an increasing focus for government policy.

The adaptation of inflation into the general Keynesian framework was based on the work of an English economist named Phillips, who discovered a close and persistent inverse relationship between rates of inflation and rates of unemployment in the nineteeth-century English data. The formulation of this relationship, called the Phillips Curve, postulates that increased demand resulting in lessened unemployment will also heighten inflationary pressures. As a consequence, there is a drawback, or tradeoff, to stimulative monetary and fiscal policies such as increased government spending, increased money growth, reduced taxes, or even currency devaluation in the form of higher inflation. A policy conflict or frustration therefore emerged. To some of the most preeminent economists the conflict was a sham, and they argued that inflation itself had little, if any, social consequences and any attempt to halt inflation would place great burdens on the economy. In the words of Yale Professor James Tobin (1972):

> What are they (the social costs of inflation)? Economists' answers have been remarkably vague.... Seldom has a society made such large immediate tangible sacrifices to avert an ill-defined, uncertain, eventual evil... certainly inflation does not merit the cliche that it is the "cruelest tax."

Nonetheless, inflation has become an increasing source of political concern. The range of policy prescriptions extends from all those fiscal policies that have the effect of reducing aggregate demand, to specific incomes policies such as wage and price controls.

Almost at its inception, Keynesian demand-oriented income/expenditure analysis faced intellectual opposition from yet another demand-oriented framework called *monetarism*. The earliest champion of the monetarist school of thought was an economist named Clark Warburton. The recent popularity of monetarism, however, must be attributed to the indefatigable efforts of Professor Milton Friedman. In his presidential address for the American Economic Association, he presented as clear an exposition of the basic tenets of monetarism as can be found. The central feature of monetarism, as in Keynesian fiscalism, is the exclusive focus on aggregate demand. The supply of goods and services is presumed to accommodate itself to any and all changes in aggregate demand. An exception is found in the analysis of the very long run, when supply plays a more prominent role (Friedman 1968).

Following Friedman's delineations, the immediate effect of an increase in the supply of money is an increase in the dollar price of bonds and a commensurate fall in interest rates. The fall in interest rates stimulates investment demand, as was also the case in Keynesian analysis. Because it takes time for investment spending to increase, the actual increase in demand does not occur at the moment of the increase in the supply of money. For the monetarist, the stimulus to demand takes on a second aspect as well. Consumption demand is augmented as well through the direct effect of excessive money balances in the hands of consumers. This effect, too, takes time to materialize.

Given sufficient time, the combined effects on aggregate demand of an increase in the supply of money will elicit an increase in output and employment. The supply of goods and services will merely accommodate this increase in aggregate demand. In due course, however, increased production of goods and services will lead to heightened wage demands, and tendencies on the part of goods and service producers to raise prices. Inflation is the end result. Therefore, in the shortest of runs, an increase in the supply of money reduces interest rates and sets the stage for an increase in aggregate demand. In the intermediate term, output increases are the direct consequence of the increased stock of money. And finally, the price level rises and output falls back to where it otherwise would have been.

Whether one concentrates on the Keynesian or monetarist form of demand analysis, nowhere in the explicit formulations does one find a distinction between the wages paid by the firm for a worker and the wages a worker receives net after tax. Likewise, the distinction between pre-tax and post-tax yields on capital is nonexistent. Basically, in demand types of analyses, people work because there are jobs, not because they are paid. Similarly, people save because their incomes are high, not because they earn an after-tax yield on their savings. Incentives on an individual basis do not play a substantive role, at least not in the short run, in demand types of analyses. As a result, macroeconomic analysis cannot be integrated with the theory of the firm or individual behavior. While the controversies between the monetarists and the Keynesians have often been heated, their domination of postwar economic thought literally has precluded classical economics. Public policy has increasingly turned to demand analysis, and the incumbent structure that accompanies such views.

Therefore, on the federal level, and on the level of state and local government, whenever the economy appears sluggish, policy makers' minds turn to increased government spending, increased money growth, reduced taxation, or currency depreciation. For state and local governments, several of these avenues are proscribed. They cannot, for example, depreciate the U.S. currency, nor can they effectuate a change in growth rate of the supply of money. As a result, state and local governments look to the output and employment effects of increased spending or reduced taxation. In some instances, they are tried in concert with specific forms of price controls. Often these controls are centered on items that cannot, without considerable difficulty, leave the jurisdiction of the governing body. Rent controls are a favorite target for state and local governments.

A CLASSICAL APPROACH TO ECONOMIC ANALYSIS

The essential tenet of classical economic analysis is that people alter their behavior when economic incentives change. If the incentives for doing an activity increase relative to alternative activities, more of the now more attractive activity will be done. Likewise, if impediments are imposed on an activity, less of the now diminished-incentive activity will be forthcoming. Basically, people have both time and resource constraints in the quest for self-fulfillment. With limited resources and time, the explicit attainment of objectives necessitates prudent management within the structure of constraints imposed by nature and people. Thus, government, with its full power of enforcement, has the capacity to alter the constraints encountered by the vast array of economic factors. Changes in the structure of these governmentally imposed constraints alter the economy's behavior.

The form of the constraints emanating from government are limited solely by the expansiveness of human imagination. Taxes, subsidies, regulation, restrictions, and requirements are but a few of the virtually endless series of possible government actions in the area of economics. The composition as well as the magnitude of government spending will also impact on the range of private activity, as will the methods of government financing. The general precepts of classical economics are founded on the role played by incentives, and the effect government actions have on those incentives.

Firms base their decision to employ their workers or acquire capital assets, in part, on the total cost to the firm of employing workers or acquiring capital, always with an eye to enhancing the value of the firm for its owners. Holding all else equal, the greater the cost to the firm of employing each worker, the less workers the firm will employ. Conversely, the lower the cost per worker, the more workers the firm will hire. Incorporated in the decision-making process are all costs associated with each worker's employment, including filing requirements, payroll taxes, rest facilities, and fringe benefits, among others. For the firm, the decision to employ is based on gross wages paid, a concept that encompasses all costs borne by the firm. A symmetric set of criteria applies equally when the decision to acquire capital is contemplated. Again, from the perspective of the firm, the explicit objective is to garner surplus value from each decision and thereby enhance the value of the firm.

The worker and the saver, on the other hand, care little about the cost to the firm of employing each worker, or acquiring each unit of capital. Of far greater concern from the worker's standpoint is how much he or she receives for providing his or her work effort, net of all deductions and taxes. Savers also do not save as a matter of social conscience. Savers basically abstain from consuming in order to earn an after-tax return on that savings. Within the classical framework, workers concentrate on net wages received, while savers are preoccupied with their yields on savings after tax. The greater net wages received, the more willing the worker is to work; the higher the net yield on savings, the greater will be total savings. Conversely, if net wages received fall, workers will find work effort less attractive and they will do less of it. Savers will also save less if the net yield to savings declines.

The difference between what it costs a firm to employ a worker or acquire a unit of capital, and what that worker or saver receives net, is the tax wedge (Fig. 1.2). From the standpoint of a single worker or a single unit of capital, an increase in the wedge has two types of effects. An increase in the wedge raises the cost to the employer in the form of higher wages paid or higher yields paid for capital. Clearly, firms will employ fewer workers and acquire less capital. On the supply side, an increase in the wedge reduces net wages received and the net yields savers receive. Again, less work effort will be supplied and there will be less savings. In sum, an increase in the wedge reduces the demand for, and the supply of, productive factors. An increase in the wedge, therefore, is associated with less employment, less investment and lower output. In dynamic formulations, as the wedge grows, output growth falls, and vice versa. Within the context of classical economics, regulation, restrictions, and requirements, along with explicit taxes, are all parts of the wedge.

In the recent past, classical economics has experienced a marked resurgence and is now presenting a formidable challenge to the hegemony of demand-side economics. This challenge results as much from the

FIGURE 1.2. The "wedge"

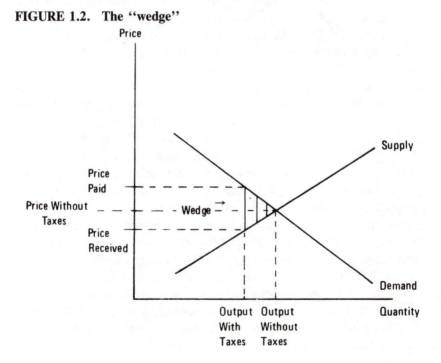

perceived failure of current economic policies as it does from the apparent elegance of the logical structures. While not precise, a review of the postwar period in the United States reveals a number of experiments that have put the various models to a test. Ironically, the imagery surrounding these tests has been diametrically opposed to the facts. The economic posture of the Kennedy administration and its aftermath in the first few years when Lyndon Johnson was president are characterized as liberal and Keynesian in orientation. The Nixon administration's policies, on the other hand, are depicted as being hardnosed and pro-business. The economic record belies these perceptions. In fact, the Kennedy era was the last time classical prescriptions were applied to the overall U.S. economy. It stands in stark relief against what had preceded and what was to follow. The Nixon era was the archtypical demand-management administration, as amply illustrated by the data. While cross-currents and contradictions were ubiquitous, there is little doubt that the Kennedy era was classical. Kennedy employed private incentives to further economic progress. By contrast, the Nixon era was one of explicit government intervention and behavior modifications by direction.

In 1963, in the Economic Report of the President, John Kennedy enunciated in a clear fashion his economic game plan. In his own words:

> To raise the nation's capacity to produce—to expand the quantity, quality, and variety of our output—we must not merely replace but continually expand, improve, modernize, and rebuild our productive capital. That is, we must invest, and we must grow. . . . As a first step, we have already provided important new tax incentives for productive investment. Last year the Congress enacted a 7-percent tax credit for business expenditure on major kinds of equipment. And the Treasury, at my direction, revised its depreciation rules to reflect today's condition. Together, these measures are saving business over $2 billion a year in taxes and significantly increasing the net rate of return on capital investments. . . . The second step in my program to lift investment incentives is to reduce the corporate tax rate from 52 percent to 46 percent. . . . the resulting increase in profitability will encourage risk-taking and enlarge the flow of internal funds which typically finance a major share of corporate investment. . . . as the total impact of the tax program takes hold and generates pressures on existing capacity, more and more companies will find the lower taxes a welcome source of finance for plant expansion. . . . the third step toward higher levels of capital spending is a combination of structural changes to remove barriers to the full flow of investment funds to sharpen the incentives for creative investment, and to remove tax-induced distortions in resource flow. . . . fourth. . .the tax program will go the heart of the main deterrent to investment today, namely, inadequate markets. Once the sovereign incentive of high and rising sales is restored, and the businessman is convinced that to-

day's new plant and equipment will find profitable use tomorrow, the effects of the directly stimulative measures will be doubled and redoubled. Thus— and it is no contradiction—the most important single thing we can do to stimulate investment in today's economy is to raise consumption by major reduction of individual income tax rates.... fifth...the Federal Reserve and the Treasury will continue to maintain...monetary and credit conditions favorable to the flow of savings into long-term investment in the productive strength of the country. (Kennedy 1963)

The game plan given birth under the Nixon presidency was different, indeed. In 1969, the tax rate on capital gains was increased. Inflation elicited illusory capital gains, illusory personal income increases, and illusory business profits, each of which incurred real tax liabilities. In 1971, the dollar was devalued and a wage and price freeze was imposed. Simultaneously, a 10 percent import surcharge was placed on goods coming into the United States; gold was officially demonetized; money growth was high; and government spending as it related to the overall economic base grew inordinately.

To avoid complications brought on by the rapid expansion of the level of defense expenditures for the Vietnam War, a direct comparison of the 1961–1966 period with the years 1969–1975 is in order. The bulk of the military expansion occurred between 1966 and 1968. The 1961–1966 period generally reflects the Kennedy era and its aftermath, whereas the 1969–1975 period is basically the Nixon era. Of interest here is that every "fiscal" policy variable initiated from a "demand management" point of view was more stimulative during the Nixon era than during the Kennedy era; just the reverse was true from a "classical" policy point of view. On the issue of inflation, the Kennedy administration maintained gold convertability, which is the essence of classical monetary policy. The Nixon administration relied on wage and price controls.

The Kennedy era's policies, if one uses a demand management framework, were literally contractionary, while Nixon's were highly expansionary (Table 1.1). Money growth during the Nixon era averaged almost 60 percent more than money growth during the Kennedy era. Government spending and the deficit both declined relative to GNP during the Kennedy era; they ballooned during the Nixon presidency. The dollar's value relative to other currencies was reduced substantially in what seemed at the time of Nixon a never ending sequence of official devaluations. Kennedy maintained the fixed dollar price of gold and dollar convertibility for official institutions.

Between 1961 and 1966, the weighted marginal tax rate on labor rose

TABLE 1.1. Demand management policy variables for the periods 1961–1966 and 1969–1975

Policy variable	1961–1966	1969–1975
Average M1 money growth (% p.a.)	3.5	5.6
Total change in government spending/GNP (%)	−0.1	4.4
Total change in deficit/GNP (%)	−0.6	5.3
Devaluation of dollar in terms of gold (% p.a.)	0.0	22.8

p.a., per annum.
Source: *Economic Report of the President*, January, 1980. Government Printing Office, Washington, D.C.

From a classical point of view, two of the relevant fiscal policy variables, marginal tax rates on labor and capital, provide a much different picture of the Kennedy and Nixon eras (see Table 1.2).

just .085 percent, half as much as during the 1969–1975 period. Moreover, between 1963 and 1965, the weighted marginal tax rates on labor declined .176 percent (Table 1.2). Similarly, the weighted marginal tax rate on capital declined in the Kennedy era, but increased during the Nixon era. Whether the focus is on the goods market or inflation, the comparison relates a record of subnormal performance for the period 1961–1975 (Table 1.3). In spite of wage and price controls, and the ensuing incomes policy apparatus, inflation and interest rates were high during the Nixon era. In spite of stimulative demand-side fiscal policy, monetary policy and trade policy, real growth was low while unemployment rose.

Kennedy had modest fiscal and monetary policies and a trade policy of gold convertibility and tariff reductions. Incomes policies were limited. Income growth was high, unemployment fell, and inflation and interest rates were low. The path of these objective economic indicators during these two periods challenge directly the demand-management framework. They coincide with the conceptual structure of classical economics.

TABLE 1.2. Classical policy variables for the periods 1961–1966 and 1969–1975

Policy variable	1961–1966	1969–1975
Absolute change (%) in average marginal tax rates on		
Labor	0.085	1.671
Capital	−1.990	3.794

Source: *"Prototype Wedge Model"*®: *Tool for Supply-Side Economics*, A Report to the Board of Directors of the American Council for Capital Formation Center for Policy Research. H.C. Wainwright and Co., Economics. Boston, September 14, 1979.

TABLE 1.3. Objective economic indicators for the periods 1961–1966 and 1969–1975

Policy variable	1961–1966	1969–1975
Average real GNP growth (% p.a.)	5.2	1.8
Average inflation in GNP price deflator (% p.a.)	2.1	6.4
Total change in the unemployment rate (%)	−2.9	5.0
Average change in the nominal S&P 500 stock index (% p.a.)	5.0	−2.1
Average 90 day treasury bill rate (%)	3.451	6.00

p.a., per annum.
Source: Economic Report of the President, January, 1980. Government Printing Office, Washington, D.C.

While stark, the comparison of Nixon's economics with Kennedy's is not out of step with the evidence generated during the rest of the post-war era. The evidence from the Carter administration through mid-1980 is corroborative of the classical model and again stands at odds with the demand-management school of thought. Carter devalued the dollar and the economy witnessed rapid monetary expansion; the price of gold has risen. However, fiscal policy, from a demand-management perspective, has been somewhat contractionary. The most telling variable during his administration is the surge in tax rates.

Recalling February 1963, one can see that fiscal policies could not have been more different. In his testimony before the House Ways and Means Committee, then Secretary of the Treasury Douglas Dillon stated:

> By increasing the reward for effort, enterprise, risk-taking, and investment, thus propelling our economy toward a faster rate of growth, and a stronger future...while a temporary revenue loss will be incurred at the outset, the stimulating effects of tax reduction and reform on the economy will give rise to subsequent revenue gains, and in the longer run the revenue producing power of our tax structure will be raised substantially. (U.S. Congress 1963)

In 1977, Walter Heller, President Kennedy's Chairman of the Council of Economic Advisors, summed it all up:

> What happened to the tax cut in 1965 is difficult to pin down, but insofar as we are able to isolate it, it did seem to have a tremendously stimulative effect, a multiplied effect on the economy. It was the major factor that led to our running a $3 billion surplus by the middle of 1965 before escalation in Vietnam struck us. It was a $12 billion tax cut, which would be about $33 or $34 billion in today's terms, and within one year the revenues into the Federal

Treasury were already above what they had been before the tax cut. Did it (the tax cut) pay for itself in increased revenues? I think the evidence is very strong that it did. (Heller 1977)

THE ELLIPSE

A comprehensive perspective on the impact of fiscal policy on economic activity from a classical point of view can be gained by including two factors of production in the analysis. For discussion purposes, these will be characterized as capital and labor.[1]

The results derived with only one factor, of course, are still applicable: An increase in the wedge increases the price paid for and reduces the price received by a factor of production, reducing both the demand for and the supply of that factor. A lower level of economic activity ensues. For example, an increase in the tax wedge on labor will raise wages paid, lower wages received, and reduce the amount of labor employed.

In a two-factor model, though, the process does not stop here. With fewer employed workers, the value of each unit of capital, from the employer's perspective, is lessened. Therefore, the demand for capital falls, less capital will be employed, and both yields paid and yields received fall. Taking the process to its final state, an increase in the tax wedge[2] on labor will lower

- output
- the quantities of both capital and labor employed;
- wages received;
- yields to capital, both paid and received.

In addition, it will raise wages paid. Similarly, an increase in the tax wedge on the returns to capital will lower

- output;
- the amount of both capital and labor employed;
- wages received and paid;
- yields received by the owners of capital.

Yields paid for capital will rise.

Within this two-factor model, containing both capital and labor as well as one market output, an increase in the tax on either factor of production has conflicting influences on total tax receipts. For example, an increase in the tax wedge on labor will mean that (1) more revenue will be collected per worker employed, thus tending to increase revenues; (2) less workers will be employed, thus lowering revenue; and (3) less capital will be employed, thus lowering revenue.

Under certain circumstances, the additional revenue collected per worker (effect 1) will dominate, and an increase in the tax wedge on labor will raise revenues. Sometimes the last two effects dominate, and less revenue will be forthcoming. The same set of conditions pertains to changes in the tax wedge on capital. In actual practice, of course, a number of additional influences are felt. With higher tax rates, there will be more tax avoidance and evasion, thus aggravating the offsetting revenue impact accompanying tax rate increases. Where possible, factor substitution will reduce the economy's reliance on the now higher taxed factor. The longer the time period allowed to elapse, the greater the offsets. The higher the initial level of tax rates, the greater will be the offsets. Overall, the relationship between tax rates and tax revenues is far from obvious. As often as not, higher tax rates yield less revenue. They always yield less output. When a tax rate increase yields higher revenues, the tax is in the normal range. When a tax rate increase leads to lower revenues it is in the prohibitive range.

One way to analyze the effects of tax rate changes is to specify the combinations of tax rate changes on capital and labor where total revenues are left unchanged. This framework is useful because it separates the issues of total spending from those of tax policies. Thus, if the taxes on labor and capital are both in the normal range, a tax rate reduction on labor will be accompanied by a tax increase on capital, or vice versa. On the other hand, a tax rate reduction on labor, which by definition would lead to higher revenues, would require a tax rate reduction on capital as well.

A representative pairing of such tax rates on labor and capital can be depicted on a two-axis graph. The horizontal axis is the tax on capital (t_k) and the vertical axis is the tax on labor (t_l). The locus of points describing the different pairings of tax rates that yield the same amount of tax revenue is named the iso-revenue line. One such line is drawn in Figure 1.3 in the form of an ellipse. The location and angle of the ellipse are purely arbitrary; the diagram is for illustrative purposes only.

Four distinct regions can be identified on the iso-revenue line. In the region from *P* to *S*, both tax rates are in their "normal" range: an increase in the tax rate on capital alone or the tax rate on labor alone will raise net revenues. Therefore, if revenues are to stay the same in the *PS* region of the iso-revenue line, an increase in either tax rate must be accompanied by a reduction in the other tax rate.

In the *PQ* region, the tax on labor is in its prohibitive range, while the tax on capital is in its normal range: an increase in the tax rate on labor loses net revenues, while an increase in the tax on capital increases net revenues. Thus, an increase in the tax rate on labor (moving up the vertical axis) must be accompanied by an increase in the tax rate on capital (moving to the right on the horizontal axis) to maintain the same level of revenues. Hence, the iso-revenue line in this region has a positive slope (rising to the right). Holding revenues constant, the higher the tax rate on labor, the higher must be the tax on capital.

QR is the region where both tax rates are in the prohibitive range. In this region, an increase in either tax rate lowers revenues. Thus, if the tax on capital is increased (movement to the right), the tax rate on labor must be reduced (movement down) to keep total revenues constant. The iso-revenue line here has a negative slope (descending to the right).

Finally, in the region *RS*, the tax on labor is in the normal range and

FIGURE 1.3. The ellipse

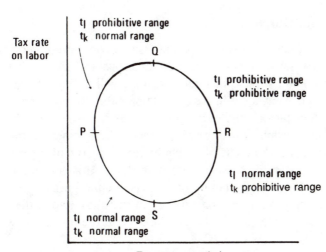

the tax on capital is in the prohibitive range. Here a rise in the tax rate on labor, which increases revenues, must be accompanied by an increase in the tax rate on capital, which lowers revenues, in order to keep total revenues constant.

In each of the three regions (*PQ, QR,* and *RS*) at least one tax rate is in the "prohibitive" range. That is, an increase in the tax rate lowers net revenues. In the range *QR*, both tax rates are in the prohibitive range. Only in the one range *PS* are both tax rates in the normal range, where an increase in either rate raises net revenues. From the relationship postulated in this tax ellipse, in any region other than *PS*, a lowering of at least one tax rate can be accompanied by a lowering of the other tax rate without reducing total revenues or spending. Only in the *PS* region does a lowering of one rate necessitate raising the other in order to maintain total revenues.

A higher level of tax revenues can be represented by a new tax ellipse inside the one just described: a lower level of revenues would be described by a larger ellipse. In all cases, four regions would exist. A maximum point of revenue exists beyond which revenues cannot be increased. Whether tax rates are raised or lowered, less revenue will be forthcoming. In sum then, a whole family of iso-revenue lines or ellipses exists, one for each level of revenue or spending. The existence of these ellipses allows for a separation of the effects of tax rates per se and total tax revenues or spending.

Tax Rates and Output

Individually unique levels of output also can be represented graphically using these same axes (i.e., tax rates on capital and labor). This time, the level of output, instead of total revenues, will be held constant.

As shown earlier, a cut in the tax rate on either factor of production will, if the other factor's tax rate is left unaltered, raise output. In order to hold output constant, if one tax rate is reduced, the other tax rate must be increased. Thus, the locus of points linking the pairs of tax rates that holds output constant must have a negative slope. This is called the *iso-output line*. In Figure 1.4 a family of these iso-output lines is given. The farther an iso-output line is from the origin (zero tax rates), the higher the respective tax rates on capital and labor, and the lower the level of output.

Combining the families of iso-revenue and iso-output lines, a number of general propositions and derivations emerge. It is apparent that there exists only one pairing of tax rates for each level of revenue (spending)

FIGURE 1.4. The iso-output line

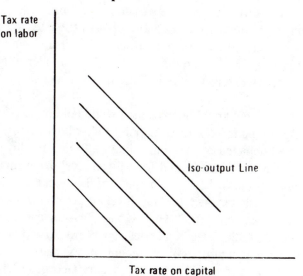

that maximizes output (Figure 1.5). It is determined by the first tangency
point between the iso-revenue and iso-output lines (the intersection point
closest to the axis) and is designated O*. A pairing of tax rates at either

FIGURE 1.5. The optimal tax mix

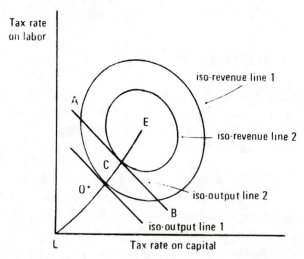

Again, it is important to remember that in the framework used up to this point, all spending
is in the form of lump-sum transfers which do not in and of themselves enhance output. Later other
forms of spending will be included.

point *A* or *B* would yield an iso-output line farther from the origin (iso-output line 2). In this case, more revenues could be raised without a loss in output by adjusting tax rates such that the paired tax rates are tangent to iso-output line 2 at point *C*. Such a pairing, of course, would yield a smaller tax ellipse inside the one diagrammed. The smaller ellipse implies more revenue (spending) while holding output constant (iso-output line 2).

Alternatively, output could be expanded while holding revenue constant by shifting the paired tax rates to point O*, which implies output at the higher level depicted by iso-output line 1. Taking the lows of the tax rate pairings that maximize output for a given level of revenue yields the output efficiency curve *EL*. This output efficiency curve designates that precise pairing of tax rates for any level of government spending whereby output is least diminished. This output efficiency curve traverses the points O* and *C*, ending where tax rates equal zero (*L*) and also where tax rates yield the maximum possible amount of revenue (*E*).[3]

The nineteenth-century U.S. economist, Henry George (1879), summarized the point of these diagrams in his book *Progress and Poverty*:

> The mode of taxation is, in fact, quite as important as the amount. As a small burden badly placed may distress a horse that could carry with ease a much larger one properly adjusted, so a people may be impoverished and their power of producing wealth destroyed by taxation, which if levied in any other way, could be borne with ease.

INCIDENCE AND BURDEN OF A TAX

The tax ellipse also may be used to explore conceptually the ultimate effects of different tax pairings on the net wages received and net yields received for each factor of production. Again, the use of the iso-revenue line allows revenue, and therefore government spending, to be held constant. The tax rate on each factor of production individually is the incidence of the tax. It is depicted explicitly by the tax rate pairings. The burden of a tax, though, is the actual change in the net wages received and net yields received due to the tax change. It must be derived.

The incidence of a tax structure is different from the burden of the same tax structures. The people on whom a tax is levied may well experience no loss in net income if they pass the tax forward to consumers or backward to suppliers. Likewise, a people on whom no tax has been levied may well suffer large net losses as a consequence of taxes levied (incidence) on others.

Within the *PS* region, an increase in the tax on capital must be accompanied by a reduction in the tax on labor. This is the condition that holds revenues constant. The increase in the tax on capital will reduce the amount of capital employed. This reduction in the demand for capital also shifts back the demand for labor. Labor pays less tax, but the reduction in the demand for labor services reduces the gross wages paid. The overall effect on net wages received on a lower pretax wage and lower taxes is ambiguous.

The farther away the tax pairing moves from the point O*, the greater is the reduction in overall output. As output falls, the net gains to labor from its tax rate cuts (which are offset by an increase in the tax on capital) will be reduced. At some point, a tax rate reduction on labor (holding revenues constant) actually may leave labor worse off. The more factors the model entertains, the less related incidence will be to burden. In the extreme, the two are unassociated. In the words of Nobel laureate Paul Samuelson (1973):

> Even if the electorate has made up its mind about how the tax burden shall be borne by individuals, the following difficult problems remain:
>
> Who ultimately pays a particular tax? Does its burden stay on the person on whom it is first levied? One cannot assume that the person Congress says a tax is levied on will end up paying that tax. He may be able to shift the tax; shift it "forward" on his customers by raising his price as much as the tax; or shift it "backward" on his suppliers (wage earners, rent, and interest receivers) who end up being able to charge him less than they would have done had there been no tax.
>
> Economists therefore say: We must study the final incidence of the tax totality of its effects on commodity prices, factor-prices, resource allocations, efforts, and composition of production and consumption. Tax incidence, thus, is no easy problem and requires all the advanced tools of economics to help toward its solution.

In more intuitive terms, as often as not, taxing capital to spare labor will damage labor. Similarly, taxing the rich is sometimes a good way to further impoverish the poor.

Various examples of the fallacy of the so-called "Robin Hood" economics exist over a broad spectrum of economic subjects. One such example pertains to the old notion that there is an inherent conflict between wages and employment on one hand, and profits and capital formation on the other. Many people have the distinct feeling that workers and capitalists are hostile entities within the economic universe. To the extent reason exists, it is widely thought that workers' ability to raise real wages comes directly out of capitalists' pool of profits. Likewise, if capitalists gain an increase in real profits, the gain must have come at the expense of the real wages of workers. Such arguments are the essence of static analysis. The vitriolic debates between national labor leaders and big business executives point up this perception. One group warns that the salvation of the United States depends entirely on the containment of labor unions. The other points to the exorbitant profits enjoyed by the undeserving robber barons at the expense of the working people in the United States. This monotonous brace of diatribes describes a world where profits and wages are mutually exclusive and inimical. Profits and wages are not, of course, mutually exclusive. Fundamentally speaking, profits and wages are complements, not substitutes.

Since 1948, the positive relationship between real after-tax economic profits and average weekly real spendable earnings is unmistakable (Fig. 1.6). Higher profits, more often than not, are associated with higher wages. Higher wages are also consistent with higher profits.

Imagine what the wages would be of a labor group such as truck drivers if there were no trucks. In order to earn a living, truck drivers need trucks to drive. Now the only way there will ever be enough trucks around for drivers is to provide people (savers and investors) with an after-tax rate of return on savings. Saving must be profitable enough (provide an incentive) to entice people either to abstain from consuming, or to work harder in order to provide the requisite real resources to acquire a capital stock of trucks.

If capital is overtaxed, there will be less capital formation and fewer trucks, and the wages of truck drivers will be low. Lowering the tax rate on capital will increase the capital stock and, more important, will raise the wages of truck drivers and other workers. High wages and high profits are far from mutually exclusive objectives. Returns to capital and returns to labor are, in fact, complements. Policies that reduce one are inimical to the other.

One such policy is the tax on capital earnings. A reduction in the rate of taxation on the earnings from capital would result in more investment, which would raise wages. Lower tax rates on wages would increase employment and thereby cause profits to rise. Capitalists and workers alike are thus helped by lower rates of taxation on either capital or income.

FIGURE 1.6. Profits and wages (1948–1979)

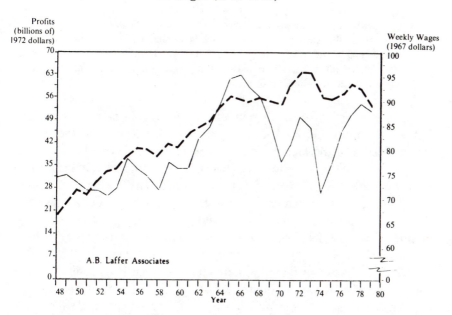

——After-tax corporate profits with inventory valuation and capital consumption adjustments in 1972 dollars.

---- Average weekly spendable earnings for private, nonfarm production or nonsupervisory worker married with three dependents, in 1967 dollars.

Source: National Income and Product Accounts. U.S. Department of Commerce, Bureau of Economic Analysis. Government Printing Office, Washington, D.C.

Within the political structure, this relationship is well known—and often ignored. In his state of the union message in 1962, President John F. Kennedy pointed out that "...a rising tide raises all boats," an explicit reference to this complementarity. In a far less sanguine vein, the same principle is referred to when discussing the "trickle-down" theory. "Trickle-down" is used to mean that if enough money is given to the rich, some of it will trickle down, very slowly, to the poor—just as molasses slowly trickles down on a crisp, fall day in New England.

To summarize, we have five basic points:

1. Changes in tax rates affect output in a direct fashion. Lower tax rates correspond to higher output.
2. Changes in tax rates affect the employment of both factors directly. Lower tax rates correspond to higher output.
3. The constellation of tax rates, holding government spending unchanged, affects

output. How taxes are collected is important, as is the total amount of taxation and spending.

4. Lowered tax rates on any one factor may or may not lower total revenue.
5. Changes in the pairing of tax rates, holding revenue unchanged, may shape the distribution of after-tax spending power, but only indirectly. As often as not, when one factor's tax rate is raised and the other's is lowered, the second factor will end up in worse economic shape.

The specific shapes of the curves and the responsiveness of the effects of tax rates and total taxation or spending depend on the innate characteristics of the factors and the production process. Those factors elastic in supply (sensitive to price changes) bear progressively less of the burden of taxation, irrespective of the incidence. The price received falls very little with the imposition of a tax wedge. This is because a small decrease in the price received would yield a large change in the quantity supplied (Figure 1.7A). Inevitably, the burden is passed to those factors that are inelastic in supply. By definition, it is these factors that have the fewest alternatives to providing their services, even if there is a reduction in the price received (Figure 1.7B).

When tax rates are lowered on inelastic factors, revenues decline. For a given reduction in a tax rate, the more elastic the supply of a factor's services with respect to net returns received, the less the overall revenue loss, or the greater the overall revenue increase.

Symmetrically, the more elastic the demand for a factor's services the greater will be the burden placed on it by any and all taxes (Figure 1.7C). This is because any change in its price leads to a large change in the quantity demanded. Inelastically supplied factors facing elastic demand bear the tax burden disproportionately, even when the taxes fall on other factors (Figure 1.7D).

Finally, the longer the time horizon, the greater will be the revenue losses from tax rate increases. With time, the mobility of most factors of production is increased. Machinery is not repaired or replaced. New job opportunities lure labor out of the taxing district, or a lack of opportunities leads to a below-average growth in employment. Thus, over time any economy becomes more sensitive to the imposition of the wedge; the elasticity of both the supply and demand for factor services increases. Revenue increases realized in the very short horizon may be more than undone over distant horizons.

More elaborate models would provide additional enrichment, but only at the expense of complexity.

FIGURE 1.7. Incidence versus burden of a wedge

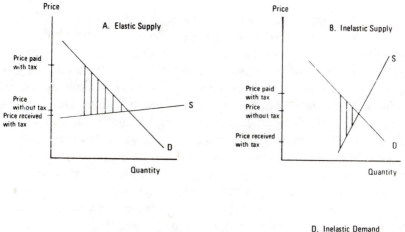

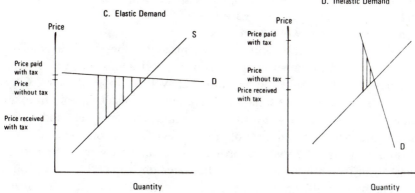

GOVERNMENT SPENDING

Up to now, the discussion has centered on the roles played by the constellation of tax rates, and the level of total taxation or spending. Fiscal effects on the overall economy also are elicited by the composition of spending. With regard to total production or output, different forms of government spending will have widely divergent consequences. There are four separate types of government spending: transfer payments, public goods, nationalized goods, and what is euphemistically referred to as "garbage goods." These four categories of public spending have different income and substitution effects. Specific requirements for qualification as a government spending recipient also will induce substitution effects.

Transfer Payments

Transfer payments are perhaps the least complex of the spending categories. With transfer payments, income effects in general would be expected to net to zero, thus leaving only substitution effects. If taxes are raised in order to give lump-sum transfers to people based solely on chance, then the taxpayers face higher tax rates and a diminution of incentives. The reduction in the incentives to work and produce will tend to make the workers supply less work effort. The other effect that comes into play results from the fact that these workers now have less after-tax income: in order to maintain a semblance of their previous living standard they must work more, not less. The desire to maintain one's standard of living is what elicits the income effect.

Therefore, for any one taxpayer, an increase in tax rates will bring about two effects that work in opposite directions. The substitiution effect will lead the taxpayer to work less while the income effect will tend to make him or her work more.

This view is widely held by economists and non-economists alike. It can be found in numerous professional publications, such as Joseph Pechman's (1980) book on taxation, as well as in Professor Lester Thurow's views on a net wealth tax. These views result directly from an attempt to aggregate a series of partial equilbrium analyses, and in the process, to ignore an entire set of effects that come out of a general equilibrium analysis. Theory does provide an explicit answer to the net effects of an increase or decrease of tax rates on work effort.

The best lay illustration of the correct general equilbrium statement was found in the *Wall Street Journal*[4]:

> ...M.I.T. economist Lester C. Thurow also speaks favorably of a net-wealth tax and the full taxation of capital gains.
>
> He argues that private capital would still be formed because every tax has an income effect and a substitution effect, and he says the former dominates the latter. If you boost the tax on wealth, people will work harder to achieve their desired level of wealth (the income effect) even as the higher tax discourages them from more work (the substitution effect). But by our reckoning, if you tax $100 from Jones, thus forcing him to work harder, and give the $100 to Smith, Smith is required to work less to achieve his desired level of wealth.
>
> The income effect washes out, and all that's left is substitution.

More technically, the answer becomes apparent from the following example:

1. For an individual taken by himself, it is clear that at zero or negative take-home wages he will work less than he would at any positive take-home wages. Therefore over the entire range of possible wages the supply of work effort is unambiguously increased by the total increase in take-home wages.

2. Within take-home wage regions, however, which may cover a wide range of take-home wages, an individual may choose to work fewer hours as take-home wages rise. In such a case the income effect of higher total take-home wages more than offsets the substitution effect of more take-home pay for the last unit of work.

To see the distinction clearly, imagine the following: a person earns pre-tax wages of $4,000 per month. He takes one month per year in unpaid vacation. He pays a flat 50 percent tax on all wages such that his take-home pay is $2,000 per month, or for the 11-month year $22,000. Let us analyze now the following two sets of circumstances:

a. He wins a once-for-all lottery of an $11,000 after-tax yearly stipend.

b. He has a permanent reduction in his tax rates to 25 percent.

Under circumstances (a), the yearly stipend, the general result will be some reduction in the number of months worked. Part of his increased income will go into more leisure consumption and thereby less time will be devoted to work. If he works the same 11 months per year under condition (a), he will receive $33,000 ([0.5 X 44,000] + 11,000) after tax and under condition (b) he will also receive $33,000 (0.75 X 44,000). If he works one month less or 10 months under (a) he will take home $31,000, while under (b) he will take home only $30,000. His lost income is greater if he takes one more month of leisure when tax rates are cut as opposed to when he received a windfall lottery. Likewise, if he works an extra month under condition (a), he will have $35,000 in take-home pay, and under condition (b) he will have $36,000 take-home.

Therefore, if we neutralize the income effect of a tax rate cut there will be more total work due simply to the substitution effect.

For any one person we cannot be sure whether the income effect dominates the substitution effect within the relevant range. What is clear is that the income effect of a tax rate reduction lowers work effort and the substitution effect raises work effort. For the economy as a whole, however, the effect of a tax rate cut can be presumed to lead to more work. If the income effects across individuals are roughly similar, then the work impact of the income effect will net to zero. The higher income accorded the worker whose tax rates are cut must be matched by a negative impact on the income of the spending recipient.

If worker output were unchanged, then a tax rate cut would lead at the same rate to a spending cut or a negative income lottery. Just as a lottery win lowers work, so a lottery net loss (usually referred to as a poll tax) would lead to increased work. Combining the two always leads to more work. This aggregate effect is equivalent to the work and output effect of our example when an $11,000 yearly poll tax is imposed simultaneously with a reduction of the income tax rate from 50 percent to 25 percent. Income at 11 months of work would raise $22,000 ([0.75 X 44,000] − 11,000), but an additional month's work would yield $3,000 net, as opposed to $2,000. Except in obviously perverse cases, more work, not less, would be forthcoming. The theoretical analysis underlying this example can be found in any number of sources. The classics are Hick's *Value and Capital* (1939) or perhaps Harberger's *Taxation and Welfare* (1974).

Transfer payments financed by increases in tax rates, therefore, do not have any net expected income effects. They do, however, yield the normal substitution effects that arise whenever tax rates are increased. These substitution effects cumulate over all taxpayers or potential taxpayers. Of course, if there are distinct differences in individual responses to income effects, then an increase in transfer payments may result in some changes due to income effects. It is important to note, however, that the determination of the net changes in income must not be confused with the incidence of the transfer payments nor with the incidence of the tax rate increases. Reliance must be placed solely on the burden of the program, and not on its incidence. Even if we knew the relative responsiveness of different groups to so-called income effects, and also knew the incidence of the transfer payments and tax rate hikes, we still would be no closer to the net income effect. It could still just as easily be positive, negative, or even zero. In all, therefore, an increase in transfer payments corresponds to a cumulative set of substitution effects and not to expected income effects. A tax increase used to finance transfer payments will lower output.

Quite frequently, an additional set of substitution effects also occurs with transfer payments. These are the so-called needs, means, retirement and incomes tests. To receive transfer payments such as unemployment compensation, food stamps, Aid for Dependent Children, Social Security benefits, housing and rent subsidies, agricultural relief, and so on, it is necessary to demonstrate need. The higher one's income, the less that person can receive. Therefore, an additional disincentive is placed in the path of work effort. Not only are people taxed if they work, but they are also paid if they don't. This further strengthens the substitution effects already discussed (Laffer 1978).

Public Goods

Government spending on so-called public goods elicits two separate and distinct effects. The first, which is called the *substitution effect*, will exert an unambiguous pressure to reduce output because of a separation of effort from reward. Taxation provides the real wherewithal to acquire public goods, and they are then distributed gratis to the recipients. Taxation per se reduces incentives and leads to lessened output.

The other effect is called the *income effect*, and in the case of public goods will lead to an even greater reduction in output, although the population will be better off. The definition of a public good is that good for which the value of the resources exacted from the population is less than the value of the government spending itself. Therefore, in value terms, the recipients receive more than the taxpayers pay. Examples might include the national highway system and perhaps some government research and development. In the case of the recipients, the receipt of value from the government will raise their level of total well-being and lead them to choose more leisure time instead of work. While for the taxpayers the opposite effect holds true, it will have a smaller impact because the value of the resources extracted is less than the value to the recipients of the goods received. Both income and substitution effects lead to lessened production. Relative to transfer payments, this form of government spending will result in higher consumption or welfare on the part of the overall population, while simultaneously yielding lower work effort. Part of the increase in total income will be used to consume more leisure.

Nationalized Goods

Nationalized goods are those goods that the government produces and sells at market prices. The government production unit also pays market wages and returns to capital. If the government's operation is precisely as efficient as private production, then there would be no difference between private and government production. There will be no substitution or income effects form this source of government spending, and therefore, it should be excluded from the analysis.

"Garbage Goods"

The final form of government spending is the so-called garbage goods. In the case of garbage goods, the government produces the product less efficiently than the private sector or, in the extreme, throws the product away. The most famous illustration of a pure garbage good was the recommendation by John Maynard Keynes that the government should hire people to dig ditches and then fill them up again. The negative connotations of the words "garbage goods" are not always appropriate. Basically, any good that the private sector would not produce or purchase on its own accord is a garbage good, irrespective of its total value to society at large. Defense spending is clearly an example of a garbage good, even though the benefits to society may be well worth the expense. For garbage goods there is a negative income effect along with the usual substitution effects from the higher tax rates. Thus, consumption or welfare will be lower for garbage goods than for transfers, while work effort will be greater.

In actual practice, these distinctions may be quite substantial in explaining the overall path of the relevant economic domain. To summarize, not only does it matter how much is collected though taxation, but also how it is collected and how it is spent.

TAXES, SPENDING, AND THE DEFICIT

Introducing spending into the general context of tax rate changes fills out the picture a little bit more fully. Focusing now on the deficit, instead of revenues, a tax rate reduction will:

1. Lessen the amount collected per unit of the lower taxed factor;
2. Increase the amount of employment for the lower taxed factor;
3. Increase the employment of other factors, and thereby their tax payments;
4. Reduce total spending as fewer people are unemployed or on welfare as, among other feed-back effects, the number of unemployed and the number of welfare recipients declines; and
5. Change the composition of spending away from transfers and garbage goods toward public goods and nationalized goods. This should have the effect of lessening the anti-output nature of government spending per unit spent. These effects, when taken only in a formal context, raise the responsiveness of the economy to tax rate changes, and heighten the chances of a well-designed tax rate reduction lowering the deficit.

The analysis, however, excludes many potentially important additional feedback effects in the system. While less amenable to formal analysis, they could, nonetheless, swing the results in favor of balancing the budget by lowering, instead of raising, tax rates. These other effects include the role and importance of tax evasion and avoidance.

Higher tax rates imply more of both tax evasion and avoidance. The more tax that is either evaded or avoided, the less revenue the government will collect per unit of the taxable base. Furthermore, it is generally true that the more evasion and avoidance that exists, the more spending the government will be required to monitor and enforce the tax codes. The existence of tax evasion and avoidance, therefore, further enhances the beneficial fiscal effects of tax rate reductions. It still remains an empirical question, however, as to what the full effects of changes in tax rates are on the overall fiscal solvency of the relevant government unit.

In any case, the important feature of the tax system is the conceptual framework on which it is based. Henry George (1879), in his chapter entitled "The Proposition Tried by the Canons of Taxation," enumerated as well as anyone the criteria by which tax policy may be analyzed:

> The best tax by which public revenues can be raised is evidently that which will closest conform to the following conditions:
>
> 1. That it bear as lightly as possible upon production—so as least to check the increase of the general fund from which taxes must be paid and the community maintained.
>
> 2. That it be easily and cheaply collected, and fall as directly as may be upon the ultimate payers—so as to take from the people as little as possible in addition to what it yields the government.
>
> 3. That it be certain—so as to give the least opportunity for tyranny or corruption on the part of officials, and the least temptation to law breaking and evasion on the part of the taxpayers.
>
> 4. That it bear equally—so as to give no citizen an advantage or put any at a disadvantage, as compared with others.

THE LAFFER CURVE

It is silly to assert that the major issue facing economic policy was never the Laffer Curve. The issue clearly is, and has been, the Laffer Curve—that is, what are the budgetary implications of tax rate changes?

The Laffer curve is, and always has been, a pedagogic device illustrating that changes in tax rates influence both the revenue collected per dollar of tax base and the very size of the tax base itself. The sophomoric notion that such a curve purports to show that cutting tax rates automatically reduces deficits should never have seduced any profound "insider."

In the abstract, lower tax rates may or may not reduce the budget deficit. In the less rarefied atmosphere of realpolitik, many factors come into play. The longer a reduction in tax rates is in existence, the more likely it is to expand total revenues. Individuals and businesses will have time to adjust. The economic vigor that accompanies a tax rate cut also tends to reduce welfare spending as workers find productive employment and businesses become more successful, necessitating less government assistance. Lower tax rates also augment the tax base by reducing the underground economy, tax avoidance schemes, and even illegal activities. Tax cuts that have no incentive effects and, therefore, increase the budget deficit on a dollar-for-dollar basis, are not tax cuts at all.

In the recording of the early 1980s, an observation as important as any feature of the tax–legislative nexus is the fact that anticipated changes in tax rates also can have a profound impact on the path of the economy. In the 1981 tax bill, the tax rate cuts were phased in. Supposedly, there was a 5 percent cut on October 1, 1981, a 10 percent cut on July 1, 1982, and a final 10 percent cut on July 1, 1983.

In truth, there is no such thing as an intra-year tax rate cut. The IRS simply cannot discriminate between income earned in January or the following December because most taxpayers report income on a calendar-year basis. As a result, the intra-year "tax cuts" were prorated across the entire year. In 1981, for example, the 5 percent cut that supposedly took effect October 1 was prorated over the calendar as a 1.25 percent tax rate reduction for the full year. Calendar year 1982 (starting on January 1, not July 1) had a cumulative 10 percent rate cut. On January 1, 1983 and 1984, the cumulative tax rate cuts were 18 percent and 23 percent, respectively (Kadlec and Laffer 1981).

The flaw in this phased-in approach to tax rate cuts is to ignore the role of incentives on individual behavior. Common sense tells us that people don't shop at a store the week before that store has a widely advertised discount sale. Prospects of lower tax rates in future years created incentives for individuals and businesses to reduce their income during 1981 and 1982 when tax rates were high, in order to realize that income in 1983 and 1984 when tax rates would be lower. The economy slowed, unemployment rose, and the deficit swelled (Fig 1.8). Ironically, the attempt to stave off deficits by delaying tax cuts, in reality, caused those very deficits to soar.

FIGURE 1.8. Unemployment and the federal deficit

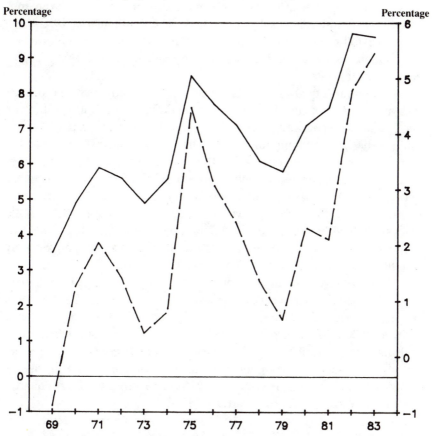

——Unemployment rate, all civilian workers.
----Federal budget deficits as a percent of GNP.
Source: National Income and Product Accounts. U.S. Department of Commerce, Bureau of Economic Analysis. Government Printing Office. Washington, D.C.; *Economic Report of the President, 1984.* Government Printing Office, Washington, D.C.

Surely the 1981 and 1982 pronouncements of the Washington savants that supply-side economics and, specifically, tax rate cuts were a failure have to be ranked as the most disingenuous nonsense. It should hardly come as a surprise to anyone that tax cuts don't work until they take effect.

What is truly astounding is the rapidity with which the economy responds to incentives. Almost as early as January 1, 1983, when the bulk of the tax cuts came into effect, the economy began to recover. The recovery, true to supply-side logic, did not foster the "roaring inflation" so confidently predicted by Walter Heller (Stein 1978), but robustly provided jobs, higher-capacity utilization, and increased productivity. Even subtle differences in incentives appear to work. The fourth-quarter 1983 slowdown was followed by a first-quarter 1984 rebound (in exact conformance with anticipated results), and then by the realization of the final 5 percent cut in tax rates.

In the fourth quarter of 1982, when the unemployment rate peaked just prior to the tax cut, the federal budget deficit, on a National Income and Products Account (NIPA) basis, peaked at an annual rate of $208.2 billion. By the fourth quarter of 1983, the rate at which red ink was being spilled had dipped some $18 billion to $190 billion. On the face of it, this didn't appear to be much of a decline, given the robust recovery during 1983. What has to be remembered, however, is that from the fourth quarter of 1982 to the fourth quarter of 1983, the tax cut itself (by static analysis) would have increased the deficit by $33 billion. Thus, the economic recovery per se reduced the federal deficit alone by approximately $51 billion.

This, however, is only one part of the story. State and local budget surpluses have experienced a veritable renaissance. In California, a projected deficit in 1983 of some $1.5 billion turned into an estimated $200 to $600 million surplus in 1984. Talk in the state, still labeled radical, projects a surplus in 1985 in the $2 billion range. California is not an isolated case. When the budgets of all state and local governments are combined, their surplus rose by over $15 billion from the fourth quarter of 1982 through the fourth quarter of 1983.

All in all, the recovery of 1983 reduced the combined federal, state, and local deficit by over $66 billion, far more than offsetting the $33 billion tax cut during that year. As if to reinforce the point, total federal receipts in 1983 rose by some 44 percent in spite of the tax rate cut. During 1982, on the other hand, total federal receipts fell by 1.5 percent. During 1982, one revenue category that bucked the down trend and actually showed a substantial increase was that group of taxpayers whose tax rate had been cut from 70 percent to 50 percent without any delay feature. Between 1981 and 1982, tax revenues from those with adjusted gross incomes of $100,000 and more increased 13.2 percent to $48.9 billion (Table 1.4) (Kemp 1984).

The deficit decline continues as the economy continues its ascent. According to the Office of Management and Budget, each percentage-point reduction in unemployment reduces the deficit by $25 billion. With fewer people unemployed, welfare expenditures decline. And with more peo-

TABLE 1.4.   Tax payments by income group 1981–1982

Adjusted gross income group (thousands of dollars)	Tax payments (millions of dollars)		Percentage change
	1981	1982	
0–10	7,974	6,967	−12.6
10–15	16,938	15,134	−10.7
15–20	22,572	19,704	−12.7
20–50	142,249	136,739	−3.9
50–100	51,015	50,655	−0.7
100–500	34,256	36,313	+6.0
500–1,000	4,101	5,694	+38.8
1,000+	4,887	6,926	+41.7

Source; "Why Tax Cuts Help the Poor: Preliminary Results of the 1982 Tax Cuts," *Special Report* House Republican Conference. Washington, D.C., April, 1984.

ple working, tax revenues grow. Hence, the continued faster-than-expected fall in the unemployment rate portends additional reductions in the deficit (Fig. 1.9).

During the first two months of this calendar year (1984), for example, the deficit as reported by the treasury declined $10 billion relative to the first two months of 1983. Possible timing differences between one year and the next make annualizing these results less than precise. Nonetheless, they point to an annualized deficit reduction for the federal government alone on the revisions in government estimates of budget deficits. Clearly, changes in tax rates are not the only policy that affects the path of the economy or deficits. Monetary policy, in particular, remains an unknown factor. A sharp rise in interest rates would contribute directly to higher deficits by increasing the cost of financing the federal government's debt. Such a rise in interest rates also could balloon the deficit by derailing the economic expansion brought about by the reduction in tax rates.

On the face of it, evidence that the economy in 1981 was operating in the prohibitive range of the Laffer Curve, where higher tax rates increase the budgetary deficit, is persuasive. As tax cuts were deferred, the economy contracted, revenues declined, and deficit forcasts were continually revised upward. With the implementation of tax rate reductions in 1983 and 1984, the economy is soaring and deficit projections are tumbling. Not only do we appear to have experienced a self-defeating tax increase in 1982, but also a self-financing tax cut in 1983 and 1984.

FIGURE 1.9. A sharp drop in unemployment

Percentage

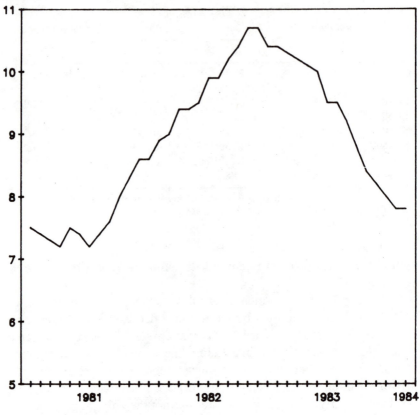

——Unemployment rate, all civilian workers.
Source: Economic Report of the President. Government Printing Office, Washington, D.C.

NOTES

1. For a mathematical derivation of the ellipse see Canto, Joines, and Laffer (1983).

2. For the purposes of this exposition, all proceeds from taxation are presumed to be returned in the form of neutral transfer payments.

3. Again, it is important to remember that in the framework used up to this point, all spending is in the form of lump-sum transfers which do not in and of themselves enhance output. Later, other forms of spending will be included.

4. *Wall Street Journal*, April 16, 1976, "Review and Outlook" section.

REFERENCES

Canto, Victor A., Douglas H. Joines, and Arthur B. Laffer. 1983. "Tax Rates, Employment, Market Production, and Welfare." In *Foundations of Supply Side Economics.* New York: Academic Press, pp. 2–24.

Friedman, Milton. 1968. "The Role of Monetary Policy," Presidential address at the 80th meeting of the American Economic Association. *American Economic Review* 58 (December):1–17.

George, Henry. 1979. *Progress and Poverty.* New York, Robert Schalkenbach Foundation, York (originally published 1879).

Hansen, Alvin. 1953. *A Guide to Keynes.* New York: McGraw-Hill.

Harberger, Arnold C. 1974. *Taxation and Welfare.* Boston, MA: Little, Brown.

Heller, Walter. 1978. "The Kemp-Roth-Laffer Free Lunch." *Wall Street Journal* (July 12, 1978, p. 70).

Hicks, John R. 1939. *Value and Capital: An Inquiry Into Some Fundamental Principles of Economic Theory.* Oxford: Clarendon Press.

Kadlec, Charles W., and Arthur B. Laffer. 1981. "The Ways and Means to an Inadequate Tax Cut." *Economic Study,* Rolling Hills Estates, CA. A.B. Laffer Associates (July).

Kemp, Jack. 1984. "Why Tax Cuts Help The Poor: Preliminary Results of the 1982 Tax Cuts." *Special Report* House Republican Conference, Washington, D.C. (April).

Kennedy, John F. 1963. *Economic Report of the President,* U.S. Government Printing Office, Washington, D.C., pp. 16–18.

Keynes, John Maynard. 1936. *The General Theory of Employment, Interest, and Money.* Boston: Harcourt, Brace.

Laffer, Arthur B. 1978. "Prohibitive Tax Rates and the Inner-City: A Rational Explanation of the Poverty Trap." *Economic Study,* Boston, H.C. Wainwright & Co. (June).

Pechman, Joseph A. 1980. *What Should Be Taxed?* Washington, D.C.: Brookings Institution.

Samuelson, Paul. 1973. *Economics.* New York: McGraw-Hill.

Stein, Nesbert. 1978. "The Real Reasons for a Tax Cut." *Wall Street Journal* (July 18, p. 20).

Tobin, James. 1972. "Inflation and Unemployment." *American Economic Review* 62 (March): 1–18.

U.S. Congress. House. Committee on Ways and Means. 1963. Douglas Dillon. *On the Special Message on Tax Reduction and Reform.* 90th Congress, Winter Session.

U.S. Congress. Joint Economic Committee. 1977. Walter Heller. *Testimony before the Joint Economic Committee.* 95th Congress, Fall Session. Quoted by Bruce Bartlett in the *National Review* (October 27, 1978, vol. 30, pp. 1333–6.)

2

Government Spending, Tax Rates, and Private Investment in Plant and Equipment

Douglas H. Joines

SUMMARY

The evidence reported here supports the contention that taxation of income from capital exerts an important effect on investment behavior. In the early 1960s, effective tax rates on income from capital were reduced. As the postwar baby-boom generation moved into the labor force, these tax cuts aided the economy in producing the new plant and equipment that would have been necessary to maintain previous growth rates of productivity and real wages. The stimulus was not sufficient, however, to prevent some fall in these growth rates. Since the late 1960s, tax rates have returned to their previous levels, and the growth rates of net investment, labor productivity, and real wages have slowed considerably. Increased taxation of the income from capital thus seems to have reduced not only the after-tax returns to capital, but those to labor as well.

May 30, 1980

The 1970s will be remembered as the decade during which the U.S. economy faltered more seriously than at any time since the Great Depression. During the first eight years of the decade, real GNP per person of working age grew at a compound annual rate barely in excess of one percent (Table 2.1). This sluggish growth occurred despite a surge in employment, which reached a record level of 97.6 million in November 1979. Not only did aggregate employment reach record levels, but the fraction of the potential work force employed also reached an all-time high

TABLE 2.1. Growth in real GNP and working-age population

Period	Growth rate of real GNP per person of working age (%)	Percentage of working-age population employed	Growth rate of population of working age (%)
1930–39	−1.07	55.5	1.23
1940–49	3.13	62.0	1.15
1950–59	3.14	65.0	0.70
1960–69	2.61	66.8	1.43
1970–77	1.08	68.9	1.64

Note: Growth rates are compound annual percentage rates of change. Working-age population is defined as total noninstitutional population of the United States aged 18 to 64, inclusive.

Source: Population data are from *Historical Statistics of the United States, Colonial Times to 1970.* U.S. Department of Commerce, Bureau of the Census, Government Printing Office, Washington, D.C., 1975 and *Current Population Reports.* U.S. Department of Commerce, Bureau of the Census, Government Printing Office, Washington, D.C., 1975. Employment data are from *Long Term Economic Growth, 1860–1970, Business Statistics,* 1977. U.S. Department of Commerce, Bureau of Economic Analysis, Government Printing Office, Washington, D.C. and the *Survey of Current Business.* U.S. Department of Commerce, Bureau of Economic Analysis, Government Printing Office, Washington, D.C. Real GNP data are from the *National Income and Product Accounts.* U.S. Department of Commerce, Bureau of Economic Analysis, Government Printing Office, Washington, D.C.

during the 1970s. In 1974, the percentage of the population aged 18 to 64, inclusive, holding market-sector jobs surpassed 70 percent for the first time in history.

How can this rapid growth in employment be reconciled with the equally sharp decline in the growth of output? One obvious explanation is that the growth of other factors of production did not keep pace with the growth of labor input. An examination of net investment in plant and equipment during the postwar period corroborates this conjecture.

The surge in aggregate employment that has occurred during the last 15 years can be attributed to two sources. The first, noted above, is the steady increase since World War II in the percentage of the working-age population actually holding market-sector jobs. The second is the rapid growth during the late 1960s and the 1970s in the pool of potential workers. During the 1950s, the working-age population grew at a compound annual rate of 0.7 percent. As those born during the postwar baby boom began to reach working age in the late 1960s and the 1970s, the growth rate of the pool of potential workers more than doubled.

In order to keep the stock of capital per worker growing at the rates experienced in the 1950s, this rapid increase in the number of workers would have necessitated an increase in the share of national income invested in plant and equipment. Economic theory suggests that, in the absence of other complicating factors, the prospect of profitable investment opportunities would have in fact elicited an increase in the share of national output devoted to net additions to the capital stock. These profitable investment opportunities would have resulted from the impending increase in the size of both the potential work force and the market for the output of those investments. Because greater investment entails a sacrifice in current consumption, however, it is unlikely that the entire burden of adjustment to a higher capital stock would have been borne immediately. It is therefore unlikely that the investment rate would have increased sufficiently to maintain the previous rate of growth of net investment (and thus capital stock) per worker. One would thus expect a slowing in the rate of growth of labor productivity and in the real wage of labor.

How well do these predictions accord with actual experience? The ratio of real gross private nonresidential fixed investment to real GNP did hold up very well in the face of the surge in the work force; it was consistently above its postwar average throughout the entire decade from 1965 through 1974, and it fell only slightly below the average from 1975 through 1977. The picture resulting from an examination of net additions to the capital stock, after allowing for depreciation of existing plant and equipment, however, is somewhat different.[1]

Net investment as a percentage of real net national product was well above its postwar average during the mid- and late 1960s. In fact, it was almost as high as it was during the immediate postwar investment boom when the capital stock was rebuilt after the real declines that had occurred during the depression and World War II. During the early 1970s, however, the net investment ratio was only slightly above its postwar average, and during the mid-1970s it was well below this average. In fact, the ratio during 1975 to 1979 was below the lowest level recorded for any other single year since World War II (Table 2.2). It thus seems that investment indeed did not increase sufficiently to keep the capital stock per worker growing at its average postwar rate.

Further evidence on this point can be obtained by examining the growth rates of labor productivity (as measured by real output per hour in private nonfarm business) and of real wages. Both productivity and real wages did grow slowly during the late 1960s and the 1970s (Table 2.3). It is particularly interesting to note that both labor productivity and real wages grew more slowly duirng the late 1960s than during the first half of that decade, even though the net investment ratio indicates that something of an investment boom began in 1964 and continued throughout the

TABLE 2.2. Ratio of real net private nonresidential fixed investment to real net national product

Period	Investment (%)
1930–39	−2.94
1940–49	1.51
1940–45	−0.30
1946–49	4.21
1950–59	2.86
1960–69	3.42
1960–63	2.40
1964–69	4.11
1970–77	2.70
1970–74	3.25
1975–77	1.79
1946–77	3.16

Note: Numbers are averages of annual figures.

Source: National Income and Product Accounts. U.S. Department of Commerce, Bureau of Economic Analysis, Government Printing Office, Washington, D.C., Tables 1.10 and 5.3.

decade. This boom was apparently insufficient to supply the rapidly growing work force with enough capital to maintain the previous rates of increase in productivity and real wages.

TABLE 2.3. Growth rates of labor productivity and real wages

Period	Productivity[a]	Real wage[b]
1950–59	2.55	2.63
1950–54	2.61	2.71
1955–59	2.48	2.55
1960–69	2.59	1.48
1960–64	3.03	1.61
1965–69	2.15	1.35
1970–77	1.56	0.79
1970–74	0.95	0.54
1975–77	2.58	1.27

Compound annual percentage rates of change.

[a]Output per hour in private nonfarm business. *Source: Handbook of Labor Statistics,* U.S. Department of Labor, Bureau of Labor Statistics, Government Printing Office, Washington, D.C., December, 1978.

[b]Average hourly earnings of production workers in manufacturing, deflated by consumer price index. *Source: Long Term Economic Growth, 1860–1970.* U.S. Department of Commerce, Bureau of Economic Analysis, Government Printing Office, Washington, D.C. and *Handbook of Labor Statistics.* U.S. Department of Labor, Bureau of Labor Statistics, Government Printing Office, Washington, D.C., December, 1978.

It thus appears from casual examination that these data are largely but not completely in accord with what economic theory would have led one to expect in the absence of other complicating factors. This suggests that some such complicating factors might have been at work and might explain the discrepancies between the predictions and the actual occurrences. The major discrepancy to be explained is: Why did investment increase in the mid-to late 1960s as predicted, but then not continue to increase at the same rate into the 1970s, a period when the work force grew at an even faster rate than it had during the 1960s?

GOVERNMENT POLICY AND CAPITAL FORMATION

As a result of the perceived "capital shortage" discussed above and also much discussed in the financial press, it is now widely recognized that one of the most important issues of public economic policy concerns how the activities of government affect private capital formation. Government has been empowered to conduct a broad range of policies that can affect even the minute details of our everyday lives. In recent years we have seen that power exercised more broadly than ever before, as programs have been enacted that extend government control into areas previously reserved for private activity. Many of these programs have potential effects on private investment decisions, whether by design or as an unintended consequence.

For example, regulations designed to protect the environment and to improve occupational health and safety standards affect the cost of doing business, thus discouraging new "productive" investment, while at the same time encouraging investments designed to meet the newly imposed requirements. Such regulations lower the stock of capital used to produce national output as conventionally measured and increase the stock of capital used to produce such things as clean air and water, which do not enter into the conventional measures of national output. It might be argued that such changes in the capital stock were fully intended by the proponents of these regulations.

The most rapidly growing of all government programs, at least as measured by budgetary outlays, are those involving transfer payments to persons. The effects of such transfer schemes on capital formation were probably not a primary consideration of those who designed the programs. But like all policies that require the expenditure of public funds, these programs do affect capital formation, however indirectly. This is because the government must somehow finance its expenditures. There are three ways in which this financing may be accomplished: by raising explicit tax revenues; by issuing interest-bearing government debt; or by "printing" money. It can be argued that each of these actions will discourage capital formation.

This chapter examines the effects on private capital formation of the first two of these methods of financing government expenditures. It thus ignores the effects of government policies, such as environmental standards, that do not entail large outlays of public funds, important as such policies might be. It also ignores the composition of public expenditures by assuming that all such spending takes the form of lump-sum payments to private citizens. This assumption is undoubtedly an oversimplification. Some public expenditures are used to acquire public capital, such as highways, which increases the productivity of private-sector investment. Other forms of government spending, most notably transfer payments, entail disincentives to private productive activity. While such incentive effects are of great importance, they are beyond the scope of this paper.

Finally, this chapter does not examine the effects of government monetary policy, in particular the "printing" of money to finance public spending, on private capital formation. This omission is not intended to imply that such effects are unimportant. It is commonly believed that excessive money creation causes inflation, and that the interaction of inflation and the tax laws increases the rate of taxation of the true economic income from capital.

The two measures of fiscal policy with which this chapter deals are the taxation of income from capital and the issuance of government debt.

THE TAX WEDGE

There is an intuitive economic proposition according to which taxation of an activity reduces the amount of that activity taking place. The tax raises the price paid by the purchaser of a good or service above the price received by the supplier and is said to drive a wedge between the two prices. This is illustrated in Figure 2.1. In the absence of a tax, the market is in equilibrium at price P_0 and quantity Q_0. Imposition of a tax of t per unit sold raises the demand price to P_d, lowers the supply price to P_s, and reduces the quantity to Q_1. The size of the wedge is $P_d - P_s$, which is equal to t.

FIGURE 2.1.   The tax wedge

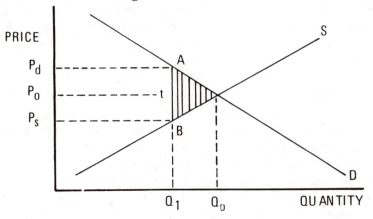

The wedge analysis can be applied to investment in physical capital as well as to other activities. This application is illustrated in Figure 2.2. Here the supply curve refers to aggregate saving out of current income (the supply of funds to the capital market). The demand curve depicts available investment opportunities (the demand for funds). The horizontal axis measures the quantity of saving and investment, and the vertical axis measures the rate of return on saving and investment. According to

FIGURE 2.2.   The effects of the wedge on investment

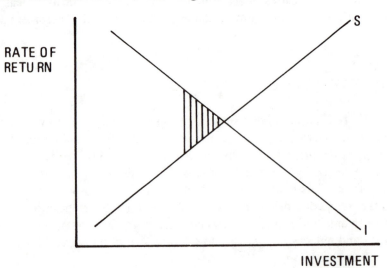

the wedge analysis, an increase in the rate of taxation of income from capital (the "tax wedge") will reduce the amount of capital formation taking place.

THE DEFICIT WEDGE

Government can also finance its expenditures by issuing debt, and such a debt issue can be viewed as a second wedge impinging on the capital market. In any period, private saving must exceed private investment by the amount of the government's debt issue. (This ignores the possibility of investing abroad or borrowing from foreigners.) Government securities compete with private securities for investors' dollars, and only those funds that are left after the sale of government bonds are available to finance the private sector's accumulation of physical capital. This "deficit wedge" is illustrated in Figure 2.3.

A government debt issue is seen to increase private saving, reduce private investment, or both. Which of these three alternatives actually occurs has been the subject of considerable debate during the last few years. The most widely held view, at least until recently, has been the "crowding out" proposition, one version of which is depicted in Figure 2.3. Before the government debt issue, private saving and private investment are equal

FIGURE 2.3. The "crowding out" of private investment

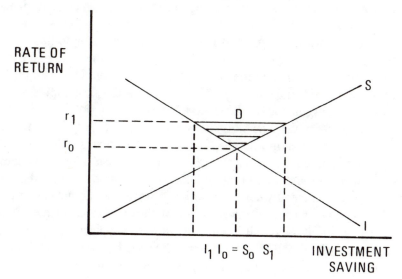

RATE OF RETURN

r_1

r_0

I_1 $I_0 = S_0$ S_1 INVESTMENT
SAVING

at $I_0 = S_0$. The interest rate is r_0. If the governemnt floats a bond issue of size D, then bond prices are bid down and the interest rate is forced up to r_1. If saving is completely insensitive to the interest rate, as in the most naive Keynesian models, the saving curve is vertical rather than having a positive slope. In this most extreme version of the crowding-out hypothesis, saving remains constant while investment falls by the full amount of the debt issue. Under any version of the crowding-out proposition, however, investment must decrease, while saving may increase or remain constant.

The crowding-out hypothesis has been called into question by those who argue that government bonds are not perceived as net wealth by the private sector and thus do not reduce private capital formation. The argument is essentially as follows (Barro 1974). Suppose the government reduces the current tax bill of every taxpayer by one dollar and finances this tax reduction by issuing bonds that bear the market rate of interest. Suppose that a lump-sum tax equal to one dollar plus interest will be levied on each taxpayer next year in order to retire the current bond issue. Will taxpayers feel wealthier today as a result of this transaction? Will they therefore increase their consumption and lower private capital accumulation? If people behave rationally, the argument goes, the answers to these questions must be no.

People will save the dollar they currently receive so as to be able to meet their increased future tax liabilities. Current saving will increase by the amount of the government debt issue and no private capital accumulation need be crowded out. This is shown in Figure 2.4. Now a debt issue of size D causes the saving schedule to shift right by an equal horizontal distance D to S'. Saving increases to S_1, investment remains constant at I_0, and the interest rate remains constant at r_0. According to this view, crowding out will occur only if the private sector does not fully take account of the future tax liabilities implied by government bonds and thus regards these bonds as a substitute for claims on physical capital.

The above argument is unobjectionable as far as it goes. But it fails to take into account the interaction between the deficit wedge and the tax wedge. The problem lies in the fact that governments seldom raise revenues through lump-sum taxes. The more common situation is that they raise revenues through distortionary taxes on economic activity; that is, through taxes that entail wedges. A deficit today is thus an indication not merely of tax liabilities tomorrow, but also of a tax wedge tomorrow. Consequently, a deficit today will reduce the incentive to acquire assets, the income from which will be subject to the implied future taxes. Such assets would include both human and nonhuman capital.

FIGURE 2.4.   Private capital accumulation

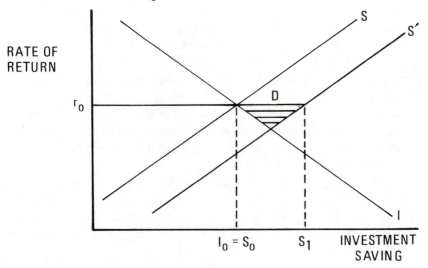

As a result, the statement that government bonds are not net wealth cannot be broadened into a statement that a government debt issue is a neutral economic policy. The latter statement follows in the Keynesian tradition of ignoring the incentive effects of fiscal policy and of concentrating only on the effects of policy upon the private sector's wealth or disposable income. According to this tradition, a current transfer payment financed by current taxes is a neutral policy, since it has no effect on disposable income. If government bonds are not net wealth, then a person following the Keynesian tradition of ignoring incentive effects would argue that a transfer financed by a government debt issue also would be neutral, since it entails no net wealth effects.[2] An adherent of the wedge model, with its emphasis on incentive effects, would argue that neither of these policies is neutral, that they both involve disincentives to productive activity.[3]

EMPIRICAL EVIDENCE

At the theoretical level, the notion of the tax wedge is very clear. At the empirical level, however, it is not at all obvious how one would go about measuring it. The construction of the effective tax rate series reported below rests on several assumptions about the U.S. tax system.

The first of these is that all taxes ultimately fall on income; that is, all taxes arise from either the generation or the spending of income. This proposition is fairly obvious when applied to personal and corporate income taxes, sales taxes, and payroll taxes, but it is equally applicable to other taxes. For example, property taxes (by far the largest source of all government revenue not accounted for by the taxes listed above) can be viewed as taxes on the flow of services produced by real property. In constructing effective economy-wide income tax rates, it is thus necessary to take account of all taxes paid in the economy and to take some comprehensive measure of income as the tax base. The income measure used here is Net National Product (NNP).

Construction of effective marginal tax rates on income from labor and income from capital requires that NNP be separated into two components, one attributable to capital and the other attributable to labor. Income attributable to capital was taken to include corporate profits, rental income of person, and net interest.[4]

The economy-wide marginal tax rate on the income from capital is the fraction of an incremental dollar of income earned by the economy's capital stock which is taken by the government in taxes. It thus depends on the marginal tax rates of the individuals receiving the incremental dollar and on the distribution of that dollar among those individuals. If we assume that each individual's share in an incremental dollar of income produced by the capital stock is equal to his or her share in existing capital income, then the economy-wide marginal tax rate is equal to a weighted average of the individual marginal tax rates, with the shares in existing capital income as weights. A similar calculation will give the economy-wide marginal rate of taxation of labor income.[5]

More specifically, the effective marginal tax rate on income from capital is taken to include three components. The first component represents the federal personal income tax. It is measured by taking a weighted average of the effective marginal federal personal income tax rates in the various income brackets, where the weight for each bracket is the fraction of total income from capital accruing to individuals in that bracket.[6] The second component is assumed to be a flat rate tax applicable only to income from capital. It is estimated by taking the ratio of property and corporate profits tax receipts to income from capital. The third component is assumed to be a flat-rate tax applicable to income from all sources. It is estimated by taking the ratio of all remaining taxes (except the Social Security tax, which is assumed to be labor-specific) to NNP. The most important of these remaining taxes, as judged by revenue raised, is sales taxes. The effective marginal tax rate on income from capital is taken to be the sum of these three components. These calculations were performed for each year from 1929 to 1975 inclusive.[7]

The deficit wedge is in principle much easier to measure. It could simply be taken to be the real government deficit per person of working age. Unfortunately, this variable is probably inappropriate for the statistical tests reported below since the size of the deficit is almost certainly determined endogenously within the economic system.[8] These tests, however, require that the investment series be explained as functions of exogenous variables. A variable that is more nearly exogenous than the deficit and can serve as a good proxy for it is real government purchases of goods and services.[9] Consequently, the ratio of such purchases (by federal, state, and local governments) to working age population is used in the following statistical tests.

Two measures of capital formation are examined. One is real gross private domestic investment in producers' durable equipment per person of working age, and the other is real gross private domestic investment in nonresidential structures per person of working age (Table 2.4).[10]

In order to determine whether the government fiscal policy variables exerted any influence on investment during the 1929–1975 sample period, regression models were estimated, relating the first differences of each of the fiscal policy variables and the first differences of the investment variables.

The statistical models (Table 2.5) perform quite well by the usual statistical standards. The following relationships were found:

• A negative contemporaneous correlation between government and both types of investment respectively. For investment in structures, this negative contemporaneous effect of an increase in goverment spending is partially offset by a postive effect one year later (Table 2.4).

• A negative correlation between current increases in both types of investment and increases in the capital income tax rate which occur one year later. Such an effect has a reasonable interpretation. Since it is future tax rates that affect the profitability of current investment, future changes in tax rates should, to the extent that they are anticipated, show an effect on current investment decisions. It may be difficult to forecast future tax rate changes over a long horizon. Reasonable predictions might be made one year ahead, however, since most tax changes work their way through Congress and state legislatures in the year before they take effect.

Quantitively, government spending exerts a statistically significant but fairly small deterrent effect on capital formation. Specifically, a perma-

TABLE 2.4. Capital formation, 1929–1975

Year	Effective marginal tax rate on capital (percentage)	Total government purchases of goods and services per person of working age (billions of 1972 dollars)	Investment in structures per person of working age (billions of 1972 dollars)	Investment in equipment per person of working age (billions of 1972 dollars)
1929	29.45	566.9	285.5	227.3
1930	27.76	607.9	237.2	177.2
1931	28.59	622.0	149.4	114.4
1932	33.12	585.5	85.2	65.2
1933	41.08	562.9	64.4	72.3
1934	41.00	632.7	68.9	92.2
1935	41.44	639.3	75.7	123.2
1936	46.20	742.7	101.6	168.9
1937	44.43	707.1	130.6	192.2
1938	41.36	760.9	101.8	131.6
1939	42.55	782.4	105.5	148.4
1940	45.12	791.7	119.7	191.0
1941	55.81	1143.7	141.9	220.6
1942	59.96	2188.3	78.9	128.4
1943	61.99	3116.2	48.9	114.0
1944	59.96	3434.2	63.2	151.7
1945	62.89	3007.6	94.4	218.5
1946	61.71	1049.9	212.0	261.6
1947	59.21	842.1	193.2	352.9
1948	52.90	929.0	203.3	361.2
1949	49.92	1051.1	194.5	308.1

Year				
1950	62.03	1058.9	207.0	334.9
1951	64.05	1428.3	221.7	347.6
1952	60.23	1705.6	220.3	336.8
1953	59.92	1806.8	239.1	359.2
1954	54.93	1635.7	248.2	335.8
1955	55.38	1583.2	265.4	376.6
1956	56.52	1586.6	292.5	386.2
1957	55.23	1654.7	290.4	391.7
1958	54.00	1738.8	271.1	333.8
1959	54.29	1739.3	273.1	367.8
1960	54.89	1738.2	289.5	374.0
1961	54.55	1813.3	290.6	360.1
1962	51.45	1894.0	302.1	393.3
1963	51.69	1917.6	298.9	414.4
1964	49.80	1947.6	319.9	458.3
1965	48.91	1975.1	373.2	527.7
1966	48.39	2124.9	393.8	589.4
1967	49.25	2263.2	374.6	568.8
1968	53.60	2325.7	376.9	593.1
1969	53.76	2267.2	388.6	620.9
1970	51.55	2173.9	371.9	583.9
1971	51.15	2131.6	356.4	566.7
1972	51.41	2127.7	357.3	624.6
1973	52.51	2088.9	376.4	707.3
1974	53.43	2098.0	346.0	717.3
1975	49.31	2102.7	297.1	612.6

Source: Historical Statistics of the United States, Colonial Times to 1970. U.S. Department of Commerce, Bureau of the Census, Government Printing Office, Washington, D.C., 1975. *National Income and Product Accounts.* U.S. Department of Commerce, Bureau of Economic Analysis. Government Printing Office, Washington, D.C.

TABLE 2.5. Statistical equations

Real gross private domestic investment in nonresidential structures per person of working age:

$$INVS(t) = 2.59 + (-0.0610 + 0.0254\ L)\Delta GXP(t)$$
$$(.51)\quad\ (-6.04)\quad\ (.249)$$

$$-206\Delta MTRK(t+1) + (1 + 0.486L)\Sigma(t)$$
$$(-2.08)\qquad\qquad\quad (3.10)$$

Real gross private domestic investment in producers' durable equipment per person of working age:

$$INVE(t) = 13.9 - 0.0248\Delta GXP(t) - 3.98\Delta MTRK(t+1)$$
$$(3.22)\qquad (-1.6)\qquad (-2.37)$$
$$+ (1 - 0.263L^2)\Sigma(t)$$
$$\quad (-1.66)$$

Independent variables: *GXP*, government (federal, state, and local) purchases of goods and services per person of working age; *MTRK*, effective marginal tax rate on income from capital; $\Sigma(t)$, random error term; *L*, lag operator defined such that $Li_x(t) = x(t-j)$ for any variable x; Δ, difference operator, defined such that $\Delta = 1 - L$; t statistic in parenthesis.

Source: compiled by the author.

nent one-dollar increase in annual government spending is associated with permanent declines of about 3.5 cents in annual investment in nonresidential structures and about 2.5 cents in annual investment in producers' durable equipment. Alternatively stated, a $10 billion increase in government spending (holding capital income tax rates constant) reduces investment in plant and equipment by about $600 million. These effects are substantially smaller than most standard discussions of crowding out would seem to suggest, constituting less than 0.5 percent of annual fixed business investment in recent years.

In contrast to the rather small effects of government spending, taxation of income from capital exerts a strong deterrent effect on capital formation. One percentage point in the effective tax rate on income from capital results in a decrease in annual investment in nonresidential structures of about two dollars per person of working age. Furthermore, it reduces annual investment in producers' durable equipment by about four dollars per person of working age. These effects are measured in 1972 dollars. Combining the two effects and converting them into an aggregate figure (using the more recent 1977 population and prices) indicates that one percentage-point increase in the tax rate reduces plant and equipment by about $1.2 billion (see Appendix B).

One further bit of evidence on the effect of tax rates on investment can be obtained by examining the ratio of investment in equipment to investment in structures. This ratio exhibits wide variation during the depression and World War II and has been much more stable since then (Figure 2.5). There is, nevertheless, a striking pattern in its movement during this seemingly stable postwar period. The ratio declined fairly steadily from 1947 to 1961, with only four of 14 positive year-to-year changes. In 1962, Congress enacted an investment tax credit that has been in effect almost continuously since then. This credit applied to investment in equipment but not to investment in structures. It seems more than coincidental that beginning in 1962, the ratio of investment in equipment to investment in structures reversed its downward drift and increased fairly steadily until the end of the sample period in 1975. During this period only three of the 14 year-to-year changes were negative. Alternatively stated, from the end of World War II until the enactment of the investment tax credit, per capita investment in structures grew at a compound annual rate of 2.7 percent, while per capita investment grew at a rate of 0.1 percent. After the enactment of the credit, however, investment in structures grew at an annual rate of only 1.2 percent while investment in equipment grew at 4.9 percent. Thus the average change in the ratio of investment in equipment to investment in structures was 0.0588 from

FIGURE 2.5. The ratio of investment in equipment to investment in structures

PERCENTAGE

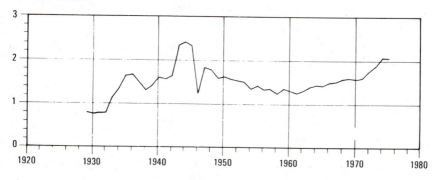

Time series plots of ratio of *INVE* to *INVS* (levels above, first differences below). The ratio of real gross private domestic investment in producers' durable equipment per person of working age to real gross private domestic investment in nonresidential structures per person of working age.
   Source: National Income and Product Accounts. U.S. Department of Commerce, Bureau of Economic Analysis, Government Printing Office, Washington, D.C.

1962 onward, compared with -0.0420 during the earlier period. By the usual statistical standards, these two numbers are quite significantly different.

It thus seems that the investment tax credit did have a noticeable effect on the composition of investment. This effect was undoubtedly contributed to during recent years by a substantial increase in the rate of inflation. Since capital must be depreciated for tax purposes, at historical rather than replacement cost, inflation tends to increase the effective tax rate on income from capital. This effect is more pronounced for long-lived assets than for short-lived ones, and thus alters the relative attractiveness of the two types of investment.

CONCLUSION

The evidence reported here supports the contention that taxation of income from capital exerts an important effect on investment behavior. In the early 1960s, effective tax rates on income from capital were reduced. As the postwar baby-boom generation moved into the labor force, these tax cuts aided the economy in producing the new plant and equipment which would have been necessary to maintain previous growth rates of productivity and real wages. The stimulus was not sufficient, however, to prevent some fall in these growth rates. Since the late 1960s, tax rates have returned to their previous levels, and the growth rates of net investment, labor productivity, and real wages have slowed considerably. Increased taxation of the income from capital thus seems to have reduced not only the after-tax returns to capital, but these to labor as well.

APPENDIX

Simulation

1. Use 1977 investment as a base.

2. One percent decrease in tax rate causes 0.67 percent increase in investment.

3. The long-run effect is 0.67 percent increase in capital stock. Assume Cobb–Douglas aggregate production function with labor share of 75 percent.

4. Then if labor supply is inelastic, this gives a 0.17 percent long-run increase in GNP and a 0.6 percent reduction in revenues (assuming that the ratio of average to marginal rates is fixed).

5. If K/L is constant, this gives a 0.67 percent increase in the long-run GNP, and a 0.14 percent reduction in revenues.

NOTES

1. Differences in the behavior of gross and net saving have been noted in Boskin (1978).

2. This rather cautious working is used to satisfy those who might argue that a true Keynesian must, by definition, believe that bonds are net wealth, since bond illusion is one of the central elements of the standard Keynesian model.

3. For a more formal treatment of these issues, see Joines (1979).

4. Alternative calculations that attributed business and professional income to income from capital did not yield materially different results.

5. These tax rates on income from labor are not reported here, but may be found in Joines (1981).

6. These weights sum to less than unity, since some income from capital escapes the federal personal income tax. Data on the federal personal income tax are taken from the *Statistics of Income* series published by the Internal Revenue Service. Other data on income and tax receipts are from the *National Income and Product Accounts*. U.S. Department of Commerce, Bureau of Economic Analysis.

7. For the sake of brevity, this description of the tax rate calculations has been greatly simplified. A more thorough description is contained in Joines (1979).

8. This is because the government cannot set tax rates, total spending, and the deficit independently of one another. For example, if the government fixes tax rates and spending, some value of national income will result. This will, in turn, imply some value for total government revenues and thus for the deficit.

9. This variable, rather than total government spending, was chosen since some items of total spending (notably, transfer payments to persons) may themselves be endogenous.

10. The three real investment series used here were obtained from the *National Income and Product Accounts of the United States 1929-74 (NIPA)*, U.S. Department of Commerce, Bureau of Economic Analysis. Government Printing Office, Washington, D.C., 1977. Table 1.2, lines 8, 9 and 10. These figures are based on the revised deflator for structures described in the August 1974 issue of the *Survey of Current Business*. The government purchases variable was obtained from line 21 of the same table. The *NIPA* contains finally revised data only for the years 1929-1972. Revised *NIPA* for 1973 were obtained from the July 1977 issue the *Survey of Current Business*. Revised *NIPA* data for 1974 and 1975 were obtained from the July 1978 issue of the *Survey of Current Business*. Each series is identified by the same table and line numbers in all these publications.

REFERENCES

Barro, Robert J. 1974. "Are Government Bonds Net Wealth?" *Journal of Political Economy,* no. 82 (November/December): 1095–1117.

Boskin, Michael J. 1978. "Taxation, Savings, and the Rate of Interest." *Journal of Political Economy,* no. 86, part 2 (April): 53–527.

Joines, Douglas H. 1981. "Estimates of Effective Marginal Tax Rates on Factor Incomes." *Journal of Business*, no. 54 (April): 191–226.

———. 1979. "Government Fiscal Policy and Private Capital Formation." Ph.D. dissertation, University of Chicago.

3

The Resolution of the Tax Debate
Paul D. Evans and Douglas H. Joines

SUMMARY

The debate over the appropriate size and shape of the tax cut now (1981) working its way through Congress can be resolved. Arguments that more stimulus is needed for business and saving to spur capital investment and hence increase productivity as opposed to reductions in personal income tax rates, ignore the evidence. Since the mid-1960s, the effective marginal tax rate on capital has remained essentially flat, while the effective marginal tax rate on labor has risen nearly 5 percent. Moreover, such arguments fail to recognize that income from capital is taxed at the personal level as well as the corporate level. It is this component of the overall tax rate on capital that has climbed in the past 15 years. Broad-based reductions in personal income tax rates would lower tax rates on both labor and capital. They would be more effective in stimulating economic growth and revenue feedback than targeted tax cuts for business, or other specialized saving incentives.

Concerns that the across-the-board reductions in personal income tax rates will heighten inflation by spurring consumption, and increase pressures in financial markets by expanding the deficit, also can be laid to rest. The question of how much of the increase in income from the tax cut people will save is misleading; it presumes incorrectly that the saving rate remains constant. A reduction in tax rates will increase the rate of return to saving, and thereby the saving rate. An increase in the saving rate, along with the rise in national income engendered by the tax cut, will lead to an increase in aggregate saving, not a reduction. An empirical analysis indicates that the Kennedy tax cuts did in fact lead to a decline in aggregate consumption relative to where it would have been in the absence of the tax cut, while saving increased more than it would have had tax rates not been cut.

Finally, a proportional tax rate cut would be more stimulative to economic activity than one directed at lower income brackets. Improved opportunities created by such growth can be far more important to the standard of living of middle- and low-income individuals than a slight decrease in their tax bill. The marriage penalty and tax rates above 50 percent on unearned income most likely are in the prohibitive range of the Laffer Curve. Immediate reductions in both tax rates should be made. Individuals in the lowest tax brackets also face very high implicit marginal tax rates due to the losses in welfare benefits associated with increases in income. Reductions in these effective rates, however, require a change in the administration of welfare programs as much as a reduction in tax rates.

July 14, 1981

During the final debates over the "compromise" package of tax cuts, a strong effort is sure to be made to shift the tax cuts toward business and away from individuals. Business tax cuts, they argue, such as investment tax credits and accelerated depreciation, as well as special incentives for saving, are needed to spur capital investment. Investment per se increases productivity and slows inflation. Across-the-board tax cuts, such as the president has proposed, will simply spur consumption and thereby tend to accelerate inflation.

These arguments, however, are flawed. They fail to take into consideration two facets of today's tax system. First, since the mid-1960s, the interaction of inflation with the progressive nature of the personal income tax code has led to a shift in the tax burden to labor from capital. This shift has occurred primarily because individuals were pushed into higher tax brackets for any given level of inflation-adjusted income. Increases in Social Security tax rates and in the Social Security wage base has also contributed to an overall increase in the effective marginal tax rate on labor. Income from capital has, in part, been sheltered by the introduction of individual retirement accounts, Keogh plans, and other shelters for income from savings. Effective corporate tax rates also have been reduced. Second, arguments for tax relief, specifically for business, ignore the fact that income from capital is taxed at the personal level as well as the corporate level. Since the mid-1960s, the proportion of the overall tax rate on capital collected through the personal income tax has grown relative to the amount collected directly by taxes on business.

Across-the-board reductions in personal income tax rates have proven to be a powerful stimulus to saving and investment. Broad-based reductions in personal income tax rates, by lowering tax rates on both labor and capital, will be effective in stimulating economic growth and saving. President Kennedy saw the role tax rates could play in shaping the economy, as he said in his 1963 Economic Report of the President:

> ...the tax program will go to the heart of the main deterrent to investment today, namely, inadequate markets. Once the sovereign incentive of high and rising sales is restored, and the businessman is convinced that today's new plant and equipment will find profitable use tomorrow, the effects of the directly stimulative measures will be doubled and redoubled. Thus—and it is no contradiction—the most important single thing we can do to stimulate investment in today's economy is to raise consumption by major reduction of individual income tax rates....

Although couched in the economic language of the mid-1960s, Kennedy's statement shows he clearly perceived the importance of personal income tax rates to increasing capital investment.

THE PATH OF EFFECTIVE TAX RATES

The observed shift in tax rates toward labor from capital is based on calculations of effective marginal tax rates on income from labor and capital (Joines 1981). All taxes in the economy can be viewed as income taxes, that is, all taxes arise from either the generation or the spending of income (Canto, Joines, and Laffer 1983). This proposition is fairly obvious when applied to personal and corporate income taxes, sales taxes, and payroll taxes, but it is equally applicable to other taxes. For example, property taxes are taxes on the flow of services produced by real property.

Effective, economy-wide income tax rates can be calculated by accounting for all taxes paid in the economy and relating them to some comprehensive measure of income as the tax base. The income measure used is Net National Product (NNP). Construction of effective marginal tax rates on income from labor and income from capital requires that NNP be separated into one component attributable to capital and another attributable to labor. Income attributable to capital was taken to include corporate profits, rental income of persons, and net interest.[1]

Calculation of Tax Rates

The economy-wide marginal tax rate on the income from capital is the fraction of an incremental dollar of income earned by the economy's capital stock that is taken by the government through taxation.[2] It depends on the marginal tax rates of the individuals receiving the incremental dollar and on distribution of that dollar among those individuals. The economy-wide marginal tax rate is equal to a weighted average of the individual marginal tax rates, with the shares in existing capital income as weights.

The effective marginal tax rate on capital income includes three components:

1. The federal personal income tax *(PCK)*. This component is a weighted average of the effective marginal federal personal income tax rates in the various income brackets, where the weight for each bracket is the fraction of total income from capital accruing to individuals in that bracket.[3]
2. A flat-rate tax applicable only to income from capital *(TK)*. It is the ratio of property and corporate profits tax receipts to income from capital.
3. A flat-rate tax applicable to income from other sources *(T)*. It is the ratio of all remaining taxes (except the Social Security tax, which is assumed to be labor-specific) to Net National Product. The most important of these remaining taxes, as judged by revenue raised, is sales tax.

The effective marginal tax rate on income from capital *(MTRK)* is taken to be the sum of these three components[4]: $MTRK = PCK + TK + T$. Similar calculations yield a measure of the effective marginal tax rate on labor income. This tax rate also has three components:

1. The federal personal income tax *(PCL)*. This component is a weighted average of the effective marginal federal personal income tax rates in the various income brackets, each weighted by the fraction of total labor income accruing to individuals in that bracket.
2. The contribution of the Social Security tax to the overall tax rate on labor income *(SSC)*.[5]
3. The tax rate *T* described above.

The effective marginal tax rate on labor income *(MTRL)* is the sum of these three components: $MTRL = PCL + SSC + T$. These calculations were performed for each year from 1929 to 1975, inclusive.[6]

Changes in the Tax Rates

Throughout the entire 1929–1975 period, the effective marginal tax rate on capital was greater than that on labor (Fig. 3.1). Both tax rates increased markedly during the 1930s as a result of the government's unsuccessful and ill-fated attempts to balance the budget through tax increases

FIGURE 3.1. Marginal tax rates on income from capital and income from labor

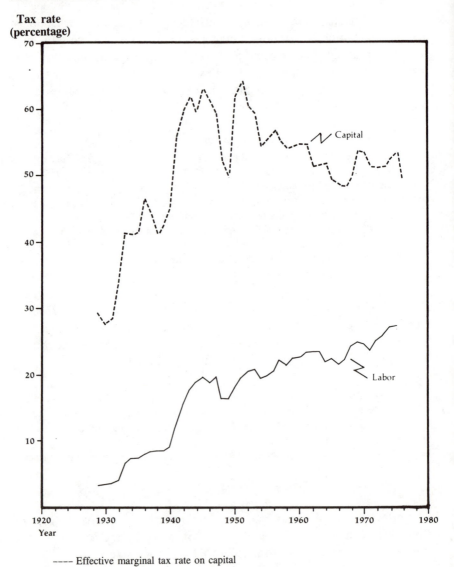

Tax rate (percentage)

---- Effective marginal tax rate on capital
——Effective marginal tax rate on labor

(Laffer 1981). The tax rate on capital, for example, rose to 46 percent in 1936 from 19 percent in 1929, while the tax on labor climbed to 8 percent from 3½ percent. During the early 1940s, when tax rates were increased to finance World War II, the tax on capital advanced to 62 percent, while the tax on labor in 1945 hit 19 percent. Beginning in the late 1940s, both series declined, reflecting the tax cuts of 1946 and 1948, but remained above their prewar levels. Both tax rates increased again in the early 1950s as the government sought more revenue to finance the Korean War. In 1951, the tax rate on capital peaked at 64 percent. The largest tax changes of recent years, the Kennedy tax cuts of the early 1960s and the Vietnam surcharge of the late 1960s, show up clearly in both series.

Since the end of the Korean conflict, the tax rate on capital has declined. The tax rate on labor, however, has continued its generally upward trend. From its trough in 1954 until 1975, the tax rate on labor increased by roughly 8 percent to a high of 27 percent. Most of this rise can be attributed to increases in the Social Security tax and personal income tax, which rose 3.5 percentage points and 3.0 percentage points, respectively (Fig. 3.2).

During the 1951–1975 period, the overall tax rate on income from capital decreased nearly 15 percent to 49 percent, as property and corporate profits taxes declined 15.6 percent (Fig. 3.3). During this period, the corporate profits tax rate was reduced to 48 percent from 52 percent, depreciation rules were liberalized, the investment tax credit was enacted, and the real value of corporate interest deductions was increased, as nominal interest rates rose because of higher anticipated inflation.[7] However, between 1951 and 1975, the "other tax" component of the tax on capital *(T)* increased 1.5 percent.

Since 1975, the last year for which all data are available, further bracket creep, dramatic increases in the Social Security tax, and reductions in the maximum tax rates on capital gains and corporate profits assure that the increase in the labor income tax rate relative to that on income from capital has continued. All these factors suggest that a reduction in labor income tax rates would provide a greater stimulus to output and employment now than at the time of the Kennedy tax cuts (Laffer 1980).

Broad-based reductions in federal personal income tax rates are the most effective way of reducing the tax rate on labor income. Such broad-based personal rate cuts would reduce the effective tax rate on capital income as well. It is the personal income tax component of overall tax on capital income that has increased steadily since the mid-1960s, offsetting the tax rate reductions on corporate income and special investment and saving incentives, such as accelerated depreciation, investment tax credits, and Keogh plans and individual retirement accounts.

FIGURE 3.2.   Components of the marginal tax rate on income from labor

Tax rate
(percentage)

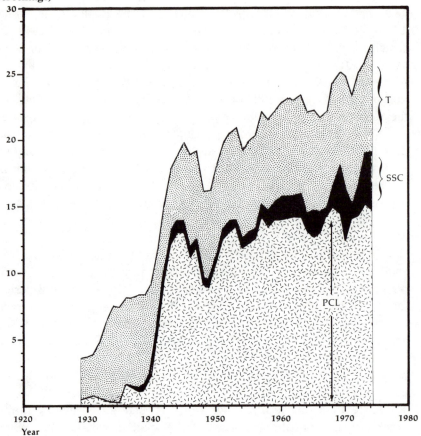

PERSONAL TAX CUTS AND SAVING

Reducing marginal personal income tax rates has three effects on saving. First, at any given level of national income, less tax revenue is raised at the reduced income tax rates. This is the effect emphasized by demand-side analyses. As a result, unless government spending is also reduced, government saving (the surplus) falls by the amount of the tax cut while

**FIGURE 3.3. Components of the marginal tax rate
on income from capital**

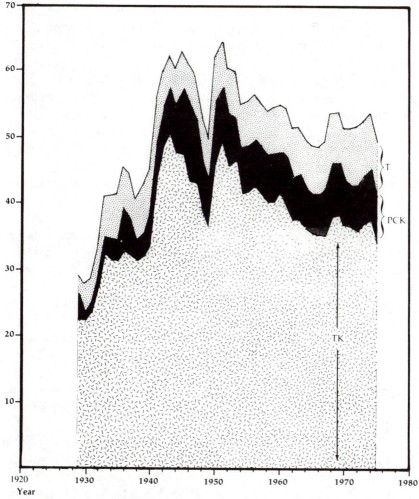

Tax rate
(percentage)

☐ The property and corporate profits tax component of the tax on capital (TK).
■ The federal personal income tax component of the tax on capital (PCK).
☒ The other taxes component of the tax on capital (T).

personal disposable (after-tax) income rises by the amount of the tax cut.
If the tax cut is permanent, households can consume more from any given
national income than they could before the tax cut. Historically, U.S.

households have consumed more than 90 percent of any permanent increase in disposable income. Focusing solely on this effect, it follows that at any given national income, private saving generally rises by less than 10 percent of a tax cut. Within this framework, reducing personal tax rates lowers total national saving (private plus government saving), because private saving would increase by less than the government's borrowing requirement, thus leaving fewer resources available to finance capital formation.

The second effect, generally ignored by demand-side analyses, is the incentive effect of the tax cut. A reduction in marginal personal income tax rates raises the real after-tax return to saving, thereby raising the saving rate—the amount that households wish to save from any given disposable income. The saving rate tends to rise because a higher real after-tax return to saving makes all of the things for which households save—their retirements, rainy days, their children's educations—more attractive.[8]

The third effect is the growth or macroeconomic effect. Both the Keynesian and supply-side approaches predict that a reduction in tax rates will stimulate the economy. However, the source of the stimulus is quite different. In the framework, the reduction in tax revenues and consequent increase in income to higher aggregate consumption, which through the multiplier effect leads to an increase in overall economic activity. In a supply-side framework, the stimulus originates in the reduction of tax rates, which yields higher rates of return to market activity and hence increased output. A higher national income implies a higher disposable income, higher tax receipts, and less spending on unemployment compensation and other income-sensitive transfer payments. The higher disposable income results in more private saving, while the higher tax receipts and lower transfer payments increase government saving (produce a smaller deficit).[9]

The following examples illustrate the first two effects and point up the differences in the predictions of demand-side and supply-side analyses. Suppose that the "compromise" 5–10–10 tax cut is enacted and goes into effect on October 1, 1981. Tax rates applicable to personal income earned in calendar year 1982 will be 10 percent below their current levels. If the tax cut did not affect national income or how the public shelters its income from taxation, federal personal income tax receipts in 1982 would be 10 percent, or $34 billion, lower than the projected $340 billion (Kadlec 1981). Holding all else constant, government saving also would be $34 billion less than projected. In the last few years, households have consumed about 93 cents of each additional dollar of disposable income. Private saving therefore would rise by only 7 percent of the $34 billion increase in disposable income, or by $2 billion. In this static analysis, national saving falls by $32 billion.[10]

Incentive (Supply-Side) Effect

An income tax cut raises the real after-tax return to saving. Consider, for example, a person who earns a nominal before-tax return of 15 percent on investments and who wishes to save for retirement 30 years hence. Suppose this person has sufficient income to be in the 70 percent bracket. The nominal after-tax return would be 4.5 percent $[15 \times (1 - 0.7)]$. If inflation is expected to average 10 percent a year for the next 30 years, the real after-tax return to saving is 5.5 percent $(4.5 - 10)$. A reduction in this household's marginal tax rate to 50 percent would raise its real after-tax return to -2.5 percent. Without the tax cut, assets lose 5.5 percent of their value each year, so that sacrificing one unit of current consumption yields $(1 - 0.055)$, or 0.18 units of retirement consumption 30 years from now. But with the tax cut, the same sacrifice would yield $(1 - 0.025)$, or 0.47 units of retirement consumption. The tradeoff between current consumption and retirement consumption improves nearly threefold, roughly the same magnitude as an increase in the price of crude oil from $10 to $30 per barrel. Just as an oil price increase of this magnitude caused dramatic changes in the pattern of energy consumption (Bollman, Canto, and Melich 1982), a similar change in the price of current consumption in terms of foregone future consumption could be expected to result in a substantial reduction in current consumption and a corresponding increase in saving. The effect just described would be smaller, though still appreciable, for all but those in the lowest tax brackets. The allegation that an across-the-board tax cut would do nothing for saving is simply not credible.

Since the 5–10–10 or some similar tax cut would so markedly improve the tradeoff between current consumption and the future goals that saving accomplishes, the fraction of disposable income saved by households should rise appreciably. An increase in the saving rate applies to all disposable income and not just to the incremental income resulting from the tax cut. For example, if households were to raise the fraction saved from 7 percent to 9 percent, and if disposable income was $2,400 billion in 1982, the higher real after-tax return to saving resulting from the "compromise" tax bill would increase saving by $48 billion (2,400 × [0.09 – 0.07]), an amount larger than the projected $32 billion decline in national saving.

Private saving can increase by more than the amount of the reduction in tax revenues. The increase in private saving is not limited to the reduction in the government's tax receipts because people can save a larger fraction of existing disposable income. The question of what fraction of the tax cut people would save is misleading. It biases the analysis against broad-based tax cuts in favor of the many specialized saving incentives that have been proposed. It is unlikely, however, that these specialized incentives would do more to stimulate saving than would an across-the-board tax cut. Simple reductions in income tax rates can provide a powerful stimulus to saving.

The Kennedy Tax Cuts and Saving

The above analysis implies that across-the-board tax rate reductions are capable of increasing national saving. The Keynesian view ignores the incentive and growth effects of such a tax cut. It assumes that the saving rate does not respond appreciably to changes in the real after-tax return to saving and that national income does not respond appreciably to changes in marginal personal income tax rates. The Reagan administration has rejected this Keynesian view, taking instead the supply-side view that the saving rate will increase in response to higher after-tax returns and that national income also will increase. The combination of a higher saving rate applied against larger income will increase aggregate private saving more than enough to offset the loss in public saving.

An analysis of the 1964–1965 Kennedy tax cut, which did not include specialized saving incentives but did include a reduction of the corporation income tax rate, suggests that national saving would rise in the aftermath of the administration's proposed tax cut. In the four years prior to the Kennedy tax cut, the fraction of disposable income (defined, unconventionally, to include retained corporate profits) devoted to private net saving was 8.37 percent. At the national incomes prevailing between 1964 and 1967, the Kennedy tax cut produced a static loss in federal tax revenues, and hence government saving, of $59.5 billion. If households had continued to save 8.37 percent of their disposable incomes between 1964 and 1967, the additional disposable income from the tax cut would have raised private saving by $5.0 billion (0.0837 × 59.5). Therefore, at the levels of national income prevailing between 1964 and 1967, national saving would have fallen by $54.5 billion (59.5 – 5.0).

Actually, households increased their saving rate to 11.1 percent of disposable income. Given the $2,061.2 billion in disposable income between 1964 and 1967, the increase in the saving rate alone increased aggregate saving by $56.5 billion. Even in the extreme case where the Kennedy tax cut is assumed to have had no effect on economic growth and hence no revenue feedback effects, the incentive effect or increase in the saving rate offset the static estimate of the increase in the deficit. The increase in the real after-tax return to saving raised national saving by a larger amount ($56.5 billion) than the increase in disposable income reduced it ($54.5 billion).

The results are even more positive when the growth or macroeconomic effects of the tax cut are included in the analysis. Various estimates suggest that national income was between 2.5 and 7.0 percent higher than it would have been without the Kennedy tax cut (Evans, 1981; Canto, Joines, and Webb 1983). Using the more conservative 2.5 percent figure, the growth in national income attributable to the tax cut increased aggregate saving another $5.7 billion ($0.025 \times 2,061.2 \times 0.111$) during the 1964–1967 period. Furthermore, tax revenues were perhaps 2.5 percent, or $20 billion, higher, and transfer payments were no doubt a few billion dollars less.[11] All told, the Kennedy tax cut probably raised saving by $30 billion over the four years from 1964 to 1967.

The Kennedy Tax Cuts and Consumption

The effect of the Kennedy tax cut on consumption can be estimated by fitting a simple Keynesian consumption function that relates consumption to disposable income. Pre-1964 data were used. As expected, "predicted" consumption tracks actual consumption quite closely during the period (1954–1963) over which the consumption function was estimated (Fig. 3.4). After the tax cut took effect, however, actual consumption (solid line) fell considerably below that predicted by the Keynesian consumption function, given the actual level of disposable income (dotted line). Individuals consumed a smaller fraction (saved a larger fraction) of their disposable income than would have been predicted using the Keynesian consumption function (i.e., the saving rate increased).

In addition to increasing the saving rate, the Kennedy tax cuts also increased disposable income. A Keynesian consumption function would have predicted lower consumption without the tax cut (and the resulting increase in income) than with the cut (dashed line). Actual consumption was lower than either of these levels predicted by the Keynesian consump-

FIGURE 3.4. Actual and predicted consumption before and after the Kennedy tax cuts

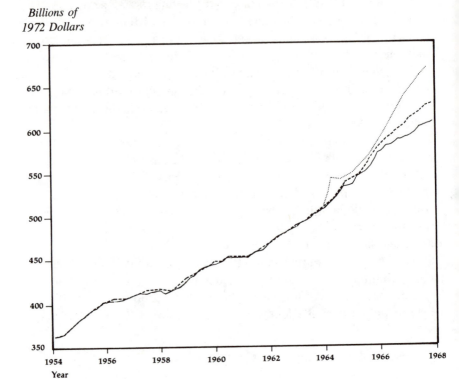

Billions of 1972 Dollars

———Actual consumption
———— Estimated consumption without a tax cut
. . . . Estimated consumption with the tax cut

tion function (which differ only in that the pre-tax cut saving rate was applied to two different levels of disposable income). Thus, not only was actual consumption lower than Keynesian analysis would have predicted (given the tax cut), it was even lower than what the Keynesian analysis would have predicted had there been no tax cut. These results provide substantial evidence that the Kennedy tax cuts reduced consumption while increasing private saving far above what it otherwise would have been.

Since the administration's proposed personal income tax cut essentially replicates the Kennedy tax cut, it is reasonable to predict that, in the event of its passage, aggregate saving would rise and consumption would decline relative to what they otherwise would have been. This kind of prediction may be somewhat risky. The U.S. economy has changed a great deal since 1964. It may respond differently to an across-the-board tax cut now from how it did to the Kennedy tax cut. For example, many critics have argued that the tax cut would not increase saving because the inflation rate is now about ten times higher than it was in 1964.

A high inflation rate does depress the real after-tax return to saving and hence the level of saving. But a reduction in personal income tax rates affects the tradeoff between current and future consumption in roughly the same way when inflation is high as when it is low. For this reason, the change in saving that the administration's tax cut would produce is likely to be in the same direction and comparable in magnitude to that produced by the Kennedy tax cut.

Despite all the changes in the economy since 1964, the best available evidence supports the administration's position that its proposed personal income tax rate cuts would raise saving more than enough to finance any short-run increase in the deficit. The critics who assert that there is no evidence to support this claim just have not looked.

A POSTSCRIPT

Shortly after the analysis above was written, Congress enacted the Reagan tax cut. Since then, three years have passed, during which households have faced considerably reduced marginal tax rates on saving. It is important to ask at this time how accurate the analysis was. In particular, did the private saving rate rise appreciably?

At first blush, the answer would seem to be no. According to the figures below, the private saving rate fell in 1981, the year Congress enacted the tax cut.

Private saving rate

Year	Percentage
1977–80	9.00
1981	8.62
1982	7.48
1983	8.05
1984I	9.95
1984II	9.86

It also fell in the following years. Although some recovery occurred in 1983, only the first two quarters of 1984 provide any evidence that the Reagan tax cut raised the private saving rate.

This answer, however, does not take into account three important influences on the saving rate. First, the Federal Reserve adopted a monetary policy in October 1979 that greatly increased the volatility of interest rates. As a result the risk of holding long-term assets rose, and households reduced their saving rates.[12] Second, a deep recession occurred during the period. Since households save in part to enable themselves to maintain consumption during bad times, it is not surprising that the saving rate fell during the deepest postwar recession.[13] Third, the Reagan tax cut was phased in. Households therefore knew that their future disposable incomes would be high relative to their current disposable incomes. For this reason, they saved less than they would have if current disposable income had been an accurate indicator of long-run, or permanent, disposable income.

Adjusting the private saving rate for the effects of changes in interest-rate volatility and of transitory disposable income yields the private saving rates below[14]:

Adjusted private saving rate

Years	Percentage
1977–80	9.00
1981	10.05
1982	10.61
1983	10.96
1984I	11.64
1984II	11.56

The adjusted private saving rate rose more than a percentage point in 1981, the year that Congress enacted the Reagan tax cut. Apparently, the anticipation of lower marginal tax rates on saving sufficed to produce this result.[15] The next two years then saw further appreciable increases in the adjusted private saving rate. Finally, it soared in the first two quarters of 1984. All told, it has risen more than 2.5 percentage points since the 1977–1980 period. This increase is nearly the same size as that following the Kennedy tax cut. The authors therefore think that experience has confirmed what they predicted in 1981.

APPENDIX A: THE TAXATION OF INCOME FROM CAPITAL

Many researchers have observed a decline in the effective corporate tax rate since the late 1950s.[16] While conceding that the rate of taxation of income from corporate capital has declined at the corporate level, Martin Feldstein and Lawrence Summers (1979) estimate that the overall tax rate on such income has risen 3.5 percentage points since the 1960s (Table 3.1). Noting that the income from corporate capital is taxed twice, they argue that taxation of corporate-source income at the personal level has increased more than enough to offset the decline in taxation at the corporate level. This claim is based on the behavior of a weighted average of legislated tax rates rather than on effective rates calculated from data on actual personal income tax collections. Our tax series on income from capital was computed using actual personal income tax collections and does not show the dramatic increase of 95 percent claimed by Feldstein and Summers (Table 3.1). Both the Feldstein–Summers corporate series and our property and corporate tax on capital series *(TK)* suggest that by the mid-1970s, the effective corporate tax rate had returned roughly to the level prevailing before the Kennedy tax cuts.[17] However, the Feldstein–Summers noncorporate series more than tripled from the mid-1950s to the mid-1970s, while our noncorporate series *(PCK)* showed only a slight increase. This discrepancy can be explained by the explicit tax avoidance of economic agents that Feldstein and Summers do not account for.

In a recent paper, Merton Miller and Myron Scholes (1978) have argued that the U.S. tax system is evolving toward a system in which income from capital is untaxed at the personal level. They argue that the current tax code includes devices such as the interest deduction, IRA and Keogh accounts, life insurance and annuity plans, and favorable capital gains treatment, which allow taxpayers effectively to shelter much of their

TABLE 3.1. Tax rates on income from capital for selected years

Year	TK	Feldstein and Summers corporate	PCK	Feldstein and Summers noncorporate	MTRK	Feldstein and Summers total
1951	49.6	—	8.0	—	64.1	—
1954	41.4	51.6	6.9	11.9	54.9	63.5
1959	40.3	49.2	6.9	13.6	54.3	62.8
1963	37.8	42.4	6.5	14.7	51.7	57.1
1964	36.4	39.1	5.9	14.2	49.8	53.3
1969	38.1	44.5	7.8	21.5	54.8	66.0
1974	37.6	56.0	7.6	38.7	53.4	94.9
1977	—	42.5	—	23.8	—	66.3

Source: Journal of Business 54 (2), 1981. University of Chicago Press.

capital income from taxation. Furthermore, the number of such devices is increasing over time. By examining only legislated tax rates rather than actual tax payments, Feldstein and Summers are unable to capture these effects, and instead rule them out by assumption. The personal tax component of our overall tax rate on income from capital, however, is based on actual tax payments and suggests that the legitimate avoidance of personal taxes may be quite important. It also suggests, however, that these effects have not actually reduced the rate of taxation of income from capital at the personal level, but have at best managed to offset such inflation-induced distortions in the tax system as bracket creep, the taxation of nominal rather than real interest payments, and the taxation of nominal rather than real capital gains. Regardless of which set of tax rate estimates is more accurate, they both indicate that to the extent that taxation of income from capital has increased since the early 1960s, it has done so largely because of an increase in the effective rate of taxation at the personal level rather than at the corporate level.

APPENDIX B

The regression equation (for 1948–1983)

$$PSR = \begin{array}{l} -0.0211 - 0.00749 \ \ln IRV\,(-1) \\ (0.0365) \qquad (0.00229) \end{array}$$

$$\begin{array}{l} -0.00045 \ \ln IRV\,(-2) - 0.00644 \ \ln IRV\,(-3) \\ (0.00294) \qquad (0.00227) \end{array}$$

$$\begin{array}{l} +0.165 \ YTR - 0.000442 \ T + 0.0173 \ \ln G\,(-1) + E \\ (0.060) \qquad (0.000142) \qquad (0.0048) \end{array}$$

$$R(2) - .723; \ S.E. = .0072; \ D.W. = 1.53$$

relates the private saving rate PSR to three lagged values of IRV, a measure of interest-rate volatility; YTR, the ratio of a measure of transitory income to private disposable income; T, a measure of the marginal personal income tax rate; $G(-1)$, real federal purchases lagged one year; and to E, the residual. Equation (3.1) was fitted using ordinary least squares; the figures in parentheses below the coefficient are standard errors.

The series YTR is defined by the equation $YTR = RY + 1.053$ $UMG + ERA/YD$, where RY is the residual from the output equation in Chapter 2; UMG is unanticipated money growth as defined there; 1.053

is the coefficient on *UMG* in the output equation; *ERA* is the transitory income generated by the phasing in of the tax cut under the Economic Recovery Act; and *YD* is private disposable income. In calculating *ERA*, it was assumed that households did not expect a tax cut before 1981III (1983 third quarter) and that thereafter they expected the Reagan tax cut to be fully implemented. It was also assumed that the tax cut changed neither income-earning nor tax-avoidance behavior. It was further assumed that households expected that their income tax payments would grow at a constant rate except for when tax rates fell. Finally, it was assumed that households discounted future taxes more rapidly than they expected income tax payments to grow. These assumptions imply that *ERA* was − $31.9 billion in 1981, − $41.8 billion in 1982, − $13.7 billion in 1983, and zero thereafter.

The adjusted private savings rates for 1977–1983 were calculated by replacing in Equation 3.1 the post-1976 *IRVs* with the value of *IRV* for 1976 and the post-1976 *YTRs* with zero. The adjusted private saving rates for 1984I and 1984II were calculated similarly. The only modification in the procedure was that, because the values of *YTR* and *E* for 1984 are not yet known, 0.165 *YTR* + *E* was assumed to be whatever made *SR* average first its 1984I value and then its 1984II value over all of 1984.

NOTES

1. Alternative calculations, which attributed business and professional income and farm income to capital, did not yield materially different results.

2. It is marginal rather than average tax rates that affect economic inventives. To the extent data availability allows, the tax rates reported here capture effective marginal tax rates.

3. These weights sum to less than unity, since some income from capital escapes the federal personal income tax. Data on the federal personal income tax are taken from the *Statistics of Income* series (Internal Revenue Service, Washington, D.C.). Other data on income and tax receipts are from the *National Income and Product Accounts* (U.S. Department of Commerce, Bureau of Economic Analysis). Since the IRS publishes the *Statistics of Income* with a lag of several years, the estimated tax rate series ends in 1975.

4. Changes in *MTRK* have been shown to be negatively related to changes in investment in plant and equipment. See Joines (1980b).

5. Note that since the Social Security tax is specific to the employment of labor, no component analogous to SSC appeared in *MTRK*. Similarly, since property and corporate profits taxes are assumed to be specific to capital, no component analogous to *TK* appears in *MTRL*.

6. For the sake of brevity, this description of the tax rate calculations has been greatly simplified. For a more thorough description see Joines (1980b).

7. The last effect occurs because higher anticipated inflation results in a higher inflation premium in corporate bond rates. Part of the "interest" payments thus really constitute principal repayment but are nevertheless deductible from corporate income. If the inflation is unanticipated and is not reflected in a premium in the corporate bond rate, then it merely results in a transfer of wealth from

creditors (bondholders) to debtors (owners of corporations).

8. The discussion of the second effect assumes that the tax cut is permanent and therefore that current and future disposable incomes rise in the same proportion. It also makes the standard assumption that household preferences between current and future consumption are homothetic. Given these assumptions, the saving rate is unambiguously an increasing function of the after-tax real return to saving. In other words, the income and wealth effects of the tax cut influence saving only by changing disposable income, while the substitution effect of the tax cut influences saving only by changing the saving rate.

9. The saving rate might increase for yet another reason. Suppose that the reduction in tax rates lowers tax receipts, that the government does not reduce spending, and that the resulting deficit is financed by issuing more government debt. This debt issue obligates the government to make future principal and interest payments whose present value is equal to the amount of the debt issue. In addition, private disposable income increases by the amount of the debt issue (i.e., by the amount of the reduction in current tax payments). Some economists argue that rational individuals will realize that this increase in the present value of their future tax payments (implied by the government's future principal and interest payments) is exactly equal to the increase in their current disposable income. Therefore, individuals will save all of the tax payments. If so, private saving will increase by the full amount of the debt issue (the reduction in government saving), leaving unaffected total national saving and the resources available for capital formation. Since the entire debt-induced increase in disposable is saved, the economy's average saving rate increases. This effect is thus empirically indistinguishable from an increase in the saving rate brought about by the incentive effect, as discussed in the text. See Barro (1976), Kormendi (1983), and Evans (1985).

10. This calculation assumes that Congress acts independently on spending, that is, spending doesn't change because of tax changes. If the tax cut actually results in deeper spending cuts, projected government saving would fall by less than $34 billion.

11. For empirical evidence on the revenue effects of the Kennedy tax cuts, see Joines (1980a).

12. See Chapter 11 of Joines (1980a), which shows that the increased interest-rate volatility also contributed greatly to the severity of the 1980–1982 recessions.

13. Formally, this paragraph states that households save a larger fraction of transitory disposable income than of permanent disposable income. The analysis of the tax cut in previous sections assumed that transitory income was zero both before and after the tax cut passed. In other words, it analyzed the private saving rate from permanent disposable income rather than from total disposable income.

14. See Appendix B for a detailed description of the adjustments.

15. The prevailing view of commentators in the major print media prior to July 1981 was that the Congress would never enact the Reagan tax cut and that the administration would therefore have to settle for much smaller reductions in tax rates. Opinion changed rapidly during July 1981, culminating in the enactment of the tax cut at the end of that month. The figure 10.05 should therefore be an average of a lower figure for the first half of 1981 and a higher figure for the last half of the year. Indeed, this is the case. During the first half, the private saving rate averaged 1.16 percentage points less than in the second half.

16. In addition to Joines, see Fama (1979), Feldstein and Summers (1979), Holland and Myers (1980), and Gonedes (1981). These measures differ slightly because of differences in the firms considered (i.e., manufacturing, nonfinancial, or all corporations) and differences in the definition of corporate income. However, all of these studies use real, inflation-adjusted income measures so that the reported tax rates capture the inflationary distortions that tend to increase effective rates of taxation of real corporate income.

17. The series reported in Fama (1979) and Gonedes (1981), however, indicate that the effective corporate rate was even lower in the mid-1970s than immediately after the Kennedy tax cuts.

REFERENCES

Barr, N. and Hall, R. 1981. "The Probability of Dependence on Public Assistance," *Economica.*

Barro, Robert J. 1976. "Are Government Bonds Net Wealth?" *Journal of Political Economy* 84 (April): 343–349.

Bollman, Gerald W., Victor A. Canto, and Kevin A. Melich. 1982. "Oil Decontrol: The Power of Incentives." *Oil and Gas Journal* 80, no. 2 (January): 92–101.

Canto, Victor A., Douglas H. Joines, and Arthur B. Laffer. 1983. "Tax Rates, Factor Employment, Market Production, and Welfare." In *Foundation of Supply-Side Economics,* edited by Victor A. Canto, Douglas H. Joines, and Arthur B. Laffer. New York: Academic Press.

Canto, Victor A., Douglas H. Joines, and Robert I. Webb. 1983. "The Revenue Effects of the Kennedy Tax Cuts." In *Foundation of Supply-Side Economics.* New York: Academic Press.

Evans, Paul D. 1985. "Do Large Deficits Produce High Interest Rates?" *American Economic Review* (March).

———. 1981. "Kemp-Roth and Saving." Federal Reserve Bank of San Francisco, *Weekly Letter* (May 6).

Fama, Eugene F. 1979. "Stock Returns, Real Activity, Inflation and Money." Working paper no. WP24, Center for Research in Security Prices, Graduate School of Business, University of Chicago (June).

Feldstein, Martin, and Lawrence Summers. 1979. "Inflation and the Taxation of Capital Income in the Corporate Sector." *National Tax Journal* 32 (December): 445–470.

Garfinkel, I., and Orr, L. 1974. "Welfare Policy and Employment Rate of AFDC Mothers," *National Tax Journal,* 27, (June): 275–84.

Gonedes, Nicholas J. 1981. "Evidence on the 'Tax Effects' of Inflation under Historical Cost Accounting Methods." *Journal of Business* 54 (April): 227–270.

Hausman, J. 1981. "Labor Supply," in H. Aaron and J. Pechman, eds., *How Taxes Affect Economic Behavior,* Brookings Institution, Washington, D.C., pp. 27–72.

Holland, Daniel M., and Stewart C. Myers, 1980. "Profitability and Capital Costs for Manufacturing Corporations and All Nonfinancial Corporations." *American Economic Review* 70 (May): 320–325.

Joines, Douglas H. 1981. "Estimates of Effective Marginal Tax Rates on Factor Incomes." *Journal of Business* 54:191–226.

———. 1980a. "The Kennedy Tax Cuts: An Application of the Ellipse." A. B. Laffer Associates (Sept. 25).

——— 1980b. "Government Spending, Tax Rates, and Private Investment in Plant and Equipment." A.B. Laffer Associates Rolling Hills Estates, CA. (May).

Kadlec, Charles W. 1981. "The Outlook at Mid-Year." A.B. Laffer Associates Rolling Hills Estates, CA. (June).

Kormendi, Roger C. 1983. "Government Debt, Government Spending, and Private Sector Behavior." *American Economic Review* 73 (December): 994–1010.

Laffer, Arthur B. 1981. "Reagan's Economic Proposals Within a Supply-Side Framework." A.B. Laffer Associates Rolling Hills Estates, CA. (March).

——. 1980. "The Ellipse." A.B. Laffer Associates Rolling Hills Estates, CA. (July). See Chapter 1, this book.

Levy, F. 1979. "The Labor Supply of Female Household Heads, or AFDC Work Incentives Don't Work Too Well," *Journal of Human Resources*, 14, (Winter): 76–96.

Masters, S. and Garfinkel, I. 1977. *Estimating the Labor Supply Effects of Income Maintenance Alternatives*, Academic Press, New York.

Miller, Merton H., and Myron S. Scholes. 1978. "Dividends and Taxes." *Journal of Financial Economics* 6 (December): 333–364.

Moffit, R., "An Economic Model of Welfare Stigma," unpublished paper, New Brunswick, N.J., Rutgers University.

Saks, D. 1975. "Public Assistance for Mothers in an Urban Labor Market," Princeton, N.J., Industrial Relations Section, Princeton University.

Williams, R. 1975. *Public Assistance and Work Effort*, Princeton, N.J., Industrial Relations Section, Princeton University.

4

The "Crowding Out" Myth

Victor A. Canto and Donald Rapp

SUMMARY

The evidence presented in this paper calls into question the popularly held view that increasing deficits lead to higher interest rates and "crowd out" private investment.

Two empirical tests are performed using data covering the period 1929–1980 to ascertain if there is any evidence that financing deficits causes crowding out and results in higher interest rates. The results show:

- Budget deficits cannot be shown to cause changes in interest rates
- Changes in interest rates cannot be shown to cause changes in real budget deficits
- Changes in interest rates do, however, partially explain changes in nominal budget deficits

Using the past as a guide, the recent increase in the budget does not necessarily reflect materially higher interest rates. On the other hand, errant monetary policy that causes higher interest rates would increase the size of the deficit. To balance the budget, the focus should be on devising a monetary policy capable of reducing interest rates quickly.

The investment implications of these findings include: (1) resources now employed to forecast changes in the budget deficit as a way to determine if changes in interest rates can be better employed elsewhere; and (2) "crowding out" should rank low on a scale of one to ten when analyzing the effect of government budget deficits on better investment alternatives.

December 30, 1981

Do government deficits cause high interest rates and thus "crowd out" private investment?

Herbert Stein, former chairman of the Council of Economic Advisors, says yes. Speaking of Ronald Reagan's decision to allow the deficit to expand, he said, "His [Ronald Reagan's] decision is ironic, but not necessarily wrong. Despite much conventional Republican rhetoric, running deficits is not a sin. Deficits do have a cost, however. They raise interest rates, crowd out private investment and slow economic growth." (Stein 1981)

George Perry, senior fellow at the Brooking Institution, agrees. He wrote, "Deficits are hardly the end of the world, and they are often not only necessary, but desirable. The large deficit that will emerge with the present recession is a case in point. But the large deficits projected for future years, even with revenues estimated on the assumption of prosperity and high employment, are a different matter. They conflict with the tight monetarist policies that the administration and the Federal Reserve are both set on pursuing.

"That monetary policy would itself result in an era of high interest rates, relieved only when the economy falls into recession. The deficits projected for fiscal policy will push those rates higher. High interest rates in turn will retard investment in plant and equipment and housing, and deepen the problems of state and local governments which must borrow for important public investments and which are already badly squeezed by reductions in federal grants." (Perry 1981)

Taking the opposite position, William Niskanen, member of the President's Council of Economic Advisors, has declared that "the simple relationship between deficit and inflation is as close to being empty as can be perceived," that there was "no necessary relationship" between deficits and money supply growth, and that the crowding-out theory was "not consistent with the evidence." (Cowan 1981)

Once created, financing the deficit requires the government to sell bonds to the public or the central bank. When the central bank purchases government securities, it monetizes the debt, or "prints money." Given the Fed's determination to keep tight control of the money supply, it is assumed that the government will cover deficits primarily by borrowing. This assumption maximizes the potential for the deficit to raise interest rates and "crowd out" private investment.

THE THEORY

Financing the government deficit by issuing debt can be viewed as an impingement on the capital markets. Ignoring the foreign market, private saving must exceed private investment by the amount of the government's debt issue. Government securities compete with private securities for investors' dollars, and only those funds that are left after the sale of government bonds are available to finance the private sector's accumulation of physical capital. Thus, deficit financing may displace private investment, or alternatively stated, deficits may "crowd out" private investment.

A government debt issue is seen to increase private saving, reduce (i.e., crowd out) private investment, or induce a combination of both of these responses. Which of these alternatives actually occurs has been the subject of considerable debate during the last few years. The most widely held view, at least until recently, has been the "crowding out" proposition, one version of which is depicted in Figure 4.1. Before the government debt issue, private saving and private investment are equal to $I_0 = S_0$. The interest rate is r_0. If the government floats a bond issue of size D then bond prices are bid down and the interest rate is forced up to r_1. The increase in interest rates stimulates saving, which moves up the savings schedule to S_1, and stifles investment, which falls along the investment schedule to I_1. The reduction in investment from I_0 to I_1 denotes the amount by which the deficit "crowds out" the private sector.

If, on the other hand, saving is completely insensitive to the interest rate, as in the most naive Keynesian models, the saving curve is vertical rather than positively sloped. In this most extreme version of the crowding-out hypothesis, saving remains constant while investment falls by the full amount of the debt issue. That is, the private sector is "crowded out" by the full amount of the deficit as opposed to the case shown in Figure 4.1, where the public sector "crowding out" of the private sector is only a fraction of the deficit. Under any version of the crowding-out proposition, however, private investment must decrease, while saving may increase or remain constant.

The crowding-out hypothesis has been called into question by those who argue that government bonds are not perceived as net wealth by the private sector and thus do not reduce private capital formation. The argument is essentially as follows (see Barro 1974). Suppose the government reduces the current tax bill of every taxpayer by one dollar and

FIGURE 4.1. How incremental government debt may crowd out private investment

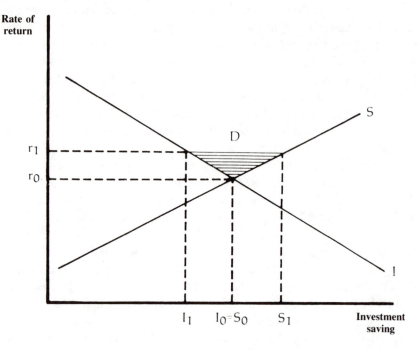

finances this tax reduction by issuing bonds that bear the market rate of interest. A lump-sum tax equal to one dollar plus interest will be levied on each taxpayer next year in order to retire the current bond issue. Will taxpayers feel wealthier today as a result of this transaction? Will they therefore increase their consumption and lower private capital accumulation?

If people behave rationally, the argument goes, the answers to these questions must be no. People will save the dollar they currently receive so as to be able to meet their increased future tax liabilities. Current saving will increase by the amount of the government debt issue. Private capital accumulation will not be crowded out (Figure 4.2). Now a debt issue of size D causes the saving schedule to shift rightward by an equal distance D to S'. Saving increases to S_1. But in this case investment remains unchanged at I_0, and the interest rate remains constant at r_0. According to this view, crowding out will occur only if the private sector does not take full account of the future tax liabilities implied by government bonds and thus regards these bonds as a substitute for claims on physical capital.

FIGURE 4.2. How incremental government debt may not crowd out private investment

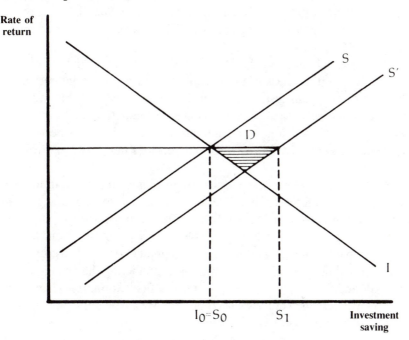

THE TESTS

Two tests are performed to determine what effect, if any, changes in the budget deficit have on interest rates. To the extent bigger deficits are associated with an increase in interest rates, crowding out is evident as well. One test is based on the work of Granger (1969). The other uses procedures developed by Sims (1972). The date utilized spans the 1929–1980 period.[1] The interest rates used were one-year yields on Treasury bills and Treasury notes.[2] Annual changes in the nominal budget deficit, the budget deficit deflated by the consumer price index, and one-year interest rates were employed in the tests.

THE EVIDENCE

The empirical results indicate that increasing budget deficits do not increase interest rates (see the Appendix at the end of this chapter for a technical explanation). There was no evidence that information on changes in past budget deficits combined with changes in past interest rates was a better predictor of changes in current interest rates than information on past interest rates alone (Granger test). These results are reported in the lower half of Table 4.1.

Moreover, changes in the "current year's" budget deficit had no statistically significant association with changes in future interest rates taken as a group (Sims test). These results are reported in Table 4.2. The lack of a causal relationship from changes in the deficit and changes in interest rates implies that government bonds are not viewed as net wealth. As a result, government borrowing, per se, does not crowd out private investment.

Next, these two tests were used to determine if increases in interest rates can explain increases in the deficit. The results for the Granger test are reported in the upper half of Table 4.3, and those for the Sims test are reported in the lower half of Table 4.4. The results indicate that changes in past values of interest rates in conjunction with past changes in the nominal budget deficit are superior at predicting the change in the current deficit than are past changes in the deficit. Similarly, changes in future budget deficits were associated in a statistically significant way with changes in current interest rates. However, no relationship was evident when the deficit was corrected for changes in the price level. These results indicate that an increase in interest rates contributes to a larger budget deficit through higher interest expense in the years following the rise in interest rates and vice versa.

Conclusions and Investment Implications

These statistical tests indicate that the recent increase in the budget deficit will not materially affect the path of interest rates. Conversely, errant monetary policy that contributes to higher interest rates is increasing the size of the deficit. Thus, current rhetoric in Washington is 180 degrees out of phase with the empirical results. Fed chairman Paul Volcker is imploring the administration to assist him in the difficult task of lowering interest rates and slowing inflation by balancing the budget. Instead, the administration should be asking Volcker to assist its efforts to reduce the deficit by devising a monetary policy capable of reducing interest rates quickly. Unless monetary policy is changed from the targeting of aggregates to a price rule, interest rates will continue to be volatile. But changes in the budget deficit will have no material impact on their overall movements.

TABLE 4.1. Regression results—Granger test*

Y	X	a^1	a^2	a^3	a^4	b^1	b^2	b^3	b^4	Constant	R
Nom Fed. Deficits	Interest Rates	-.0044 (.028)	-.0937 (.619)	-.3001 (2.04)	0.9584 (.374)	-73956 (.438)	-396830 (2.47)	-123560 (.640)	236610 (1.32)	-889.44 (.433)	.341
Interest Rates	Nom. Fed Deficits	-.0801 (.468)	-.0976 (.600)	-.0076 (.039)	.1415 (.777)	.0000 (.313)	.0000 (.140)	.0000 (1.553)	.0000 (.413)	.0026 (1.249)	.115
Real Fed. Deficits	Interest Rates	.2712 (1.732)	-.1631 (1.03)	-.1965 (1.25)	0.1458 (.942)	-791.7 (.373)	-2168.4 (1.09)	516.23 (.220)	3843.5 (1.77)	-2.738 (.105)	.301
Interest Rates	Real Fed. Deficits	-.0556 (.327)	-.1361 (.851)	-.0667 (.355)	.1053 (.593)	.0000 (.075)	.0000 (.490)	.0000 (1.06)	.0000 (.781)	.0028 (1.33)	.083
Nom. Total Deficits	Interest Rates	-.0791 (.493)	-.1505 (.995)	-.3207 (2.22)	-.0428 (.280)	-46874 (.274)	-384460 (2.35)	-53635 (.269)	272590 (1.48)	-181.92 (.088)	.375
Interest Rates	Nom. Total Deficits	-.0804 (.470)	-.1004 (.611)	.0009 (.005)	.1610 (.870)	.0000 (.698)	.0000 (.510)	.0000 (.961)	.0000 (.560)	.0028 (1.32)	.099
Real Total Deficits	Interest Rates	.2236 (1.432)	-.1700 (1.09)	-.1997 (1.31)	-.1378 (.902)	-681.83 (.321)	-2407.8 (1.21)	1090.3 (.459)	4088.5 (1.83)	.1585 (.006)	.304
Interest Rates	Real Total Deficits	-.0581 (.341)	-.1324 (.827)	-.0700 (.368)	.1138 (.633)	.0000 (.006)	.0000 (.506)	.0000 (.852)	.0000 (.699)	.0028 (1.33)	.074

*$\Delta Y_t = \Sigma a(i) \Delta Y(t\text{-}i) + \Sigma b(i) \Delta X(t\text{-}i) + e_t$

Source: compiled by the author.

TABLE 4.2. Regression results—Sims test

Y	X	a(-1)	a(-2)	a(-3)	a(-4)	a(0)	a(1)	a(2)	a(3)	a(4)	Constant	R
Nom. Fed. Deficits	Interest Rates	-11632 (.048)	-381770 (1.76)	-110750 (.510)	246260 (1.28)	94188 (.381)	22659 (.093)	-91640 (.429)	-202890 (1.03)	142160 (.790)	-613.73 (.234)	.2722
Real Fed. Deficits	Interest Rates	-1289.4 (.375)	-3597.0 (1.17)	-380.38 (.124)	369.98 (1.35)	-357.5 (.102)	-1154.9 (.335)	-1114.1 (.368)	-1314.4 (.470)	2062.6 (.808)	-55.937 (.015)	.1490
Nom. Total Deficits	Interest Rates	-35237 (.139)	-458460 (2.03)	-66045 (.292)	303150 (1.51)	72388 (.280)	90861 (.358)	-32434 (.146)	-152790 (.743)	178220 (.949)	-640.94 (.234)	.2796
Real Total Deficits	Interest Rates	-1460.5 (.427)	-4273.7 (1.40)	-104.96 (.034)	4127.6 (1.52)	-616.98 (.177)	-823.3 (.240)	-852.9 (.284)	-992.17 (.357)	2178.9 (.860)	.13137 (.004)	.1679
Interest Rates	Nom. Fed. Deficits	.0000 (.911)	.0000 (.950)	.0000 (.565)	.0000 (.848)	.0000 (1.03)	.0000 (.652)	.0000 (1.36)	.0000 (.477)	.0000 (2.13)	.0011 (.581)	.2932
Interest Rates	Real Fed. Deficits	.0000 (.781)	.0000 (.694)	.0000 (.454)	.0000 (1.04)	.0000 (1.27)	.0000 (.309)	.0000 (.629)	.0000 (.464)	.0000 (1.99)	.0008 (.459)	.2120
Interest Rates	Nom. Total Deficits	.0000 (.579)	.0000 (.586)	.0000 (.169)	.0000 (.510)	.0000 (.581)	.0000 (.489)	.0000 (1.58)	.0000 (.009)	.0000 (1.89)	.0008 (.474)	.2932
Interest Rates	Real Total Deficits	.0000 (.596)	.0000 (.513)	.0000 (.248)	.0000 (.916)	.0000 (1.06)	.0000 (.403)	.912 (.912)	.0000 (.099)	.0000 (1.92)	.0008 (.411)	.2118

$\Delta Y_t \ \Sigma a(i) \Delta X(t-i) + u(t)$

Source: compiled by the author.

82

TABLE 4.3. Regression results—Granger test (joint significance of independent variable)

Y	X	F(4,38)*
Nominal Federal Deficits	Interest Rates	2.38
Real Federal Deficits	Interest Rates	1.41
Nominal Total Deficits	Interest Rates	2.29
Real Total Deficits	Interest Rates	1.58
Interest Rates	Nominal Federal Deficits	0.69
Interest Rates	Real Federal Deficits	0.34
Interest Rates	Nominal Total Deficits	0.52
Interest Rates	Real Total Deficits	0.25

*Confidence value of the F statistic.
Confidence level: 99%, 3.87; 95%, 2.63.
Source: compiled by the author.

The central challenge facing the administration is how to prolong the current period of rapid economic growth while reducing interest rates. Slightly higher tax rates in 1985 will dampen the pace of economic expansion. Indexing for inflation will virtually eliminate bracket creep due to nominal gains in income. But real income gains due to productivity increases will still push individuals into higher tax brackets. In addition, the combined employer–employee Social Security tax rate rises 0.3 percentage points to 14 percent on January 1. Moreover, both fiscal and

TABLE 4.4. Regression results—Sims test (joint significance of future variable)

Y	X	F(4,33)*
Nominal Federal Deficits	Interest Rates	0.43
Real Federal Deficits	Interest Rates	0.20
Nominal Total Deficits	Interest Rates	0.36
Real Total Deficits	Interest Rates	0.19
Interest Rates	Nominal Federal Deficits	2.21
Interest Rates	Real Federal Deficits	1.48
Interest Rates	Nominal Total Deficits	2.42
Interest Rates	Real Total Deficits	1.66

*Critical value of the F statistic.
Confidence level: 99%, 3.96; 95%, 2.67.
Source: compiled by the author.

monetary policy debates will continue to be preoccupied by the never ending assertions that deficit reduction is the key to lower interest rates.

Such assertions, however, reverse cause and effect. The empirical evidence, such as it exists, suggests the proper description of the relationship is that higher interest rates lead to bigger deficits. The surge in deficits, both in the mid 1970s and again in 1982 and 1983, were preceded by sharp rises in interest rates. Symmetrically, deficit declines were preceded by a sharp drop in rates (Figure 4.3). The rise in the average Treasury-bill rate in 1984 presages an increase in the deficit during the coming year. Symmetrically, if the recent decline in rates holds, deficit projections will of necessity undergo downward revisions.

The key investment implications include:

FIGURE 4.3.   Interest rates and the deficit, 1970–1984

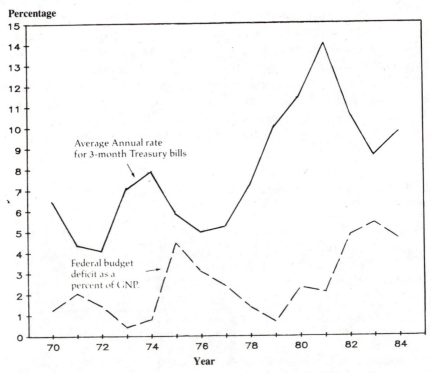

Source: Economic Report of the President. U.S. Government Printing Office, Washington, D.C. *Selected Interest Rates.* Statistical Release, U.S. Federal Reserve System, *Survey of Current Business.* U.S. Department of Commerce, Bureau of Economic Analysis.

- Forecasts of changes in the budget deficit, even if correct, will not be good indicators of change in interest rates. Resources employed in this way could be better utilized in other ways;
- Projected budget deficits should be given little if any consideration in the decision to buy or sell interest-sensitive securities;
- "Crowding out" should not be of material concern when analyzing the effect of government deficits on investments in plant and equipment;
- Projected budget deficits should be given little if any consideration when making investment decisions with respect to securities of companies intensive in the use or production of capital equipment.

APPENDIX

The coefficients in the Granger test are reported in Table 4.1. The Granger test requires the data to exhibit stationary characteristics, a requirement satisfied by differencing the series (only first difference was required). Diagnostic checks on the residuals of the estimated regressions failed to uncover any evidence of serial correlation.[3] The F statistic reported in Table 4.3 tests the joint significance of the lagged values of X, given lagged values of Y. The hypothesis that deficit spending does not cause changes in the level of interest rates cannot be rejected at the 1 percent level of significance. Similarly, the hypothesis that changes in the interest rates do not cause changes in the deficit cannot be rejected at the 5 percent level. Notice, however, that the result for the deficit in current dollars does suggest the possibility of a causal relationship going from interest rates to the deficit (in nominal, i.e., current dollars).

To further investigate the economic relationship between deficit and interest rates, the Sims procedures are implemented. The coefficient and estimated regression are contained in Table 4.3, which reports the F statistics corresponding to the Sims test. These tests investigate the joint significance of the future coefficients. If the sets of future coefficients are significantly different from zero, then Y causes X. The results reported in Table 4.3 replicate those of the Granger test (the bottom half of Table 4.3 corresponds to the upper half of Table 4.1). The hypothesis that interest rates are exogenous to the deficit cannot be rejected at the 1 percent significance level. In contrast, although interest rates do not cause changes in the real deficit, they do appear to cause changes in the nominal deficit.

NOTES

1. The data are available on request from the authors.
2. Where annual instruments were not available, yields on the next closest maturity were annualized.
3. In the case for the regressions reported in Tables 4.1 and 4.2, any of the autocorrelations of residuals up to 12 lags exceeded the two standard error limit. Furthermore, in each case the Box–Pierce statistic was well below its expected value under the null hypothesis of zero autocorrelations. These results are also available from the authors on request.

REFERENCES

Barro, Robert J. 1974. "Are Government Bonds Net Wealth?" *Journal of Political Economy* 82 (November/December): 1095–1117.

Cowan, Edward. 1981. "Reagan Aides Defend Deficits." *New York Times* (December).

Granger, C.W.J. 1969. "Investigating Causal Relations by Econometric Models and Cross-Spectral Methods." *Econometrica* 3 (July): 424–438.

Perry, George L. 1981. "Reaganomics' First Year A Failure." *Los Angeles Times* (November 15).

Sims, C.A. 1972. Money, Income and Causality." *American Economic Review* 62 (September); 540–552.

Stein, Herbert. 1981. "Reagan Should Take A Lesson From Stockman." *Los Angeles Times* (November 15).

5

Government Deficits and the Fiscal Policy Debate

Douglas H. Joines

SUMMARY

Projected deficits exceeding $200 billion have intensified the fiscal policy debate. However, the focus on fiscal year 1983 and 1984 deficits, per se, is misplaced. The debate fails to consider four issues essential to a complete analysis of the importance of deficits to the fiscal health of the government and to the economic recovery:

1. Deficits are important primarily because of their implication for future tax rates; empirical evidence indicates that large deficits do not lead to higher inflation or interest rates.
2. Although the projected deficits are large, in real terms and relative to the size of the economy, they are far from unprecedented. Current deficits do not constitute a threat to economic recovery.
3. Deficits are an important and essential part of a well-designed fiscal plan. Their role is to bring about an optimal distribution of the tax burden over time. Changing tax rates to balance budgets on a yearly or even cyclical basis is inferior to maintaining a stable tax rate over very long time periods.
4. Given the state of the economy, the deficits are an appropriate use of fiscal policy.

A recovery more nearly approximating the postwar norm would reduce the projected persistent or "structural deficits" to tolerable levels with no changes in tax rates or expenditure programs. The prudent course of action is to forego tax increases until the strength of the recovery is known. Raising tax rates would threaten the vitality of the recovery, the essential ingredient to reduction of the long-run deficit.

February 3, 1983

The latest prognostications over the size of future budget deficits has intensified the current debate over the effect of these deficits on interest rates, inflation, and thereby the recovery. Taken at face value, the 1982 record deficit of $111 billion ($128 billion, including federal agency borrowing debt) and this year's projected deficit of more than $200 billion appear to push fiscal policy into the uncharted regions of fiscal irresponsibility. Visages of persistent, "structural deficits" in excess of $100 billion call into question the very long-run credit-worthiness of the federal government.

As a result, the administration's 1984 budget calls for further reductions in various entitlement programs, personal income tax increases in the form of elimination of some deductions, and higher Social Security payroll taxes. A contingent, $146 billion, three-year tax increase may also begin in 1986.

The Democratic response eschews further domestic spending reductions in favor of reductions in defense expenditures. Tax increases, too, are deemed necessary. The 1983 tax cut would be canceled. Indexation of the personal income tax schedules for inflation, which would eliminate the automatic tax increase associated with bracket creep, would be abolished.

To date, however, the fiscal policy debate has failed to recognize four essential points:

1. Deficits matter because of their implication for future tax rates. Virtually all empirical evidence indicates that concerns over the deficit's impact on interest rates, inflation rates, and capital formation are exaggerated.
2. Although large, the deficits in real terms and relative to the size of the economy are far from unprecedented. Moreover, the federal debt held by the private sector relative to GNP at the end of fiscal year 1982 was 25 percent below its 1960 level.
3. Deficits are an important and essential part of a well-designed fiscal plan. Balancing the budget every year is not optimal. Nor are "structural deficits" as high as $65 billion in today's economy inconsistent with long-run fiscal stability. Assuming 5 percent inflation and 3 percent average real growth, such deficits would simply maintain the current ratio of debt to GNP.
4. Given the state of the economy, the deficits are an appropriate use of fiscal policy. The key to deficit reduction lies in economic recovery and lower interest rates.

THE EFFECTS OF GOVERNMENT DEFICITS

Deficits do matter; they can have a direct effect on equity values. Deficits are nothing more or less than an increase in government liabilities to the private sector. They represent an exchange of current resources for the promise of future repayment of principal plus a premium for deferred consumption. The total of these promises is government debt. The importance of debt lies in its implication for future tax liabilities and tax rates on the private sector.

Each additional dollar of debt commits the government to collect future tax revenues with a present value of $1.00, or to reduce future government spending by a like amount. Unless a current debt issue stimulates present and future output by an amount sufficiently large to increase revenues through a broader tax base or reduce expenditures through a decline in unemployment, an increase in the debt implies higher future tax rates as well. As a result, the current market value of future earning streams subject to the now higher expected tax rate will be lower, reducing the market value of equity securities. The size of deficits projected by the administration is important because of its implications for future tax rates.

In addition, the experiences of Mexico, Brazil, and other developing countries are vivid examples of how deficits can bring governments into default. Deficits can be too big. The larger the ratio of public debt to gross national product (GNP), the larger the fraction of GNP the government will have to tax away to meet debt service payments. As illustrated by the Laffer curve, however, there is a limit to the government's ability to generate tax revenue (Fig. 5.1). It is therefore possible that the ratio of public debt to GNP can grow so large that the government will

FIGURE 5.1.   How the debt service requirement can exceed the government's capacity to raise revenues

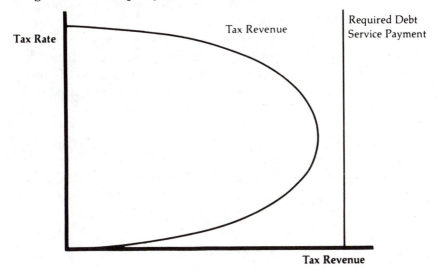

Tax Revenue

be unable to meet its debt service payments. Like private individuals and corporations, governments can default.

A government default can take the form of outright repudiation of its debt, or it can occur through more subtle means of debasement. The most obvious form of debasement is through monetization, whereby the government prints money to buy back part of its debt. This is merely exchange of a non–interest-bearing government liability for an interest-bearing one. The resulting increase in the money supply leads to inflation, which erodes the real value of the government's monetary liabilities. It can thus be viewed as a tax on the holders of money. If, as with the United States, the government's interest-bearing debt is denominated primarily in its own currency, unexpected inflation also erodes the real value of the public debt. To the extent that such debasement is anticipated, however, purchasers of government debt protect themselves by including an inflation premium in nominal interest rates.

Much of the concern over recent deficit projections arises from fears either of monetization or of equally severe consequences that will follow if the debt is not monetized. It is widely believed that if the government is forced to borrow large sums, the Federal Reserve will come under irresistible pressure to monetize at least a portion of the new debt, thus setting off another round of inflation. If the Fed does successfully resist this pressure, then the heavy government borrowing will supposedly keep real interest rates high, crowd out private investment in plant and equipment, and stifle economic recovery.

These fears are exaggerated. It is not mandatory that the Federal Reserve monetize a portion of new federal debt. Most empirical studies conclude that there has been little or no monetization of past deficits (Niskanen 1978; Barro 1977). Unless the projected deficits would raise the debt-to-GNP ratio to such unprecedented levels that debt service payments could not be made, there is little historical evidence to suggest that inflation need be a major problem. The fact that countries such as Japan and Germany have run larger deficits relative to GNP than now contemplated in the United States, and have had lower inflation and interest rates than has the United States, supports this view (Laffer 1980).

If monetary policy does not accommodate the Treasury's borrowing, then what of the consequences for interest rates, capital investment, and economic recovery? Once again, there is little empirical evidence that links deficits and interest rates (Canto and Rapp 1981). Instead, the research suggests that an increase in government borrowing elicits an offsetting increase in private saving. This increase in saving prevents both a rise in real interest rates and a crowding out of investment in plant and equipment. While there is some evidence of a statistically significant deterrent effect of deficits on capital expenditures, this effect is much smaller than most discussions of crowding out would lead one to believe. In particular, a statistical analysis of fiscal policy and capital formation in the United States between 1929 and 1975 indicates that, holding tax rates constant, a one-dollar increase in government purchases of goods and services is associated with a reduction of investment in goods and services of only six cents.[1]

THE ACTUAL SIZE OF THE DEFICIT

Given the sheer magnitude of the projected deficits, it is important that they be viewed in a historical context that corrects for the change in the price level, the growth in the economy, and the effect of inflation on the real value of goverment debt.

Correcting for Inflation

Merely expressing past deficits (inclusive of federal agency borrowing), in constant, end-of-1982 dollars, provides an important perspective on the severity of the current deficit. In nominal dollars, the 1982 cash deficit of $128 billion is by far the biggest, exceeding the previous record of $66.4 billion reached in fiscal year 1976. But when the 1976 deficit is expressed in constant, fourth-quarter 1982 dollars, it is equal to $118 billion (Fig. 5.2).

Moreover, there is historical precedent even for the $200 billion-plus deficit projected for the current year. In today's dollars, the largest deficit by far occurred in 1943, when it exceeded $320 billion. Deficits also exceeded $200 billion in 1944 and 1945 (Fig. 5.2).[2]

Correcting for the Economy's Growth

Taking into account the economy's growth yields even more striking results. In 1943, the federal government deficit totaled 29 percent of GNP, more than four times greater than that for the $225 billion deficit projected for FY 1983 (Fig. 5.3).

It is also evident that, while large, the current deficits are not out of the ordinary for previous contractions. In the aftermath of the 1974–1975

FIGURE 5.2.   The cash deficit* in constant and current dollars, 1929–1988

Billions of dollars

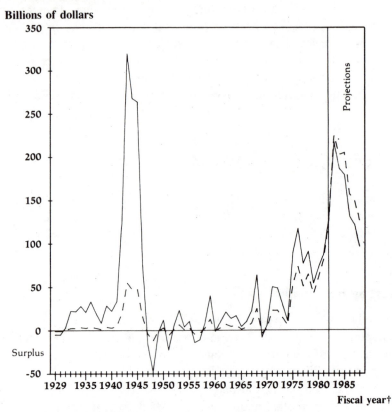

Fiscal year†

*inclusive of federal agency debt
†fiscal year ending June 30 through 1981, thereafter ending September 30
——— Deficit in constant, 4th quarter 1982 dollars
– – – – Deficit in current dollars.
Source: Budget of the United States Government, Fiscal Year 1984. Executive Office of the President, Office of Management and Budget, U.S. Government Printing Office, Washington, D.C., January 31, 1983.

recession, for example, the deficit hit 4.3 percent of GNP, compared to 3.3 percent during fiscal year 1982. And in the depression year 1934, the deficit totaled 5.6 percent of GNP, equal to $167 billion in today's economy, even though government then was much smaller relative to the economy (Fig. 5.3).[2]

Correcting for the "Inflation Premium"

Finally, the current realized and projected deficits are overstated by substantial proportions because of the treatment of interest expense. Net

FIGURE 5.3.   The cash deficit* as a percentage of GNP, 1930–1988

Percentage

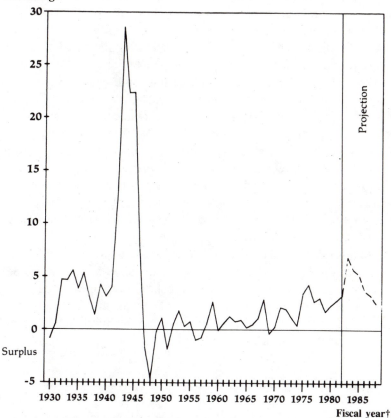

*inclusive of federal agency debt
†fiscal year ending June 30 through 1981, thereafter ending September 30
——— Deficit as a percentage of GNP
- - - - Administration projection
Source: Budget of the United States Government, Fiscal Year 1984. U.S. Government Printing Office, Washington, D.C., January 31, 1983.

interest expense totals $100 billion, or 12 percent of projected 1983 outlays, making servicing of the debt the third largest expenditure item in the budget. This expenditure item, however, includes compensation to lenders for the effects of inflation on the real value of their bonds. This portion of the interest expense is, in reality, a repayment of principal on the loan. For example, with 10 percent inflation, the inflation-adjusted value of a $100,000 debt falls to $90,000 after one year. If interest rates are, say 13 percent, then $10,000 of the $13,000 in interest payments is, when properly accounted for, a repayment of principal.

A similar adjustment should be made when computing the government's deficit. An amount equal to the inflation-induced decrease in real value of the government's outstanding debt should be subtracted from the actual cash deficit. U.S. government debt held by the public, excluding the debt held by the Federal Reserve at the end of fiscal year 1981, totaled $661.5 billion at the end of FY 1982. During the fiscal year, the GNP deflator advanced 5.6 percent. Thus, $37 billion ($661.5 billion x 5.6 percent) of last year's $128 billion deficit represented a repayment of principal to existing debt holders (Table 5.1).[3]

With this final adjustment, the apparent magnitude of the current and projected deficit appears much more manageable (Fig. 5.4). Last year's $128 billion deficit, for example, shrinks to $91 billion, which is just over 3 percent of GNP. Moreover, this calculation implies that, given the rate of inflation projected in the administration's latest budget, any cash deficit below $40 billion is, in inflation adjusted terms, a surplus. A real deficit of 2 percent of GNP, a quite reasonable level for recession years based on historical standards, would be approximately $100 billion.[4]

Thus, it is clear that the 1982 deficit and even the projected 1983 deficit are far from being so large as to drive the United States toward default, require monetization, or crowd out capital investment. The question as to why incur deficits at all, however, remains unanswered. Since deficit finance does not allow a society to avoid the burden of taxation, its use must be justified on other grounds.

THE ROLE OF GOVERNMENT DEBT

Deficits can be used to bring about an optimal distribution of the tax burden over time.

TABLE 5.1. "Repayment of principal" due to inflation

	1982 ($ billions)	1983 ($ billions)
Debt held by public at beginning of fiscal year[a]	794.4	929.3
Less debt held by Federal Reserve	132.9	141.0[b]
Net debt held by public	661.5	788.3
Inflation rate	5.6%	5.0%
Repayment of principal	37.0	39.4

[a]Includes federal agency debt.

[b]Assumes 6 percent growth in federal debt held by Federal Reserve banks.

Source: Budget of the United States, Fiscal Year 1984; U.S. Government Printing Office, Washington, D.C., January 31, 1983. *Federal Reserve Bulletin.* U.S. Government Printing Office, Washington, D.C.

FIGURE 5.4. The cash deficit* and real deficit*
(billions of constant dollars), 1930–1988

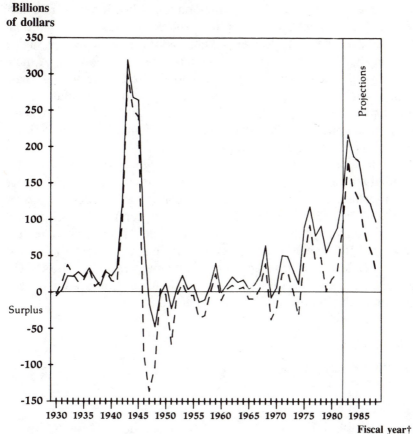

*inclusive of federal agency debt
†fiscal year ending June 30 through 1981, thereafter ending September 30

——— Deficit in constant 4th quarter 1982 dollars
---- Deficit adjusted for decrease in value of government debt due to inflation expressed in
     constant, 4th quarter 1982 dollars
Source: Budget of the United States Government, Fiscal Year 1984. U.S. Government Printing Of-
fice, Washington, D.C. January 31, 1983.

The Optimal Tax

When a tax is imposed, it drives a wedge between the prices paid by
the consumer and those received by the supplier. As a result, output falls.
The total loss in welfare to the economy is the value of the foregone output
to the consumer less the cost of its production. This loss is equal to the
shaded triangular area known as the "wedge."[5] Revenues raised by the

tax are represented by the area equal to the tax rate times the tax base (Figure 5.5).

Simple geometry leads to two important insights. If the tax rate doubles: (1) Government revenue less than doubles. A less than proportionate increase is due to the decline in output associated with the now higher tax rate. (2) The loss in economic welfare more than doubles. A more than proportionate increase is due to the simultaneous increase in the base of the triangle (the tax rate) and also the height (loss of output). These two simple facts have profound implications for the manner in which the government collects revenue over time. These implications can be illustrated by considering a very simple scenario.

Suppose that over a two-year period the government must raise a specified amount of revenue from a tax on apples (for simplicity, ignore present-value considerations and assume that the government requires a fixed dollar sum to be collected over the two years). Also assume that the demand and supply curves for apples do not change from one year to the next. If the government levies the same tax rate in year 1 as in year 2, it will collect equal revenue in each of the two years (Fig. 5.6A). The constant tax rate will result in the same welfare costs of taxation in each year, or double the welfare loss experienced in year 1.

FIGURE 5.5.   The burden of a tax

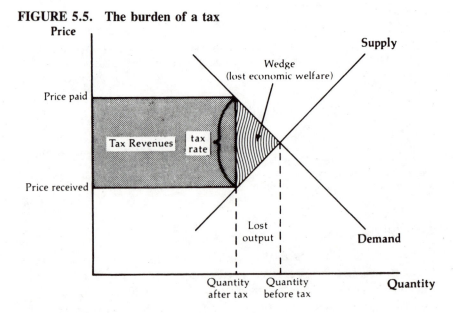

FIGURE 5.6.   How changing tax rates change the total tax burden

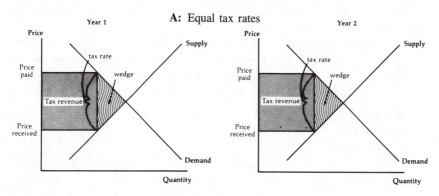

A: Equal tax rates

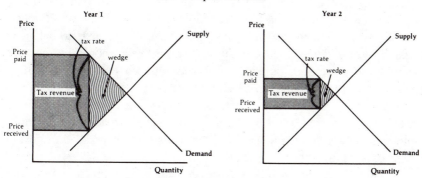

B: Unequal tax rates

Now suppose that instead of levying equal tax rates in each of the two years, the government decides to double the tax rate in year 1. Since doubling the tax rate less than doubles tax revenue, an additional tax will have to be imposed in year 2 in order to collect the same amount of total revenue (Fig. 5.6B). Such an approach yields the same revenue. But the loss in welfare is much greater. Doubling the tax rate in year 1 more than doubled the welfare loss in that year alone. Since revenues were not doubled, an additional loss of welfare also was incurred in year 2.

In order to minimize the welfare cost of collecting a given amount of revenue, tax rates would have to be constant over the two periods. Tax rates would not be higher or lower now than they need to be in the long run. Tax rates would be raised or lowered only if some unforeseen event arose that permanently required more or less revenue, respectively. Moreover, the now higher (or lower) tax rates would then be maintained indefinitely. Temporary tax increases or temporary tax cuts reduce total welfare.

This principle of tax policy also has implications for the role of the deficit. In our previous two-period example, suppose that the government planned to spend more in year 2 than in year 1. Since its optimal policy is to collect equal revenue in the two periods, this would imply a surplus in year 1 and a deficit in year 2. The appropriate deficit is whatever is required to reconcile the pattern of the government's expenditures with the pattern of its receipts.

As an alternative, imagine that the government plans to spend equal amounts in the two years but, because of a "recession" in year 1, output and revenues are lower than in year 2. Revenues are unequal in the two years even though tax rates are equal. With equal spending in the two years, this implies a deficit in year 1 and a surplus in year 2.

The point is that even if it is desirable to "balance" the government's budget over the business cycle, no attempt should be made to balance it year by year.[6] The deficit (or surplus) in any year should be whatever is required to smooth out the difference between the desired paths of government receipts and expenditures. If desired expenditures tended to increase rather than remain constant during a recession, the countercyclical swings in the deficit would be even sharper. In addition, the absolute magnitude of these swings would grow as the normal level of government expenditure became larger.

These results are much more general than the simple example used to illustrate them. It is possible to construct other examples in which the slopes as well as the locations of the demand and supply curves change over the business cycle. Such shifts could conceivably cause optimal tax rates to vary either procyclically or countercyclically, but there is little reason to believe that any government could in practice measure these shifts accurately enough to implement such variations in tax rates, or even to determine whether the variations should be procyclical or countercyclical. Any deviations from constant tax rates would be a distinctly hit-or-miss proposition, and there is no strong presumption in favor of anything other than constant tax rates over the cycle. The resulting countercyclical swings in the government deficit constitute a rational use of debt financing by the government.[7]

The Implications for Current Policy

The pattern of deficits resulting from application of this "rational theory of government debt" is very similar to that which would occur if the government always adopted a full-employment balanced budget. But its premise is quite different. According to the Keynesian theory of aggregate demand management, the degree of fiscal stimulus provided by government is measured by the size of the full-employment deficit, not the actual deficit. A balanced budget would be fiscally neutral. By contrast, the rationale for maintaining constant tax rates over time has nothing to do with providing fiscal stimulus to the economy. It is a policy for minimizing the unavoidable distortions of taxation.[8]

There are three direct implications of this analysis for the current policy debate:

1. The income tax cuts scheduled for 1983 should be advanced to January 1.[9] In fact, the cuts should have been designed to take effect in one stage rather than in three.
2. No temporary tax should be imposed, including the prepared income tax surcharge.
3. The projected near-term deficits, to the extent that they are a by-product of the recession, should not be of concern. The deficits require corrective action only to the extent that they are inconsistent with some relevant definition of budget balance over the long term. The appropriate definition of long-run balance is not merely the equality between receipts and expenditures on the unified budget. A budget balanced in inflation-adjusted terms will appear in deficit on a cash basis whenever inflation is positive.

THE APPROPRIATE LONG-RUN DEFICIT

The appropirate long-run average deficit should be judged by its effect on the real value of government debt. It is the deficit which, if it occurred year after year, would cause the real government debt to change in the desired manner. If the government on average ran a real deficit of zero, then the real stock of government debt would remain roughly constant. If, at the same time, population were growing, the real per capita government debt would eventually approach zero. If real GNP were growing, the ratio of government debt to GNP also would approach zero.

If a constant, real per capita public debt is desired, a real deficit equal to the population growth rate times the real stock of government debt would have to be incurred on average each year. With a long-run average population growth rate of 1.5 percent per year and an average inflation rate of 5 percent, a fiscal 1983 cash deficit in excess of $50 billion would be consistent with constant real per capita government debt.

In order to maintain a constant ratio of public debt to GNP, a cash deficit equal to the stock of public debt times the growth rate of nominal GNP is required on average every year. If real GNP grew an average of

3 percent per year, and inflation were 5 percent, this would require a fiscal 1983 cash deficit in excess of $65 billion. Lower cash deficits would result in effective repayment of part of the public debt, either in real per capita terms or relative to GNP.

A strategy to maintain a given ratio of public debt to GNP must also take into account the near certainty of military and economic emergencies that require sudden and large additions to the debt. This pattern has marked U.S. history from the inception of the country. Gross federal debt amounted to about $80 million in 1789 and had fallen to $65 million by 1860. During the Civil War, the federal debt rose sharply to $2.75 billion and then declined gradually to slightly over $1 billion at the beginning of World War I, which precipitated another sharp increase. The federal public debt stood at about $25 billion in 1919, declined to about $15 billion by 1931, and rose to somewhat over $40 billion by 1941. During World War II, the public debt increased sixfold to $240 billion, and today it stands in excess of $800 billion. The pattern seems fairly clear; until the post–World War II era, large increases in the public debt were the result of financing major wars. The primary exception to this rule was the substantial increase in the debt during the Great Depression of the 1930s.

Since dealing with an extreme national emergency can be viewed as an investment in the long-term well-being of the country, it is only appropriate that the cost be amortized over a correspondingly long period. For the government to pursue a pay-as-you-go policy would impose an enormous burden on individuals paying taxes at that time. Public debt allows part of this burden of taxation to be shared by future generations. It also allows tax rates to remain relatively constant over time.

If national emergencies requiring large debt issues are expected to recur periodically and the ratio of debt to GNP is to have some limit, then this ratio has to be reduced during "normal" times.[10] For example, imagine a strategy which assumes that an emergency will occur every 50 years which raises the debt-to-GNP ratio from its 1940 level to the level prevailing at the end of World War II and that fiscal policy is designed to reduce the debt-to-GNP ratio to its 1940 level over the remainder of the 50-year period. To implement this strategy with a 3 percent real growth rate, the government would have to run a real deficit equal to 0.70 percent of GNP on average. In actuality, the World War II debt was paid back at a much more rapid rate. By 1960, the debt-to-GNP ratio was slightly below its 1940 level. A strategy calling for beginning each emergency with the lower debt-to-GNP ratio that prevailed in 1929 implies an average real surplus of 0.34 percent of GNP.

If national emergencies occurred more frequently than every 50 years or if real GNP grew more slowly than 3 percent per year, then a smaller deficit or a larger surplus would be required to achieve the target debt-to-GNP ratio. The exact real deficit or surplus required depends on the real growth rate of GNP, the target debt-to-GNP ratio, and the time allowed for reaching the target. Table 5.2 contains the real surplus implied by various values of these parameters. Which of these figures is most relevant depends on one's beliefs as to the likely frequency and severity of national emergencies and the growth rate of real GNP. Our most reliable evidence suggests that the average long-run growth rate of real GNP is between 3.0 and 3.5 percent per year.[11] This still leaves a fairly wide range of values for the real deficit or surplus.

If the government consistently chooses a real deficit that is smaller than optimal, it will repay the debt (relative to GNP) at too fast a rate. Too much of the burden of the debt will be borne now and too little will be spread over time. Tax rates during this period will be above their optimal long-run level. The optimal real deficit will be consistent with a zero cash deficit only by accident. In times of sustained high inflation, an optimal real deficit (or surplus) will almost certainly correspond to a substantial average cash deficit.

During periods of stable prices, it might be optimal to run a cash surplus on average in order to achieve an adequate reduction in the real debt, although a cash (and real) deficit might still be optimal, even with zero inflation. In any given year, the optimal deficit will differ from its aver-

TABLE 5.2. Real surplus or deficit ($-$) as a percentage of GNP required to achieve target debt to GNP action

Years allowed to reach target	Annual percentage growth rate of real GNP						
	1.0	1.5	2.0	2.5	3.0	3.5	4.0
	Target: 1940 ratio of government debt to GNP						
50	0.618	0.268	−0.069	−0.392	−0.704	−1.004	−1.294
40	0.953	0.596	0.250	−0.086	−0.411	−0.726	−1.632
	Target: 1929 ratio of government debt to GNP						
50	1.304	1.036	0.786	0.554	0.339	0.139	−0.045
40	1.772	1.493	1.230	0.982	0.748	0.528	0.321

Source: compiled by the author.

age value if unemployment is above or below average. Naive pursuit of a balanced cash budget on a year-by-year basis, or even on average, will result in good fiscal policy only by accident.

CONCLUSION

The large deficits and slow output growth of recent years have increased the privately held stock of government debt as a ratio to GNP. If the administration's projections are correct, the debt will grow to about 30 or 31 percent of GNP in 1983. This is still considerably below the 41.3 percent recorded in 1960. The administration's projections imply that the debt-to-GNP ratio will grow at a decreasing rate until 1988, when the debt will total about 36 percent of GNP (Fig. 5.7). The pattern of steadily declining cash deficits over time implies that the debt-to-GNP ratio would itself begin to decline around the end of the decade. The deficits contained in the 1984 budget would thus not saddle the economy with a debt burden of unprecedented proportions. Nor are they a threat to the sustainability of the recovery. A debt-to-GNP ratio in 1960 significantly higher than those comtemplated in the administration's budget did not preclude rapid economic growth through most of the subsequent decade.

If the administration fails to get the spending reductions and revenue called for in its 1984 budget, and if its economic growth assumptions are correct, then there will be large and growing deficits and a steadily increasing debt-to-GNP ratio. By 1988, the deficit would exceed $300 billion, and the debt-to-GNP ratio would be above 40 percent (Fig. 5.7). A debt-to-GNP ratio that grows too large is undesirable. It implies that the government must eventually either default or subject the economy to a crushing tax burden in order to service the debt. If accepted at face value, the baseline deficit projections are a threat to fiscal stability and long-run economic growth. They portend much higher future tax rates, and much slower economic growth and sharply lower equity values.

However, all of the administration's deficit projections are based on a rather dismal view of the economy's ability to recover quickly from the current recession. The average growth rate of GNP between now and 1988 is expected to be only slightly below that for the average postwar recovery. But very little of that growth is expected to occur during 1983. This slow recovery scenario has a large effect on near-term deficit projections, and an even larger effect on forecasts of future deficits. Under the forecast, a one percent shortfall in 1983 GNP means one percent less GNP

FIGURE 5.7. Federal debt held by the private sector* as a percentage of GNP, 1930–1988

Percentage

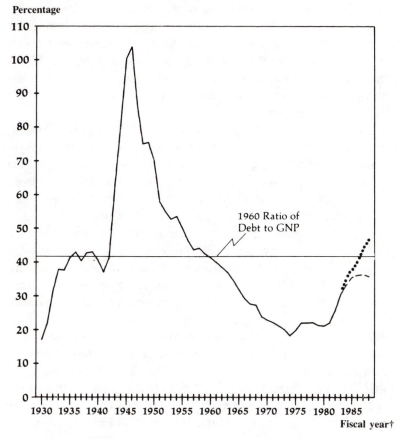

*government and agency debt held by the public less that held by Federal Reserve Banks
†fiscal year ending June 30 through 1981, thereafter ending September 30
——— Stock of debt divided by GNP
– – – – Administration projection
. . . . Baseline projection
Source: Budget of the United States Government, U.S. Government Printing Office, Washington, D.C. January 31, 1983; *Treasury Bulletin,* U.S. Department of Treasury, Government Printing Office, Washington D.C.; *Federal Reserve Bulletin.* Board of Governers of the Federal Reserve System, U.S. Government Printing Office, Washington, D.C.

forever. Furthermore, the extra debt that must be issued implies higher interest expense in the future. This is why the administration asserts that most of its upward revision of deficit projections for 1983 through 1988 is due to unexpectedly low 1982 GNP.

The administration's near-term growth assumption, and therefore its projections for both near-term and future deficits, are unduly pessimistic. First, projected GNP growth is below the average for postwar recoveries. Second, the recovery tends to be stronger the more severe the preceding recession, and this recession has itself been worse than the postwar average. Finally, the Office of Management and Budget (OMB) has overestimated deficits in previous recoveries. Forecasts are rarely on target, and a stronger-then-predicted recovery seems distinctly more likely than a weaker-than-predicted one.

If the recovery turns out to be more in line with the postwar norm, and if the administration gets its spending reductions and revenue increases, then the deficit will quickly fall to levels low enough to keep the debt-to-GNP ratio from rising. Furthermore, it is not even clear that those spending reductions and revenue increases would be needed to reach sustainable long-run deficits within an acceptably short time.

Given the uncertainty surrounding the near-term economic growth assumptions, and the degree to which all future deficit projections depend on these growth assumptions, the prudent course is to defer any tax increases until the pace of the recovery is evident. A temporary tax increase now followed by tax cuts later would be deleterious to the economy. Such a strategy would increase unnecessarily the economic welfare loss associated with tax policy, as well as threaten the rapid recovery that is central to alleviating future deficits. By contrast, if the recovery turns out to be anemic, such a strategy would lead to only a small increase in the debt-to-GNP ration between now and 1986. This is a risk worth taking in order to ensure that taxes are not raised unnecessarily. It is also far less risky than the alternative of significant new tax increases.

A POSTSCRIPT

It is interesting to compare the events that have occurred since this chapter was written in early 1983 with the predictions made at that time.

The economic recovery during 1983 and 1984 was much stronger than the administration and most private economists predicted. Real output grew at a 6.8 percent rate in calendar year 1984, the fastest in over 30 years. Real GNP for 1984 was $1,639 (measured in billions of 1972 dollars), or about 5.5 percent higher than the $1,555 billion forecast by the administration in its January 1983 budget message.

The administration did not obtain all the spending cuts and revenue increases requested in that budget message. Nevertheless, actual outlays for fiscal year 1984 were $11 billion less than forecast by the administration under the assumption that it would obtain those cuts. Outlays were $45 billion less than the baseline projection. Revenues, on the other hand, were $7 billion higher than the administration projected under the assumption that it would obtain all its requested revenue increases and $18 billion more than the baseline projection. As a result of the lower-than-expected outlays and higher-than-expected receipts, the deficit (including off-budget outlays for fiscal year 1984) was $185 billion. This is $18 billion less than the administration forecasted and $64 billion less than the baseline projection.

Since the deficit turned out to be smaller than expected, the debt also grew less than had been forecasted. Combined with the rapid economic recovery, this meant that government debt owned by the private sector stood at only 31.4 percent of GNP at the end of fiscal year 1984. This compares with figures of 32.6 percent and 33.9 percent implied by the administration and the baseline projections, respectively.

The ratio of debt to GNP is thus below the trajectory in Figure 5.7 which showed it reaching a peak of 36 percent in 1988 before beginning to decline. Despite this encouraging performance, one cannot assume that the debt-to-GNP ratio will peak at less than 36 percent in 1988 and then begin to decline. One reason why the ratio is below earlier projections is that real output has grown very fast. It is possible that the administration's failure to obtain all its requested program cuts in fiscal 1984 will affect the level of government spending in future years. If this effect were sufficiently large, it would cause the deficit to remain above $200 billion until the end of the decade and beyond. This in turn could cause the ratio of debt to GNP to continue to rise above 36 percent and to continue increasing after 1988. The administration recently predicted that without further spending cuts, the deficit would be $215 billion in fiscal 1986 and $232 billion in fiscal 1987. This compares with projections of $157 billion and $152 billion contained in the January 1983 budget message. If the latest projections are correct, then deficit reductions of about $60 billion in 1986 and $80 billion in 1987 would be required if the debt-to-GNP ratio is to start declining by 1988. If these deficit reductions are achieved, the debt should reach a peak of somewhat less than 36 percent of GNP.

NOTES

1. This view is based on the assumption that taxpayers recognize that if the government issues more debt, it must raise enough additional revenue in the future to service the debt. Therefore, they

increase their current saving in order to be able to pay the increased future taxes and still maintain future consumption. For a more complete discussion of this hypothesis, see Joines (1980). See also Barro (1974). Note that if the traditional view is correct, and deficits do crowd out private capital formation, then such a deficit-induced reduction in investment will lower future GNP, and thus the future tax base. This further limits the government's ability to service the debt and increases the likelihood of default.

2. Years used in measuring deficits denote 12-month periods ending on June 30 of the year indicated. Until 1976, this corresponded to the federal government's fiscal year. GNP is based on calendar years.

3. The analysis changes slightly if the inflation is not fully anticipated. Suppose that investors had anticipated none of the 5.6 percent inflation and had incorporated no inflation premium into interest rates. The government's interest expense and its cash deficit would have been correspondingly lower. The real value of its outstanding debt would still have depreciated by $37 billion, since the loss in purchasing power does not depend on whether inflation is anticipated or not. This amount can be viewed as the revenue from a 5.6 percent wealth tax on government bonds, and it is just as real as a tax on income or expenditure.

4. If inflation changes, the actual cash deficit will in general move less than one-for-one with the cash deficit required to maintain a constant real value of government debt. This is so because the government's interest payments on outstanding long-term debt will not adjust to changes in expected inflation. The sensitivity of the actual cash deficit to inflation will be higher, the larger the share of short-term debt is of the total government debt. The average maturity of U.S. government debt is actually quite short. Half the deficit is refunded in 15 months.

5. The value to consumers of the lost output is the area under the demand curve between the quantities with and without the tax. The cost of producing this output is the area under the supply curve between the quantities with and without the tax. The net loss to the economy is the shaded triangle, commonly referred to as consumer and producer surplus. For a more detailed explanation of these concepts, refer to a standard intermediate microeconomics text, such as McCloskey's *The Applied Theory of Price* (1982), Chapter 10.

6. Different notions of long-run budget balance, or balance over the business cycle, were discussed above. It is sufficient to note here that the relevant definition of balance need not imply equality of receipts and expenditures as measured by the administrative budget, the unified budget, or any other set of commonly published numbers. Due to inflation, a budget balanced on a cash basis might result in reductions in the real value of government debt.

7. For a more formal treatment of the notion of varying the deficit so as to keep expected tax rates constant, see Barro (1979).

8. Some people have argued against frequent changes in tax rates on the grounds that these fluctuations increase the uncertainty faced by economic agents in trying to plan for the future. This chapter has totally ignored such effects, although they might well be important. To the extent that these effects exist, they reinforce the arguments made here. In addition, even if economic agents can forecast tax rate changes with perfect certainty, an expected change in rates distorts decisions as to the timing of economic activity and the realization of income.

9. If the new, lower tax rates will raise less revenue than the public desires the government to spend in the long run, then one might argue that all or part of the cut should be canceled. However, it is highly likely that the upper reaches of the personal income tax schedule are in the prohibitive range of the Laffer Curve, and failure to reduce them would hold down rather than increase revenue. If more revenue is needed in the long run, then it could be more efficiently raised by restructuring the tax code than by raising rates across the board. Some form of restructuring, such as a flat rate tax, might well be desirable, regardless of the revenue required by the public. This chapter takes the structure as given and merely argues that rates should not be varied countercyclically.

10. If each national emergency caused a permanent increase in the debt-to-GNP ratio, ultimately the magnitude would exceed the economy's ability to service it, to say nothing of paying it off.

11. Data extracted from the U.S. Department of Commerce, Bureau of Economic Analysis, *Long-Term Economic Growth, 1860-1970.*

REFERENCES

Barro, Robert J. 1979. "On the Determination of the Public Debt." *Journal of Political Economy*, 87 (October): 940–71.

—— 1977. "Unanticipated Money Growth and Unemployment in the United States." *American Economic Review*, 67 (March): 101–115.

—— 1974. "Are Government Bonds Net Wealth?" *Journal of Political Economy*, 82 (November/December): 1095–1117.

Canto, Victor A., and Donald Rapp. 1981. "The Crowding Out Myth." A. B. Laffer Associates Rolling Hills Estates, CA. (December). See Chapter 4 of this book.

Joines, Douglas H. 1980. "Government Spending, Tax Rates and Private Investment in Plant and Equipment." A. B. Laffer Associates Rolling Hills Estates, CA. (May). See Chapter 2 of this book.

Laffer, Arthur B. 1980. "Memo to the Reagan Transition Team: A Return to Conversability." A. B. Laffer Associates Rolling Hills Estates, CA. (December).

McCloskey, Donald N. 1982. *The Applied Theory of Price*. New York: Macmillan.

Niskanen, William A. 1978. "Deficits, Government Spending, and Inflation: What is the Evidence?" *Journal of Monetary Economics*, 4 (August): 591–602.

U.S. Department of Commerce. Bureau of Economic Analysis. *Long-Term Economic Growth, 1860–1970*. U.S. Government Printing Office, Washington, D.C., 1973.

6

The Complete Flat Tax

Arthur B. Laffer

SUMMARY

The Complete Flat Tax sets forth a simple yet comprehensive plan for tax reform. It calls for the elimination of the federal personal income tax, corporate income tax, Social Security (OASDHI) payroll tax, and estate and gift taxes as well as some lesser taxes. Two single-rate taxes would take their place: one, a business value-added tax, and the other, a personal income tax. With a minimum amount of deductions, including mortgage payments and charitable contributions, a tax rate of 11.5 percent would immediately produce slightly more revenue than all the excluded taxes. Implementation of the Complete Flat Tax would, in due course:

- Elevate real GNP by between 8 percent and 15 percent above where it otherwise would have been;
- Produce additional government revenues of $40 billion before allowing for the Laffer Curve effect and of between $84 billion and $122 billion after taking into account the economic expansion implied by the Complete Flat Tax;
- Reduce government spending by reducing the number of people in need of government assistance;
- Move the federal budget toward balance;
- Restore hope and opportunity to the economically disadvantaged.

The Complete Flat Tax is as politically attractive as it is economically efficient. The Complete Flat Tax is likely to become the successor to the Kemp/Roth tax cut as the focal point of the debate over fiscal policy and the structure of the tax system.

February 22, 1984

THE COMPLETE FLAT TAX

This proposal sets forth a simple yet comprehensive plan for tax reform. All but a small number of federal taxes would be eliminated, including the present personal income tax, corporate income tax, Social Security (OASDHI) payroll tax, and estate and gift taxes as well as some lesser taxes. Two single-rate flat taxes would take their place, one on business and one on personal income. With a minimum amount of deductions, a tax rate of 11.5 percent would immediately produce slightly more revenue than all the excluded taxes and, in short order, would produce substantially higher revenues even without a Laffer Curve effect. Additionally, there would be increased revenues due to the Laffer Curve effect itself. According to simulations based on generally accepted estimates of the economic responses to lower marginal tax rates, the Complete Flat Tax would, in due course, elevate GNP by between 8 percent and 15 percent. This expansion of the economy implies additional tax revenues of between $44 billion and $82 billion.

Why a Flat Tax

The theory of incentives provides the basis for the concept of a flat-rate tax, which is so-called because a single tax rate applies equally to all sources of income and does not change as a result of the taxpayer's volume of income. Any exemptions, deductions, differential rates or progressivity would, as a matter of linguistics, preclude the name "flat rate." They also represent a deviation from the principles of efficient taxation. Such exceptions to the even application of a single tax narrow the tax base, lead to a higher tax rate, make for greater complexity and increase tax avoidance.

Incentives can be either positive or negative. They are alternatively described as carrots and sticks or pleasure and pain. Whatever their form, people seek positive and avoid negative incentives. If a dog is beaten, for example, the animal's whereabouts will not be known, but the dog is certain not to be where the beating took place. If, however, a dog is fed, we know exactly where the dog will be. The principle is simple enough: If an activity should be shunned, a negative incentive is appropriate and vice versa.

In the realm of economics, taxes are negative incentives and government subsidies are positive incentives, subject to all the subtleties and intricacies of the general theory of incentives. People attempt to avoid taxed activities—the higher the tax, the greater their attempt to avoid. As with all negative incentives, no one can be sure how the avoidance will be carried out.

In the case of taxable income, people try to shift income from higher-taxed categories to lower-taxed categories. They purchase tax shelters and, in the extreme, they may even earn less income or literally evade the strictures of the IRS at considerable personal risk. Because taxation in some form is necessary to sustain government spending, one canon of taxation has always been to have the largest possible tax base coupled with the lowest possible tax rate. By so doing, people are provided the least opportunity to avoid paying taxes and the lowest incentive to do so. In the words of Henry George: A good tax should "bear as lightly as possible on production—so as least to check the increase of the general fund from which taxes must be paid and the community maintained." He also went on to say that a tax should "be easily and cheaply collected...so as to take from the people as little as possible in addition to what it yields government."

A number of tax proposals over the years have attempted to reform one specific tax or another. Such reform attempts, however, are doomed at the outset. There can be no presumption even that the overall tax code will benefit from the most earnest of efforts to rectify one specific tax in a sea of flawed taxes. Interactive effects of all taxes taken in concert are barely imaginable when only one tax is viewed in isolation. True tax reform must take into account the entire tax code. Sincere efforts directed toward remedies of one specific tax are inherently tragically flawed by their lack of completeness.

In the realm of federal taxation, three taxes account for the bulk of revenues: personal income taxes, corporate profits taxes, and federal payroll taxes. They alone account for about 85 percent of total federal revenues (Table 6.1). Therefore, any flat-rate tax proposal should incorporate all three forms of taxation.

In the recent political era, most attention has been paid to the current state of disarray of the personal income tax. It is widely recognized that in spite of the statutory progressivity of the tax codes, deductions,

TABLE 6.1. Tax receipts by major category (fiscal year 1983)

Tax	Revenue (millions of dollars)	Percentage of total revenue
Individual income taxes	288,938	48.1
Corporate income taxes	37,022	6.2
Old age survivors, disability, and health insurance (OASDHI)	182,961	30.4
Total income and federal payroll taxes	508,921	84.7
Estate and gift taxes	6,053	1.0
Other taxes and budget receipts	85,589	14.3
Total budget receipts	600,563	100.0

Source: Department of the Treasury. *Treasury Bulletin.* Government Printing Office, Washington, D.C.

exemptions, and exclusions of all sorts have rendered the actual income tax neither fair nor efficient. The wealthy don't pay their fair share of taxes. The legislative process has made available tax shelters, deferrals, and various other tax-avoidance schemes to those with access to fancy accountants and high-priced lawyers. People struggling to become wealthy who can neither afford nor have access to such inequitable devices pay taxes after taxes, rarely getting the rewards they so rightfully deserve. The current income tax does not redistribute income and would be more appropriately designated a lawyer's and accountant's employment act.

In today's economy, the personal income tax is not alone in its failure to serve its appointed task. The corporate profits tax also has become a farce. Lobbyists have seduced a solicitous Congress time and again to substitute nonsense for common sense. Businesses that make highly desirable products and conserve our precious natural resources without adhering to the dictates of sophisticated tax counsel are taxed at incredibly onerous rates. If, on the other hand, a business squanders resources, makes a lousy product, retains gilded lobbyists and tax lawyers, and thereby reports horrendous losses, it stands a good chance of qualifying for government subsidies and most assuredly doesn't pay for the government it uses.

Equally as flawed are Social Security (OASDHI) payroll taxes. These taxes are notoriously regressive and yet account for $183 billion in revenues and unmeasured lost opportunities. "Unearned income" is not subject to the payroll tax, nor in 1984 are annual incomes in excess of

$37,800. Any reform of the overall tax structure must redress the inequities of the payroll tax. Adding to the list of ill-conceived and poorly executed taxes would be inheritance taxes, excess profits taxes, and numerous others.

To date, major flat-rate tax proposals have been tragically flawed. By failing to incorporate payroll taxes into the reform proposals, any flat-rate tax is demonstrably inequitable and patently unfair. Attempting to redress the equity issue by levying differential rates or permitting extensive deductions, exemptions and exclusions miss the whole point of a flat-rate tax. Refusing to fold the payroll tax into a flat-rate tax will also fail in providing the poor with actual relief. Comfortable images will once again have supplanted careful logic.

Perhaps the single most serious problem with the current tax system is the immense distortions introduced by the existing business tax code. Not only has the business tax code caused high unemployment and low productivity growth, but, even as this has occurred, government revenues from business taxes have dwindled.

The practical difficulties inherent in any proposed flat-rate tax scheme mandate far more consideration than would, at first glance, appear necessary from the uncomplicated nature of the theory.

Conflicting Notions

In reality, issues of equity, solvency, and efficiency can conflict with the notion of a flat-rate tax. Should, for example, the poor pay the same proportion of their income in taxes as do the rich? How about drinking, smoking, and gambling as activities versus charities, clean living, and conservation? Should all be taxed at the same rate? Even beneficial activities may, if necessary, succumb to a tax to provide the state with the requisite revenues. Clearly, considerations other than economic efficiency are of great importance. To reiterate the essential point, a piecemeal approach to tax reform will not work. Thus, a flat-rate income tax is of little consequence unless considered in conjunction with other taxes.

Tax Categories

Today, even a summary of federal budget receipts requires page after page of entries in ever smaller type to catalog a myriad of specific taxes. In total, many of these taxes raise little revenue. Their cost to the economy in terms of record keeping and collection represents an unnecessary burden. In general, all of these taxes should be eliminated forthwith.

Judicial fees, railroad and federal retirement funds and the like, however, are revenues associated with the provision of a specific good or service to the payee. They are more analogous to a payment for a specific identifiable service than a tax and as such should be retained. Customs duties, which are an arcane code unto themselves involving international relations, fall outside the purview of this proposal. Yet, even they should be considered in conjunction with the overall tax code.

The unemployment system, which varies from state to state in terms of both benefits and tax rates and also because of its state-specific nature, should be left intact in any purely federal tax reform. As a matter of practice, states, more often than not, use the federal tax codes as the starting point for developing their own statutes. As such, any federal tax reform will, perforce, lead to numerous state reforms.

Excise taxes on alcoholic beverages, tobacco products, firearms, and munitions also should be retained. It must be presumed that Congress, when it passed these specific taxes, did so with the intent of discouraging their use rather than raising revenue. These are the so-called "sin taxes."

One last major source of revenue comes from the Federal Reserve Bank. Because the Federal Reserve requires banks to hold non–interest-bearing deposits at Federal Reserve Banks, and then lends these funds at market rates of interest, the central bank's profits are absolutely enormous. What the Federal Reserve Bank doesn't spend it turns over to the treasury. These policies are an integral part of monetary policy and, thus, are not included in this proposal.

In total, the above categories designated as being outside the purview of a flat-rate tax base contributed $61.3 billion in federal revenues during fiscal year 1983 (Table 6.2).

As part of an overall tax simplification tax reform, all other taxes and sources of budgetary revenues should be repealed (Table 6.3). In their stead would be two flat taxes of equal rates: a flat-rate personal income tax and a flat-rate business value-added tax.

Deductions

The tax base for both individuals and businesses has been eroded over the last 20 years by the enactment of numerous exemptions and deductions. In addition, a profusion of tax credits serves to reduce the effective tax rate paid by some taxpayers on this already reduced tax base while

TABLE 6.2.   Revenue categories maintained

Classification	Receipt symbol	FY 1983 revenues (millions of dollars)
Railroad Retirement Accounts		2,805
Unemployment Insurance		18,799
Federal Employees' Retirement Contribution		4,358
Civil Service Retirement and	8,135.21	
Disability Fund		78
Excise taxes:		
Federal alcohol tax		5,537
Federal tobacco tax		4,136
Land and Water Conservation Fund,		
motorboat fuels tax, National Park Service	5,005.3	24
Tax on pistols and revolvers,		
bows and arrows	5,029.1	31
Tax on firearms	5,029.2	63
Tax on fishing rods, creels, reels,		
artificial lures, baits and flies	5,138	34
National Recreational Boating Safety		
and Facilities Improvement Fund	5,171	25
Deposits, internal revenue,		
collections for Puerto Rico	5,737	326
Deposits, internal revenue,		
collections for Virgin Islands	5,738	neg*
Transfers from general fund, Black		
Lung Benefits Revenue Act taxes	8,144.1	494
Transfers from general fund of amounts		
equal to certain taxes, Hazardous		
Substance Response Trust Fund	8,145.1	230
Transfers from general fund, Inland		
Waterways Revenue Act taxes	8,861.1	29
Customs Duties		8,655
Miscellaneous Receipts and Taxes:		
Deposits, Duties and Taxes, Puerto		
Rico, United States Customs Service	5,687	72
Deposits Internal Revenue Service,		
collections for child support	5,734	1
Receipts from Monetary Power		14,492
Fees for Permits, Regulatory and		
Judicial Services		681
Fines, Penalties and Forfeitures		323
War Reparation and Recoveries under		
Military Occupations		4
Gifts and Contributions		26
Total Budget Revenues Maintained		61,223

*Negligible; estimate based on *1981 Treasury Combined Statement.*

Source: Department of the Treasury. *Treasury Bulletin.* Government Printing Office, Washington, D.C.

TABLE 6.3. Taxes to be repealed

Classification	FY 1983 revenues (millions of dollars)	
Individual income taxes	288,938	
Corporate income taxes	37,022	
Federal payroll taxes		
Old age survivors, disability and health insurance	182,961	
Total income and payroll taxes repealed		508,921
Gift and estate taxes	6,053	
Selected excise and other taxes	24,366	
Total other taxes repealed		30,419
Total taxes repealed		539,340

Source: Department of the Treasury. *Treasury Bulletin.* Government Printing Office, Washington, D.C.

doing nothing to reduce the tax burden on individuals or businesses who are otherwise in identical economic circumstances. Such credits reduce the government's tax receipts and the average tax rate while leaving marginal rates unchanged. In short, tax credits in virtually all forms are counterproductive.

In addition, the business tax base should be broadened to include the value-added of labor as well as the value-added of capital and land. Great care, however, should be taken to make certain that value-added, as it wends its way through numerous businesses, is taxed once and only once. Double, triple, and even higher multiples of taxation in our current business tax code, no matter how well concealed, have cost our society unconscionable quantities of lost output and lost employment opportunities.

Border Tax Adjustments

The business value-added tax on traded goods should be levied in a manner similar to that of major U.S. trading partners. As such, the business value-added tax should be rebated on goods and services exported and should be imposed on imported goods and services at the point of entry. This border tax adjustment will assure equitable and fair competition both within the U.S. market and in world markets.

CALCULATION OF THE TAX BASE

Specifically, the tax base for individuals, businesses and independent contractors would be calculated as follows.

Personal Income Tax

Taxable income for all individuals, save independent contractors

1. Take income from all sources—wages, salaries, interest income, dividends, net capital gains (short-term and long-term), royalties, fees, and so on.
2. Subtract charitable contributions.
3. Subtract mortgage interest payments.
4. Subtract receipts of Social Security, unemployment benefits, and other transfer payments specifically designated as tax exempt.
5. The resultant figure is the taxable income base.

Taxable income for independent contractors

To receive a business taxpaying identifying number for an individual requires explicit federal permission, which should be based on the recipient's demonstrated special employment circumstances that would warrant such treatment.

1. For the independent contractor possessing a taxpaying identifying number, the tax base for personal income tax purposes is the dollar value of total sales (including, but not restricted to, personal services) less:

   - Purchases from other businesses and independent contractors bearing taxpaying identifying numbers of items used exclusively to generate sales and revenues.
   - Purchases of imported goods or services, with the requisite import taxpaying identifying number, used exclusively to generate sales and revenues.
   - Depreciation of pre–flat-rate tax-depreciable assets at their regular depreciation schedules.

2. Subtract charitable contributions.
3. Subtract mortgage interest payments.
4. Subtract receipts of Social Security, unemployment benefits, and other transfer payments specifically designated as tax exempt.
5. The resultant figure is the independent contractor taxable personal income base.

The personal income tax base for fiscal year 1983 is estimated as follows:

	(billions of dollars)
Personal income	2,691.3
Plus capital gains[a]	32
Less charitable contributions[a]	(34.0)
Less mortgage interest payments[a]	(71.5)
Less transfer payments (tax exempt)	(401.4)
Less imputed rent[b]	(67.0)
Equals tax base for personal income	2,149.4

[a]Estimate based on deductions in 1981 individual income tax returns.

[b]Estimate based on 1981 imputed rents reported in the July 1983 issue of *Survey of Current Business*.

Business Value-Added Tax

Taxable value-added for business

1. For all entities possessing a business taxpaying identifying number, including independent contractors, the tax base is the total dollar value of all sales during the tax period less:

   - All purchases from entities that possess a taxpaying identifying number (including independent contractors).
   - All purchases of imported goods with the requisite import taxpaying identifying number.
- Depreciation of pre–flat-rate tax-depreciable assets at their regular depreciation schedules.
- Bad debts incurred.
- Charitable contributions.
- No other deductions are permitted.

2. The resultant figure is the value-added tax base.

The business value-added tax base for fiscal year 1983 is estimated as follows:

	(billions of dollars)
Final sales	3,254.3
Less business investment	
Fixed nonresidential	(339.1)
Business-fixed residential[a]	(24.6)
Depreciation[b]	(352.2)

Business transfers[c]	(15.2)
Increase (+ if decrease) in business inventories	25.5
	2,548.7

[a]Estimate based on all farm structures and 20 percent of nonfarm structures.
[b]Capital consumption allowance without capital consumption adjustment.
[c]Charitable contributions plus bad debts.

In subsequent years, the depreciation allowed for fixed assets purchased before implementation of the flat tax will decline to zero. At that point, the analogous tax base for the value-added tax would be $2,900.9 ($2548.7 + $352.2) billion.

The Tax Rate

The tax rate is derived by dividing targeted revenues by the total tax base. On a statistical basis, with no increase in average tax rates and using fiscal year 1983 as a guide, requisite flat-tax revenue would be $539.2 billion on a combined tax base of $4,698.1 billion (Table 6.4). On this basis, the flat-tax rate would be 11.48 percent applied to both taxable personal income and business value-added. The appropriate tax rate for independent contractors would be 22.96 percent applied to their tax base.

Every percentage point increase in the tax rate on a statistical basis would yield an additional $47 billion. Based on the larger tax base implied by the eventual exhaustion of preexisting depreciation, the implied flat-tax rate would be 10.68 percent ($539.3 ÷ $5050.3).

Economic Growth Effects

Implementation of the Complete Flat Tax would augment economic growth for several reasons. First, the dramatic reduction in marginal tax rates would increase incentives to work, save, and invest.

Changes in marginal tax rates are important because they change incentives to demand and supply work effort and capital. For example, firms base their decisions to employ workers, in part, on their total cost to the firm. Holding all else equal, the greater the cost to the firm of employing each additional worker, the fewer workers the firm will employ. Conversely, the lower the marginal cost per worker, the more workers the firm hires. For the firm, the decision to employ is based on gross wages paid, a concept that encompasses all costs borne by the firm.

Workers, on the other hand, care little about the cost to the firm of employing them. Of concern from a worker's standpoint is how much the

TABLE 6.4. Calculation of flat-tax rate

	Tax base + budget revenues (billions of dollars)
Tax base, personal income	2,149.4
Plus tax base, business value-added tax	2,548.7
Total tax base	4,698.1
FY 1983 targeted budget revenue	600.6
Less budget revenues elsewhere obtained	(61.2)
Requisite flat-tax revenues	539.3
Flat-tax rate = revenues tax base = 539.3/4,698.1 = 11.48 percent	

Source: Compiled by the author.

worker receives for providing work effort, net of all deductions and taxes. Workers concentrate on net wages received. The greater net wages received, the more willing a worker is to work. Conversely, if net wages received fall, workers will find work effort less attractive and they will do less of it.

The difference between what is costs a firm to employ a worker and what that worker receives net, is the tax wedge. From the standpoint of a single worker, a tax cut has two types of effects. Because a decrease in marginal tax rates lowers the cost to the employer in the form of lower wages paid, clearly, firms will employ more workers. On the supply side, a reduction in marginal tax rates raises net wages received. Again, more work effort will be supplied. In sum, tax rate cuts increase the demand for, and the supply of, productive factors. In dynamic formulations, as tax rates fall, output growth increases, and vice versa. Regulations, restrictions, and requirements, along with explicit taxes, are all parts of the wedge.

With the Complete Flat Tax, average tax rates will remain approximately constant for a given GNP. However, the rewards for incremental work by labor, the employment of additional capital, and the more efficient combination of the two will all be higher with the flat tax. As a result, more employment output and production would be expected. Economic growth rates would accelerate until these effects are fully incorporated into the workings of the economy.

An estimate of the growth-augmenting effects of the Complete Flat Tax was derived using a simple general equilibrium model for the economy. (A mathematical derivation of the model, an explication of its parameter estimates, and the simulation results are reported in Appendix A.) A range of responses to lower marginal tax rates for capital and high-skilled and low-skilled labor were taken from the economic literature. The more responsive economic agents are to the change in tax rates, the greater will be the economic growth effects of implementing a flat tax.

A series of forecasts was made based on different assumptions as to the responsiveness of the economy to the reduction in marginal tax rates implied by the Complete Flat Tax. Based on parameters near the low end of the spectrum, the level of GNP would be expected to increase by approximately 8 percent. If, however, the responsiveness of capital and labor to lower tax rates were at the values most economists consider to be at the high end of the spectrum, implementation of the Complete Flat Tax would elevate real GNP by approximately 15 percent.

An estimate of the revenue effects of this growth rate can be calculated by expanding the tax base by 8 percent and 15 percent, respectively, and multiplying this increase in the tax base by a tax rate of 11.5 percent. This Laffer Curve effect of the Complete Flat Tax would provide between $44 billion and $82 billion in additional revenues.

Thus, implementation of this tax reform would likely increase revenues within three years by between $84 billion and $122 billion due to both the expansion of the economy and exhaustion of preexisting depreciation. In addition, the rapid increase in aggregate output and employment associated with adoption of the Complete Flat Tax would reduce automatically entitlement expenditures associated with the unemployed, including unemployment benefits, Aid to Families with Dependent Children, and food stamps. In this case, savings would be realized by reducing the number of recipients rather than cutting the benefits to those in need.

Taken all together, adoption of the Complete Flat Tax, could, by itself, provide most if not all of the "down payment" on the deficit called for by the president, while establishing the preconditions for realization of a budget balanced not on the backs of the taxpayer, but through the dynamics of a healthy, robust economy.

APPENDIX A: ESTIMATION OF THE EFFECTS OF THE COMPLETE FLAT TAX ON ECONOMIC ACTIVITY

An increasing amount of attention has recently been devoted to the effect of alternative tax structures on the pattern of economic activity, on the level of taxable economic activity, on employment, and on the aggregate amount of revenues generated by the tax system. A static, one-sector, three-factor model is developed in order to analyze the effects of taxes imposed purely for the purpose of generating revenues.[1]

Mathematical Derivation of the Model

The model presented is a highly simplified one. While we call our three factors of production capital, high-skilled labor, and low-skilled labor, we do not distinguish one as fixed and the other as variable. Since the model is static, we do not attempt to analyze the process of capital formation.[2] Instead, we assume that at any point there exist fixed stocks of capital and labor and that these stocks must be allocated either to household production or to market-sector production.[3]

Three factors all combine in the market sector according to a Cobb–Douglas production function to produce the market good Q:

$$Q = K^{(1-\alpha_1-\alpha_2)} L^{\alpha_1} H^{\alpha_2} \qquad\qquad 6.1$$

Where $(1-\alpha_1-\alpha_2)$, $\alpha_1\alpha_2$ denote the partial output elasticities of capital (K), low-skilled labor (L), and high-skilled labor (H), respectively, and $0<(1-\alpha_1-\alpha_2)<1$; $0<\alpha_1<1$; and $0<\alpha_2<1$. The market good, capital and both kinds of labor, are inputs into the household production process. Capital and labor thus have identical analytical properties, except that they are not perfect substitutes in either market or household production.

We assume that factors employed in the market sector are paid their marginal products and that the rental rate received by capital (R^*) and the wage rates received by low-skilled and high-skilled labor $(W^*$ and $S^*)$ differ from the rates paid because of the taxation of factor income:

$$R^* = R(1-t_K) \qquad\qquad 6.2$$
$$W^* = W(1-t_L) \qquad\qquad 6.3$$
$$S^* = S(1-t_H) \qquad\qquad 6.4$$

Where R, W, and S denote the gross-of-tax rental rates on capital, low-skilled labor, and high-skilled labor, and t_K, t_L, and t_H are the tax rates on an income from capital, low-skilled labor, and high-skilled labor, respectively. The gross-of-tax factor payments are denominated in terms of the market good.

A change in the rates of W to R and/or S to R will change the ratios of high-skilled and low-skilled labor to capital demanded by firms for reproduction of any level of market goods. One of the characteristics of the Cobb–Douglas production function is the constancy of the shares of the factors of production. Accordingly, the demand for the various factors and the optimal factor proportions are

$$K^d = (1 - \alpha_1 - \alpha_2) \frac{Q}{R} \qquad 6.5$$

$$L^d = \alpha_1 \frac{Q}{W} \qquad 6.6$$

$$H^d = \alpha_2 \frac{Q}{S} \qquad 6.7$$

$$\frac{K^d}{L^d} = \frac{(1 - \alpha_1 - \alpha_2)}{\alpha_1} \frac{W}{R} = \frac{(1 - \alpha_1 - \alpha_2)}{\alpha_1} \frac{W^*}{R^*} \frac{(1 - t_K)}{(1 - t_L)} \qquad 6.8$$

$$\frac{L^d}{H^d} = \frac{\alpha_1}{\alpha_2} \frac{S}{W} = \frac{\alpha_1}{\alpha_2} \frac{S^*}{W^*} \frac{(1 - t_L)}{(1 - t_H)} \qquad 6.9$$

$$\frac{K^d}{H^d} = \frac{(1 - \alpha_1 - \alpha_2)}{\alpha_2} \frac{S}{R} = \frac{(1 - \alpha_1 - \alpha_2)}{\alpha_2} \frac{S^*}{R^*} \frac{(1 - t_K)}{(1 - t_H)} \qquad 6.10$$

Where K_d, L_d, and H_d denote the demand for capital, low-skilled labor, and skilled labor services, respectively. A change in the ratio of W^* to S^* and S^* to R^* will cause a change in the ratio of high-skilled labor to low-skilled labor demanded by household for the production of any level of the household commodity. In addition, an increase in the absolute levels of W^*, S^*, and R^* will cause households to substitute market goods for high-skilled and low-skilled labor. In other words, an equiproportionate increase in W^*, S^*, and R^* causes households to supply more labor to the market sector. Specifically, we assume that the supply functions take the following form[4]:

$$K^S = A_K \left(\frac{R^*}{S^*}\right)^{\sigma_L} \left(\frac{R^*}{W^*}\right)^{\sigma_S} R^{*\epsilon} \qquad 6.11$$

$$L^S = A_L \left(\frac{W^*}{S^*}\right)^{\sigma_L} \left(\frac{W^*}{R^*}\right)^{\beta} W^{*\epsilon} \qquad 6.12$$

$$H^S = A_H \left(\frac{S^*}{W^*}\right)^{\sigma_S} \left(\frac{S^*}{R^*}\right)^{\beta} S^{*\epsilon} \qquad 6.13$$

It is assumed that the government derives its revenue entirely from proportional taxes on factor income, that the budget is always balanced, and that revenue collections are returned to the economy in a neutral fashion so that no income effects are generated.[5]

Combining Equations 6.11, 6.12, and 6.13, the ratio of factors supplied to the market sector are

$$\frac{K^S}{L^S} = \frac{A_K}{A_L} \left(\frac{R^*}{W^*} \right)^\sigma \text{ where } \sigma > 0 \qquad 6.14$$

$$\frac{L^S}{H^S} = \frac{A_L}{A_H} \left(\frac{W^*}{S^*} \right)^\sigma \qquad 6.15$$

$$\frac{K^S}{H^S} = \frac{A_K}{A_H} \left(\frac{R^*}{S^*} \right)^\sigma \qquad 6.16$$

Where σ, the partial elasticity of substitution in factor supply is assumed to be positive and defined as $\sigma = \sigma_L + \sigma_s + \beta + \epsilon$.

Equation 6.14 says that the ratio of capital to low-skilled labor supplied to the market sector depends only on the after-tax low-skilled wage–rental ratio. On the other hand, Equation 6.8 says that the proportion of capital to labor demanded by the market sector depends only on the gross-of-tax wage–rental ratio. Combining the two equations, one can solve the level of gross and net-of-tax wage–rental ratio as a function of the tax rates:

$$\frac{W^*}{R^*} = \left[\frac{A_K}{A_L} \frac{\alpha_1}{(1-\alpha_1-\alpha_2)} \frac{(1-t_L)}{(1-t_K)} \right]^{\frac{1}{1+\sigma}} \qquad 6.17$$

$$\frac{W}{R} = \left[\frac{A_K}{A_L} \frac{\alpha_1}{(1-\alpha_1-\alpha_2)} \right] \left[\frac{A_K}{A_L} \frac{\alpha_1}{(1-\alpha_1-\alpha_2)} \frac{(1-t_L)}{(1-t_K)} \right]^{\frac{\sigma}{1+\sigma}} \qquad 6.18$$

Combining Equations 6.9 and 6.15 one can solve for the equilibrium net-of-tax low-skilled/high-skilled wage ratio and the gross-of-tax low-skilled/high-skilled wage ratio:

$$\frac{W^*}{S^*} = \left[\frac{A_H}{A_L} \frac{\alpha_1}{\alpha_2} \frac{(1-t_L)}{(1-t_H)} \right]^{\frac{1}{1+\sigma}} \qquad 6.19$$

$$\frac{W}{S} = \left[\frac{A_H}{A_L} \frac{\alpha_1}{\alpha_2} \right]\left[\frac{A_H}{A_L} \frac{\alpha_1}{\alpha_2} \frac{(1-t_L)}{(1-t_H)} \right]^{-\frac{\sigma}{1+\sigma}} \quad\quad 6.20$$

Similarly, combining Equations 6.10 and 6.17 one can solve for the equilibrium values of the net-of-tax high-skilled labor wage–rental ratio and the gross-of-tax high-skilled labor wage–rental ratio:

$$\frac{S^*}{R^*} = \left[\frac{A_K}{A_H} \frac{\alpha_2}{(1-\alpha_1-\alpha_2)} \frac{(1-t_H)}{(1-t_K)} \right]^{\frac{1}{1+\sigma}} \quad\quad 6.21$$

$$\frac{S}{R} = \left[\frac{A_K}{A_H} \frac{\alpha_2}{(1-\alpha_1-\alpha_2)} \right]\left[\frac{A_K}{A_H} \frac{\alpha_2}{(1-\alpha_1-\alpha_2)} \frac{(1-t_H)}{(1-t_K)} \right]^{-\frac{\sigma}{1+\sigma}} \quad\quad 6.22$$

Equations 17 to 22 show that the net-of-tax and gross-of-tax relative factor costs depend on the factor tax rates, the factors supply elasticities, and the output elasticities of the factors.

It can be shown that if producers maximize profits, the cost function of the market good will also be of the Cobb–Douglas form:

$$1 = \left(\frac{R}{(1-\alpha_1-\alpha_2)} \right)^{1-\alpha_1-\alpha_2}\left(\frac{W}{\alpha_1} \right)^{\alpha_1}\left(\frac{S}{\alpha_2} \right)^{\alpha_2} \quad\quad 6.23$$

where the market good has been defined as the numeraire.

Rearranging Equation 6.23 and substituting for the gross-of-tax relative factor costs (Equations 6.18 and 6.22), one can solve for the gross-of-tax rental rate.

$$R = (1-\alpha_1-\alpha_2) \frac{A_K}{A_L}^{-\alpha_1}\left[\frac{A_K}{A_L} \frac{\alpha_1}{(1-\alpha_1-\alpha_2)} \frac{(1-t_L)}{(1-t_K)} \right]^{\frac{\alpha_1\sigma}{1+\sigma}} \times$$

$$\left(\frac{A_K}{A_H} \right)^{-\alpha_2}\left[\frac{A_K}{A_H} \frac{\alpha_2}{(1-\alpha_1-\alpha_2)} \frac{(1-t_H)}{(1-t_K)} \right]^{\frac{\alpha_2\sigma}{1+\sigma}} \quad\quad 6.24$$

Substituting Equation 6.24 into Equation 6.18 one can solve for the gross-of-tax wage rate for low-skilled workers:

$$W = \alpha_1\left(\frac{A_K}{A_L} \right)^{(1-\alpha_1)}\left[\frac{A_K}{A_L} \frac{\alpha_1}{(1-\alpha_1-\alpha_2)} \frac{(1-t_L)}{(1-t_K)} \right]^{\frac{-(1-\alpha_1)\sigma}{1+\sigma}} \times$$

$$\quad\quad 6.25$$

$$\left(\frac{A_K}{A_H}\right)^{-\alpha_2}\left[\frac{A_K}{A_H}\frac{\alpha_2}{(1-\alpha_1-\alpha_2)}\frac{(1-t_H)}{(1-t_K)}\right]^{\frac{\alpha_2\sigma}{1+\sigma}}$$

Similarly, substituting Equation 6.24 into Equation 6.22 one can solve for the gross-of-tax wage rate for high-skilled workers:

$$S=\alpha_2\left(\frac{A_K}{A_L}\right)^{-\alpha_1}\left[\frac{A_K}{A_L}\frac{\alpha_1}{(1-\alpha_1-\alpha_2)}\frac{(1-t_L)}{(1-t_K)}\right]^{\frac{\alpha_1\sigma}{1+\sigma}}\times$$

6.26

$$\left(\frac{A_K}{A_H}\right)^{(1-\alpha_2)}\left[\frac{A_K}{A_H}\frac{\alpha_2}{(1-\alpha_1-\alpha_2)}\frac{(1-t_H)}{(1-t_K)}\right]^{\frac{-(1-\alpha_2)\sigma}{1+\sigma}}$$

Substituting Equations 6.2, 6.3, 6.4, 6.24, 6.25, and 6.26 into the factor supply equations, one can determine the equilibrium quantities of each factor:

$$K^S=A_K\left(\frac{A_K}{A_L}\right)^{-\alpha_1\epsilon}\left(\frac{A_K}{A_H}\right)^{-\alpha_2\epsilon}[(1-\alpha_1-\alpha_2)(1-t_K)]^\epsilon\times$$

6.27

$$\left[\frac{A_K}{A_H}\frac{\alpha_2}{(1-\alpha_1-\alpha_2)}\frac{(1-t_H)}{(1-t_K)}\right]^{\frac{\alpha_2\epsilon\sigma-\sigma_L}{1+\sigma}}\times$$

$$\left[\frac{A_K}{A_L}\frac{\alpha_1}{(1-\alpha_1-\alpha_2)}\frac{(1-t_L)}{(1-t_K)}\right]^{\frac{\alpha_1\epsilon\sigma-\sigma_S}{1+\sigma}}$$

$$L^S=A_L\frac{A_K}{A_L}^{(1-\alpha_1)\epsilon}\frac{A_K}{A_H}^{-\alpha_2\epsilon}[\alpha_1(1-t_L)]^\epsilon\left[\frac{A_H}{A_L}\frac{\alpha_1}{\alpha_2}\frac{(1-t_L)}{(1-t_H)}\right]^{\frac{\sigma_L}{1+\sigma}}\times$$

6.28

$$\left[\frac{A_K}{A_L}\frac{\alpha_1}{(1-\alpha_1-\alpha_2)}\frac{(1-t_L)}{(1-t_K)}\right]^{\frac{\beta-\epsilon(1-\alpha_1)\sigma}{1+\sigma}}\times$$

$$\left[\frac{A_K}{A_H}\frac{\alpha_2}{(1-\alpha_1-\alpha_2)}\frac{(1-t_H)}{(1-t_K)}\right]^{\frac{\epsilon\alpha_2\sigma}{1+\sigma}}$$

$$H^S = A_H \left(\frac{A_K}{A_L}\right)^{-\alpha_1\epsilon} \left(\frac{A_K}{A_H}\right)^{(1-\alpha_2)\epsilon} [\alpha_2(1-t_H)]^\epsilon \left[\frac{A_H}{A_L} \frac{\alpha_1}{\alpha_2} \frac{(1-t_L)}{(1-t_H)}\right]^{\frac{-\sigma_S}{1+\sigma}} \times$$

$$6.29$$

$$\left[\frac{A_K}{A_H} \frac{\alpha_2}{(1-\alpha_1-\alpha_2)} \frac{(1-t_H)}{(1-t_K)}\right]^{\frac{\beta-\epsilon(1-\alpha_1)\sigma}{1+\sigma}}$$

$$\left[\frac{A_K}{A_L} \frac{\alpha_1}{(1-\alpha_1-\alpha_2)} \frac{(1-t_L)}{(1-t_K)}\right]^{\frac{\epsilon\alpha_1\sigma}{1+\sigma}}$$

The equilibrium level of market output as a function of the tax rates is obtained by substituting Equations 6.27, 6.28, and 6.29 into Equation 6.1:

$$Q = A_K \left(\frac{A_L}{A_K}\right)^{\alpha_1(1+\epsilon)} \left(\frac{A_H}{A_L}\right)^{\alpha_2(1+\epsilon)} [(1-t_K)(1-\alpha_1-\alpha_2)]^\epsilon \times$$

$$6.30$$

$$\left[\frac{A_K}{A_H} \frac{\alpha_2}{(1-\alpha_1-\alpha_2)} \frac{(1-t_H)}{(1-t_K)}\right]^{\frac{(1+\epsilon)\alpha_2\sigma-\sigma_L}{1+\sigma}}$$

$$\left[\frac{A_K}{A_L} \frac{\alpha_1}{(1-\alpha_1-\alpha_2)} \frac{(1-t_L)}{(1-t_K)}\right]^{\frac{(1+\epsilon)\alpha_1\sigma-\sigma_S}{1+\sigma}}$$

Parameter Estimates

The various parameters in the model can be classified by the following four categories:

1. Factor's share of output (factor's partial output elasticities)
2. Marginal tax rates on factor incomes
3. Labor supply elasticities
4. Scaling factors

Factor's Share of Output

Capital's share of output $(1-\alpha_1-\alpha_2)$. Capital's share of output (income from capital divided by GNP) may be estimated from the National Income and Product Accounts. It varies from year to year. In what follows, capital's share of output $(1-\alpha_1-\alpha_2)$ takes the following value: 0.25.

High-skilled and Low-skilled Labor Share of Output (α_1, α_2). The sum of capital, high-skilled labor, and low-skilled labor's share of total output must, by definition, add up to one. It thus follows that labor's (high-skilled and low-skilled) share of output will be one minus capital's share of output.

Allocation of labor's share of output to high-skilled and low-skilled workers is a more complicated task. First, an operational definition of high-skilled and low-skilled labor is needed. Second, a way to separate the labor and non-labor income for each type of worker is required. Once these steps are taken, high-skilled and low-skilled labor income can be determined. Such an approach, however, is outside the scope of this study. As a result, output share for high-skilled and low-skilled labor was assumed. For low-skilled labor, the share is assumed to be 25 percent. For high-skilled labor, 50 percent of GNP was used, so that total labor output summed to 75 percent of GNP.

Marginal Tax Rates on Factor Incomes

Tax Rates on Income from Capital (t_K). There are several estimates of historical average marginal tax rates on income from capital. A comparison of the various series can be found in Joines (1981). In 1975, the last year for which Joines' data is available, Joines estimates the marginal tax rate to be 49.31 percent. Since then, the Reagan tax cuts have been enacted. Therefore, calculations based on these values will tend to overstate the increase in GNP due to the reduction in marginal tax rates on income from capital.

Marginal Tax Rates on Low-Skilled Labor (t_L). Although the current legislated tax rates include a zero bracket, employees and employers are subject to Social Security and other payroll taxes. Sales taxes may also have a marginal impact on labor income. Individuals work to consume and thus a sales tax reduces the value of pretax wages in a manner quite similar to an income tax. Payroll taxes combined with sales taxes on finished goods suggest a minimum marginal tax rate of 15 to 20 percent.

In addition, public assistance (welfare) programs have "means" and "income" tests as eligibility criteria. Benefits are inversely related to income from private sources. The reduction in benefits as income rises implies de facto marginal tax rates which may exceed 100 percent in some instances. In what follows, a 90 percent maximum rate will be assumed (Laffer 1984).

The previous discussion suggests that there may be two distinct ranges of marginal tax rates for low-skilled labor. One will be for those who are currently working and who do not qualify for social welfare programs. Their marginal tax rate will be determined by their combined federal, state, and local tax rates. The other tax range will be for the low-skilled who are not working and who receive welfare benefits. This group faces a substantially higher effective marginal tax rate because of the loss of unemployment and other welfare benefits. Since our analysis is not concerned with this second group in what follows, it is assumed that the income level of the low-skilled is sufficiently low to be facing a 20 percent tax rate on labor income.

Marginal Tax Rates on High-Skilled Labor (t_H). The marginal tax rate on high-skilled labor was estimated to be 27.35 percent. This estimate is Joines' estimate for the U.S. labor force, which would tend to underestimate the average marginal tax rate on high-skilled labor. In addition, Social Security tax rates and wage base have been increased significantly since 1975. However, the Reagan tax cuts have lowered marginal tax rates. To the extent these effects cancel out, the 27.35 percent rate is a good estimate for the marginal tax rate on high-skilled labor.

Elasticity Parameters

Partial Elasticity of Substitution (s). Empirical estimates of the elasticity of substitution between capital and labor differ across empirical studies. The bulk of these studies suggest an elasticity of substitution in the neighborhood of one, with some studies estimating a value as low as 0.5 and others as high as 1.5 (see Boskin, 1978 and Evans, 1983). Most of these studies estimate the elasticity of substitution between capital and all forms of labor.

The model developed in this study, however, distinguishes between high-skilled and low-skilled labor. To the extent that there is substitution between these two types of labor, the aggregate elasticity of substitution reported in other studies may underestimate the partial elasticity of substitution between the various factors of production. For this reason we will consider a wider range of estimates for the partial elasticity of substitution (s). The values used range from 0.5 to 1.5.

Labor Supply Elasticities (E_{LW}^S, E_{HS}^S). There are a considerable number of empirical studies that provide estimates of labor supply elasticities. The studies differ in the way the wage is measured, the time period, and functional forms estimated. They also differ as to whether they account for labor participation rates, government spending, and so on. Most of these studies report a low labor supply elasticity for prime age males and a positive elasticity for females. Finnegan's (1962) occupational study estimated labor supply elasticities of craftsmen and clerical workers to range from −0.29 to +0.42. In Boskin's (1973) study using U.S. cross-sectional data accounting for sex, race and age, the labor supply elasticity for prime age males was estimated to be −0.07. More recently, the review of Borjas and Heckman (1978) on the labor supply elasticities of prime age males reported that the estimated elasticities range from −0.19 to −0.07. The negative elasticity suggests a backward-bending labor supply curve. That is, an increase in the after-tax wage rate reduces the supply of labor.

The estimates for female labor supply elasticities are more often positive and can often be large in magnitude. Killingsworth (1983), using U.S. cross-sectional data, estimates female labor supply elasticities ranging between 0.20 and 0.90. Similarly, Boskin's (1973) study accounting for race, sex, and age estimated labor supply elasticities as high as 1.60 for black elderly women. This much greater sensitivity to tax rates by females indicates that when both husband and wife work, more often than not the marginal income will be that of the wife. In fact, the empirical evidence on labor supply suggests a fairly low supply elasticity for husbands and a much higher one for wives. One possible reason for this asymmetrical result is the costs associated with husband and wife both adjusting their hours of work. In order to minimize these costs, it would be optimal for the family to adjust its taxable income by changing the hours worked by the wife.

The next step in the analysis is to obtain an aggregate labor supply elasticity for each class of labor. One way to obtain an estimate for the aggregate supply elasticity is to take into account the median income of males and females as well as the ratio of males to females in the labor force. Given these data, a weighted average of the labor supply elasticity could be calculated. The weighting scheme could be expanded to incorporate age, race, and other characteristics of the labor force. Alternative calculations suggest that for high-skilled labor, a range of elasticity from a low of 0.10 to a high of 0.6 is reasonable. The time-series estimates of Lucas and Rapping (1970) suggest a short-run aggregate labor supply elasticity ranging from 1.35 to 1.58.

Various studies on how Aid to Families with Dependent Children affects the supply of labor suggest that the availability of social welfare benefits reduces the supply of labor. The estimates of the labor supply elasticities for the people receiving welfare are fairly large. In fact, some of the studies suggest a labor supply elasticity in excess of three (Table 6.5).

Based on the reported empirical evidence, the parameter ranges for high-skilled and low-skilled labor are assumed to be as follows:

Labor supply elasticity	Range
High-skilled	0.10 to 0.6
Low-skilled	0.04 to 1.4

The development of the model shows that the factor supply elasticities for the high-skilled and low-skilled labor (E_H and E_L, respectively) can be expressed in terms of the parameters in the model:

$$E_{HS}^S = \sigma_S + \beta + \epsilon \qquad 6.31$$

$$E_{LW}^S = \sigma_L + \beta + \epsilon \qquad 6.32$$

Similarly, the elasticity of substitution can be expressed as

$$\sigma = \sigma_L + \sigma_S + \beta + \epsilon \qquad 6.33$$

From these equations, one can solve for the values of σ_S and σ_L implied by the elasticities. That is:

$$\sigma_L = \sigma - E_{HS}^S \qquad 6.34$$

$$\sigma_H = \sigma - E_{LW}^S \qquad 6.35$$

Finally, from Equations 6.31 and 6.33 one can also show that

$$E_{HS}^S - \sigma_S = \beta + \epsilon \qquad 6.36$$

Similarly, from Equations 6.32 and 6.33:

$$E_{LW}^S - \sigma_L = \beta + \epsilon \qquad 6.37$$

The formulation assumes that own effects dominate cross effects. That is:

$$E_{LW}^S > \sigma_L \qquad\qquad 6.38$$

$$E_{HS}^S > \sigma_S \qquad\qquad 6.39$$

Equation 6.39 combined with Equation 6.34 yields the following restriction on the magnitude of the parameters:

$$E_{HS}^S > \sigma_L = \sigma - E_{HS}^S \qquad\qquad 6.40$$

Thus,

$$2E_{HS}^S > \sigma \qquad\qquad 6.41$$

Similarly, by combining Equations 6.35 and 6.38, it can be shown that

$$2E_{LW}^S > \sigma \qquad\qquad 6.42$$

The parameter measuring the overall response from non-market to market activity (ϵ), is assumed always to be positive. In what follows we will assume ranges from 0.25 to 2.0. Thus, given $\beta + \epsilon$ and the values for ϵ, the implied value for β can be determined.

Scaling Coefficients

A_H, A_L, and A_K denote scaling factors which are determined by the initial conditions. The values for these coefficients were chosen such that the overall supply of labor (L^S and H^S) and capacity utilization (K^S) is of the same order of magnitude as actually occurs in the United States. These estimates were obtained by substituting what we considered to be the most likely parameter values into the following equations:

$$RK^S = \text{income from capital} \qquad\qquad 6.43$$

$$WL^S + SH^S = \text{compensation to employees} \qquad\qquad 6.44$$

where the income from capital and compensation to employees figures were taken from the *Survey of Current Business*, and the expressions for RK_S, WL_S, and SH_S are derived from the model.

Given these equations and the factor share assumptions, values for the scaling factors were derived.

TABLE 6.5. Labor supply analyses of AFDC

Study	Population analyzed	Data used [a]	Dependent variable	Program variables [b]	Specification [c]	Results
Recipient Behavior						
Garfinkel–Orr (1974)	Female AFDC recipients	Aggregates on 50 states, 1967	Employment rate	G, T, SA, allowable deductions, work test	OLS	Elasticity of employment rate w.r.t. G is −0.7, T is −0.7, SA is 0.3, deductions is 0.2
Saks (1975)	As above	AFDC Survey for NYC, 1967	Participation	G, T	OLS, GLS	Elasticity of partic. w.r.t. G is −0.94, T is −3.29
Williams (1975)	As above	National AFDC survey, 1968	Employment rate, hours, participation	G, T	OLS	Elasticity of employ, rate, hrs., and partic. w.r.t. G is −0.76, −1.11, −1.14; for T, −46, −.99, −1.19
Female Head Behavior						
Masters–Garfinkel (1977)	All female heads of fam. with children	SEO, 1967; PSID, 1972	Hours, employment dummy	G, T, administrative variables	OLS on full and low wage samples	G and T have no consistent impacts

Levy (1979)	As directly above	PSID, 1968	Hours, 3 categories	G, T, SA, deductions	Multinomial logit	Range of elasticity of hrs. w.r.t. G is −0.9 to −1.5; T is 0.19 to 0.65, SA is −0.01 to −0.08
Moffitt (1980a)	As directly above	PSID, 1975	Hours	G, T	Maximum likelihood jointly on hours and participation in AFDC	G has large negative impact, but T has very weak impact on hours worked
Barr-Hall (1981)	As directly above	SEO and Sur of AFDC recipients, both	Dependence = benefits ÷ (benefits + earnings), 4 categories	G, T	Multinomial logit	Degree of dependence varies directly with G, inversely with T
Hausman (1981)	As directly above	PSID, 1975	Hours	G, T	Maximum likelihood	G and T have large negative impacts on hours worked

[a] All are cross section studies. PSID, Panel Survey on Income Dynamics; SEO, Survey of Economic Opportunity.
[b] G, guarantee; T, tax rate; SA, set-aside.
[c] OLS, ordinary least squares; GLS, generalized least squares.

Source: Reprinted from Sheldon Danziger, Robert Haveman, and Robert Plotnick. 1981. "How Income Transfer Programs Affect Work, Savings, and the Income Distribution: A Critical Review." *Journal of Economic Literature.* 19 (September): 975–1028.

Simulation Results

This section analyzes the simulation results obtained by using the mathematical model developed in this appendix. The parameter values for the elasticity of substitution (σ), and labor supply elasticity for low-skilled and high-skilled individuals (E_{LW}, E_{HS}, respectively) capture the range of parameters found in the economic literature. The model developed in the previous section imposes some restrictions on the combined magnitude of the three elasticities. These three elasticities (σ, E_{LW}, and E_{HS}) determine all of the other parameters in the model. The last column reports the percentage change in GNP that would result from substituting the flat-rate tax proposed in this chapter for the current tax structure.

Since the model developed is a static one, the percentage changes in GNP may be interpreted as steady-state gains in the economy.

The results reported in Table 6.6 suggest that the flat-rate tax proposal most likely will result in a significant increase in GNP. Only in two cases does GNP decline. (The decline is less than 1 percent.) This decline can be attributed to the fact that, using our calculations, the marginal tax rate in low-skilled labor is increased to 23 percent from 20 percent. The increase in tax rates will tend to reduce employment of that factor. In addition, for this set of parameter values, we assume that the labor supply elasticity is relatively more responsive; hence, it will tend to dominate the results.

At the other extreme, when all elasticity parameters are fairly large (i.e., very responsive to incentives), the tax rate reduction on most of the factors of production will elicit a phenomenal response. Our model estimates the economic response in this area could be as high as 28.9 percent.

The low estimate for GNP is based on the elasticity values at the low end of the spectrum: the partial elasticity of substitution between capital and labor (σ) equals 0.5, the high-skilled labor supply elasticity (E_{HS}) equals 0.2, and the low-skilled labor supply elasticity (E_{LW}) equals 0.4. Given these values, the change in GNP is approximately 8 percent.

Similarly, the high estimate for GNP is based on elasticity values near what most economists consider the high end of the spectrum: the partial elasticity of substitution between capital and labor equals 1.0, the high-skilled labor supply elasticity equals 0.4, and the low-skilled labor supply elasticity equals 0.8. Given these values, the change in GNP is approximately 15 percent.

TABLE 6.6. Simulation results

obs	σ	E_{HS}^{S}	E_{LW}^{S}	σ_L	σ_H	ϵ	β	$\dfrac{\Delta GNP}{GNP}$
01	0.500000	0.200000	0.400000	0.300000	0.100000	0.100000	0.000000	8.029108
02	0.500000	0.200000	0.400000	0.300000	0.100000	0.000000	0.100000	7.405169
03	0.500000	0.400000	0.400000	0.100000	0.110000	0.100000	0.200000	-0.409362
04	0.500000	0.400000	0.400000	0.100000	0.100000	0.200000	0.100000	-0.167438
05	1.000000	0.100000	0.900000	0.900000	0.100000	0.000000	0.000000	21.45601
06	1.000000	0.200000	0.900000	0.800000	0.100000	0.100000	0.000000	19.17739
07	1.000000	0.200000	0.900000	0.800000	0.100000	0.000000	0.100000	18.14232
08	1.000000	0.400000	0.900000	0.600000	0.100000	0.100000	0.200000	12.55001
09	1.000000	0.400000	0.900000	0.600000	0.100000	0.200000	0.100000	13.60107
10	1.000000	0.600000	0.900000	0.400000	0.100000	0.100000	0.400000	5.922628
11	1.000000	0.600000	0.900000	0.400000	0.100000	0.200000	0.300000	6.973690
12	1.000000	0.600000	0.900000	0.400000	0.100000	0.300000	0.200000	8.040745
13	1.000000	0.600000	0.900000	0.400000	0.100000	0.400000	0.100000	9.123793
14	1.000000	0.400000	0.800000	0.600000	0.200000	0.100000	0.100000	15.21839
15	1.000000	0.600000	0.800000	0.400000	0.200000	0.100000	0.300000	8.591010
16	1.000000	0.600000	0.800000	0.400000	0.200000	0.200000	0.200000	9.577951
17	1.000000	0.600000	0.800000	0.400000	0.200000	0.300000	0.100000	10.58089
18	1.000000	0.600000	0.600000	0.400000	0.400000	0.100000	0.100000	13.92777
19	1.500000	0.200000	1.400000	1.300000	0.100000	0.100000	0.000000	28.91313
20	1.500000	0.200000	1.400000	1.300000	0.100000	0.000000	0.100000	27.60335
21	1.500000	0.400000	1.400000	1.100000	0.100000	0.100000	0.200000	23.61123
22	1.500000	0.400000	1.400000	1.100000	0.100000	0.200000	0.100000	24.93056
23	1.500000	0.400000	1.200000	1.100000	0.300000	0.100000	0.000000	27.37364
24	1.500000	0.400000	1.200000	1.100000	0.300000	0.000000	0.100000	26.16646

Source: Compiled by the author.

135

APPENDIX B

The Treasury proposal for a modified flat tax, submitted to the president by Treasury Secretary Donald Regan on November 27, 1984, joins several other bills now before Congress. Most notable among these other proposals are the Bradley–Gephardt "Fair Tax" bill (Sen. William Bradley [D-NJ] and Rep. Richard Gephardt [D-MO] and the Kemp–Kasten "FAST Tax" bill (Rep. Jack Kemp [R-NY] and Sen. Robert Kasten [R-WI]).

The similarities between the Treasury proposal, Kemp–Kasten, and Bradley–Gephardt are more numerous than the differences. All three tax simplification proposals embody the concepts of revenue-neutrality and fairness. This ensures that tax reform will not be used as a vehicle to raise taxes, that average tax rates will remain the same, and that the changes in the tax codes will leave the distribution of the tax burden essentially unchanged by adjusted gross income class.

One area of concern is to what extent the Treasury's proposal would raise effective tax rates on production. The depreciation schedules offered by the Treasury provide slower than straight-line schedules. The risk is that even with the lower top corporate tax rate of 33 percent and indexation for inflation, business will be forced to depreciate equipment at a rate far below its true economic life, thereby increasing the effective tax rate on capital.

Moreover, a significant portion of the additional monies raised through corporate taxes are to be used to reduce non-marginal tax rates on personal income, specifically, an increase in the standard deduction and personal exemptions. This change in the constellation of tax rates decreases the efficiency of the tax system.

Capital Gains

An increase in the top capital gains tax rate to 35 percent from 20 percent also would decrease the efficiency of the tax code, although the negative effects are not nearly as great as suggested by the rate increase taken in isolation. Changes in the capital gains tax rate have to be analyzed in conjunction with the changes in the corporate income tax rate. Imagine, for example, that the capital gains tax was eliminated, but that the tax rate on business was elevated to 100 percent. Clearly, there would be no capital gains to realize, so the lower rate would be of no consequence.

Interest Deduction

The Treasury's proposal picks sound middle ground in its treatment of interest deductions. The home mortgage interest deduction is maintained. But, deductions for other non-business interest expense would have been eliminated by Kemp–Kasten and only allowed up to the amount of net investment income by Bradley–Gephardt. Both of these proposals would have discriminated against the young and workers with modest incomes that had yet to accumulate any assets, including a home. Clearly a wealthy individual with a million dollars in assets would still be able to write off the interest expense associated with purchasing, say, a Rolls Royce. But someone who lived in an apartment and had accumulated no assets would be unable to deduct the interest associated with the purchase of, say, a used car.

By allowing interest deductions up to $5,000 above net investment income, the Treasury proposal eliminates this bias against those of modest means while reducing the exploitations of interest expense in tax shelters. At a 15 percent rate, for example, an individual could deduct interest payments on up to $33,333 of additional debt.

The Tax Schedule

Finally, the personal income tax code proposed by the treasury recognizes at least in part the existence of federal payroll tax. For joint returns, the 15 percent marginal tax rate is effective for taxable income up to $31,800. For a family of four with no itemized deductions, the 15 percent rate would apply on adjusted gross income up to $39,800 ($31,800 + $8,000 in personal exemptions) (Fig. 6.1A). This schedule provides a near perfect overlap with the combined employer–employee federal payroll tax rate of 14 percent on (in 1985) the first $39,600 in wages. Thus, for a family of four taking only the standard deduction, the combined effective tax rate is 14 percent up to adjusted gross income (AGI) of $11,800 ($8,000 in personal exemption plus a zero bracket amount of $3,800) 29 percent (14 percent payroll tax plus 15 percent income tax) between AGI of $11,800 and approximately $40,000, 25 percent between AGI of approximately $40,000 and $71,800, and 35 percent thereafter (Fig. 6.1B). Thus, the tax schedule is, in reality, quite close to a flat tax.

Such an approach is quite similar to the schedule embodied in the Kemp–Kasten and Bradley–Gephardt bills (Fig. 6.1C, D). That such tax schedules are now the center of the fiscal policy debate is strong evidence of the revolution that has taken place in the conceptualization of tax policy.

FIGURE 6.1.   The modified flat tax for a family of four taking the standard deduction

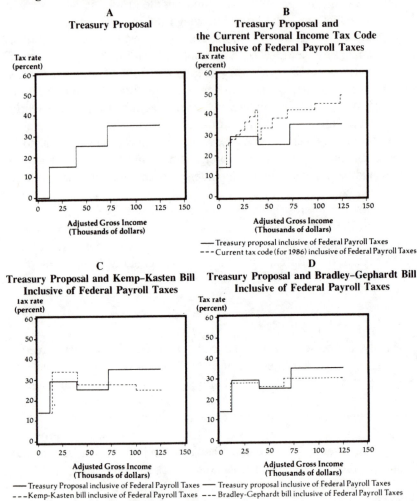

A
Treasury Proposal

B
Treasury Proposal and
the Current Personal Income Tax Code
Inclusive of Federal Payroll Taxes

——— Treasury proposal inclusive of Federal Payroll Taxes
– – – Current tax code (for 1986) inclusive of Federal Payroll Taxes

C
Treasury Proposal and Kemp–Kasten Bill
Inclusive of Federal Payroll Taxes

D
Treasury Proposal and Bradley–Gephardt Bill
Inclusive of Federal Payroll Taxes

——— Treasury Proposal inclusive of Federal Payroll Taxes   ——— Treasury proposal inclusive of Federal Payroll Taxes
– – – Kemp-Kasten bill inclusive of Federal Payroll Taxes   – – – Bradley-Gephardt bill inclusive of Federal Payroll Taxes

Source: Los Angeles Times, New York Times, Wall Street Journal.

NOTES

1. More accurately, our model has only one market output. It is, in fact, a two-sector model in the sense that it has a household production sector which also employs capital and labor in proportions that depend on their relative costs.

2. For dynamic models that treat capital formation as the outcome of an intertemporal utility maximization process, see Canto (1977) and Joines (1979).

3. For a discussion of household production see, for example, Becker and Ghez (1975).

4. Notice that the labor supply functions yield positive own-price factor supply elasticities:

$$E_{LW}^S = \frac{W^*}{L} \frac{\partial L}{\partial W^*} = \sigma_L + \beta + \epsilon > 0$$

$$E_{HS}^S = \frac{S^*}{H} \frac{\partial H}{\partial S^*} = \sigma_S + \beta + \epsilon > 0$$

The cross-price elasticities, however, could be either positive or negative:

$$E_{LS}^S = \frac{S^*}{L} \frac{\partial L}{\partial S^*} = -\sigma_L \gtrless 0$$

$$E_{HW}^S = \frac{W^*}{H} \frac{\partial H}{\partial W^*} = -\sigma_H \gtrless 0$$

5. For simplicity we assume that:

    a. government expenditures take the form of transfer payment to individuals, receipt of which is unrelated to factor supply;

    b. there is no waste or inefficiency on the part of the government;

    c. taxes and transfers are costless to collect and distribute, respectively.

Under these conditions, government spending will have no net income effect, only a substitution effect, due to the relative price changes resulting from the taxes. Joines (1979) and Canto (1977) develop a similar analysis of government fiscal policy in which the possibility of deficit financing is presented. Canto and Miles (1981) consider the possibility of income effects resulting from different types of government expenditures, collection costs, and the government efficiency level.

REFERENCES

Becker, G., and G. Ghez. 1975. *The Allocation of Time and Goods Over the Lifecycle.* New York: Columbia University Press, for the National Bureau of Economic Research.

Borjas, G., and J. Heckman. 1978. "Labor Supply Estimates for Public Policy Evaluation." *Proceedings of the Industrial Relations Research Association,* pp. 320–331.

Boskin, M. 1978. "Taxation, Savings and the Rate of Interest." *Journal of Political Economy* 86 (April):3–27.

———. 1973. "The Economics of the Labor Supply." In *Income Maintenance and Labor Supply,* edited by Glen G. Cain and Harold W. Watts. Chicago, IL: Rand McNally.

Bradley, B., and R. Gephardt. 1983. "Fact Sheet on the Bradley–Gephardt 'Fair Tax Act of 1983'" Press Release (May).

Canto, V. 1977. "Taxation, Welfare and Economic Activity." Ph.D. dissertation, University of Chicago.

Canto, V. and M. Miles. 1981. "The Missing Equation: An Alternative Interpretation." *Journal of Macroeconomics* 3 (Spring): 247–269.

Danziger, S., R. Haveman and R. Plotnick. 1981. "How Income Transfer Programs Affect Work, Savings, and the Income Distribution: A Critical Review." *Journal of Economic Literature* 19 (September): 975–1028.

Davis, A., with V. Canto, C. Kadlec, A. Laffer, and J. Rogers. 1983. "A Productive Employment Program Utilizing the Marginal Economy." A.B. Laffer Associates Rolling Hills Estates, CA. (June).

Evans, P. 1983. "Fiscal Policy and the Labor Market." In *Foundations of Supply-Side Economics*, edited by V. Canto, D. Joines, and A. Laffer, pp. 104–123. New York: Academic Press.

Finnegan, T. 1962. "Hours of Work in the United States—A Cross-Sectional Analysis." *Journal of Political Economy* 70 (October): 450–470.

Hall, R., and A. Rabushka. 1982. "A Simple Income Tax with Low Marginal Rates." Hoover Institution, Stanford University (July).

Joines, D. 1981. "Estimates of Effective Marginal Rates on Factor Incomes." *Journal of Business* 54, 2: 191–226.

———. 1979. "Government Fiscal Policy and Private Capital Formation." Ph.D. dissertation, University of Chicago.

Killingsworth, M. 1983. *Labor Supply*. New York: Cambridge University Press.

Laffer, A. 1984. "The Tightening Grip of the Poverty Trap." *Policy Analysis* (Cato Institute) 1, 41 (August): 1–22.

———. 1981. "Government Exactions and Revenue Deficiencies." *Cato Journal, 1,* no. 1 (Spring): 1–21.

Lucas, R., and L. Rapping. 1970. "Real Wages, Employment and Inflation." In *Microeconomic Foundations of Employment and Inflation Theory,* edited by E. Phelps et al., pp. 257–305. New York: W.W. Norton.

U.S. Department of Commerce. Bureau of Economic Analysis. *Survey of Current Business.* U.S. Government Printing Office, January, 1984.

7
The Tightening Grip of the Poverty Trap
Arthur B. Laffer

SUMMARY

A tragedy of immense proportions is in the making. The recent tightening of eligibility requirements for the receipt of food stamps, Aid to Families with Dependent Children, and the like has created effective tax rates on the poor well in excess of 100 percent. Today, if a family of four with a single adult increases its earnings to $1,200 a month from zero, the loss of welfare benefits plus the bite of taxes shrink the family's total spending power by $46—an average effective tax rate of over 100 percent. Parsimony has turned the "safety net" of a moral society into an immoral labyrinth of need and income tests that uses poverty to entrap the poor.

The Enterprise Zone legislation designed by the Reagan administration will do little, if anything, to free the poor from this poverty trap. This legislation suffers from a disregard for the impact of incentives on human behavior. In the name of frugality, this new law would continue to squander the precious capabilities and futures of the nation's poor.

Policy must be redirected so that prosperity does not remain quarantined in the suburbs. Economic recovery should be allowed to spread to the barrios and ghettos that comprise the inner city. Implementation of the following five-point program within designated Enterprise Zones would be a step in that direction:

• Reduce effective tax rates resulting from "needs," "means," and "income" tests that sometimes exceed 100 percent by relaxing eligibility requirements for entitlements

- Eliminate payroll taxes on wages below $10,000 per year earnings.
- Eliminate or reduce the teenage minimum wage.
- Reduce the corporate tax rate to 10 percent.
- Require economic impact statements for all new and existing regulations and other government strictures.

April 29, 1983

THE "SAFETY NET"

Over the past 16 years, a "safety net" has been created for the disadvantaged and unemployed in our society. Food stamps, rent subsidies, medical care, and direct income supplements in the form of Aid to Families with Dependent Children (AFDC) are all available to alleviate the worst hardships of poverty. Since 1968, transfer payments to persons have increased more than sevenfold to $403 billion. Even after adjusting for inflation, transfer payments have more than doubled. While much of this increase has occurred in Social Security and other government-funded retirement programs, the growth in transfer payment programs aimed specifically at the poor and disadvantaged tells much the same story. In 1983, expenditures for AFDC, food stamps and the like totaled $105.6 billion—nearly three times the amount spent in constant dollars in 1968 (Fig. 7.1).[1]

Nonetheless, in the persistent effort to achieve parsimony in conjunction with fairness and equity, each of these programs has stringent criteria for its recipients. For those who receive AFDC, there is an "income" test which, after four months, reduces this benefit, dollar-for-dollar, on earned income above $75 per month. AFDC benefits can be sheltered from this 100 percent tax by expending that amount on child care. Similar "means" and "income" test strictures apply to recipients of food stamps, housing subsidies, unemployment compensation, and the like. These criteria of eligibility were designed to ensure that only the truly needy would receive the help they so desperately lacked. Excluding people in progressively higher income groups meant that funds would not be squandered on those who were less in need.

While these retirement, means, income, unemployment, and other "need" tests may be rationalized on both moral and budgetary grounds,

FIGURE 7.1.   Growth in transfer payments to the poor and disadvantaged, 1950–1982

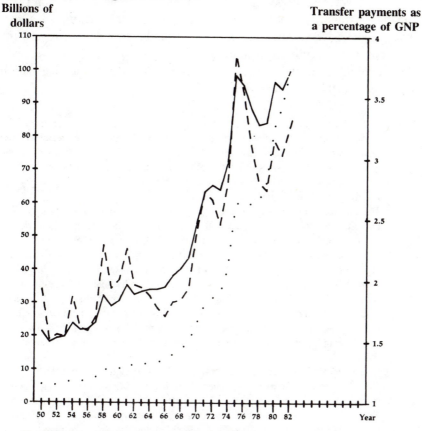

—— Unemployment, AFDC and other benefits in 1982 dollars
– – – Unemployment, AFDC and other benefits as a percent of GNP
· · · · Unemployment, AFDC and other benefits in nominal dollars

Source: U.S. Department of Commerce. Bureau of Economic Analysis. *National Income and Product Accounts.* Government Printing Office, Washington, D.C.

they have marked, perverse effects on economic incentives of the poor. When combined with payroll and income taxes, the phased reduction of welfare benefits meant that spendable income actually rose very little as gross wages increased to $1,600 per month. With the tightening of eligibility requirements for food stamps and AFDC, spendable income (total spending power) actually declines as gross wages rise to $1,300 per month.

A Flawed Enterprise Zone Proposal

The Enterprise Zone legislation offered by the administration is incapable of freeing the inner city from this poverty trap. It reflects a misplaced fear of losing nonexistent revenues and a complete disregard for the impact of incentives on individual behavior.

There are four major weaknesses in the Enterprise Zone legislation supported by the administration.[2]

1. The bill discriminates against employers currently located in the Enterprise Zone. Under the proposed legislation, disbursement of tax credits will be greater to those businesses with greater additions to the payroll. This works to the disadvantage of already existing businesses relative to new companies which, by definition, have base wages equal to zero. Newly relocated firms can pass these savings on by hiring more workers or paying more competitive salaries.

2. The bill discriminates against low-wage individuals currently working in the Enterprise Zone by offering substantial tax incentives over a seven-year period to "Economically Disadvantaged Individuals" (EDI). Certification as an EDI requires, among other things, a 60-day period of unemployment and a record of having received, or being eligible to receive, welfare assistance. The tax incentives narrow the employer–employee wedge for certified individuals. As a result, at the same wage received, a certified individual costs an employer less. Or, at the same wage paid by the employer, wages received by the certified individual will be higher. The net result is to increase incentives among low-wage individuals to become unemployed until they become certifiable as "Economically Disadvantaged Individuals."

3. Investment tax credits increase incentives to locate capital equipment in the zone. Once the capital is in place, however, there is no additional incentive to operate it, compared to capital in place anywhere else in the United States or the world. The investment tax credit will distort the type of operations located in the inner city toward those intensive in the use of capital equipment, rather than those intensive in the use of capital. This does not solve the problem of inadequate demand for low-wage labor.

4. The provisions of the bill are too complex. Reporting requirements, record keeping, and so on, discriminate against small local entrepreneurs in favor of large corporations with existing legal and personnel departments.

CASE STUDY: A LOS ANGELES FAMILY

The net effect on spendable income of the combination of "need" tests and taxes for an inner-city family of four in Los Angeles is shown in Table 7.1. The family is assumed to have one adult and three dependent children. In addition, it is assumed that the family avails itself of the

TABLE 7.1. The effect of taxes and "income" tests on family spendable income from wages and welfare benefits

Monthly gross wages($)	Net family spendable income($)	Increase in spendable income($)	De facto marginal tax rate(%)
0	1,125	na	na
100	1,172	47	53
200	1,219	47	53
300	1,215	−4	104
400	1,204	−11	111
500	1,245	41	59
600	1,285	40	60
700	1,307	22	78
800	1,300	−7	107
900	1,305	5	95
1,000	1,201	−104	204[a]
1,100	987	−214	314[b]
1,200	1,034	47	53
1,300	1,078	44	56

na: not available.

[a]The increase in marginal tax rates is due to elimination of $133 in food stamp benefits between gross wages of $900 and $1,000.

[b]The sharp increase in marginal tax rate is due to elimination of $374 in AFDC benefits between wages of $1,000 and $1,100.

Source: Department of Social Security, Los Angeles; County Welfare Office, Department of Social Services; Housing Authority of the City of Los Angeles

maximum city, county, state, and federal welfare benefits to which it is entitled, based on its income. These benefits include AFDC, food stamps, MediCal (California's Medicaid) and housing subsidy.

The impact of incremental increases in gross wages of $100 per month has been calculated up to $1,600 per month (Table 7.1). The wage figure is the total cost to the firm of employing one person. The income figures thus include employer contributions to Social Security and unemployment insurance contributions.

Several biases exist that cut in a number of directions, but the central point is obvious. Marginal tax rates for inner-city inhabitants are prohibitively high. Over the entire range from zero wages to $1,600 per month (equivalent to a gross paycheck of $1,463 per month), the family's monthly spendable income rises by $69. This corresponds to an average tax "wedge" of 95.7 percent. More shocking is that between zero wages and $1,200 per month, the family loses $46 in monthly spendable income—an average tax in excess of 100 percent.

This loss in net spendable income is concentrated between monthly wages of $700 and $1,200 per month. As monthly wages paid rise by $500, the family loses its entitlement to $385 in AFDC benefits and $9 in food stamps. In addition, the housing subsidy is reduced by $23 and the value of medical benefits declines an estimated $130. At the same time, the family's tax liabilities increase by a total of $161—$8 in state income and disability insurance taxes, $68 in payroll taxes, and $85 in federal income tax. (Details of these calculations can be found in the Appendix at the end of this chapter.)

The net result is to impose an effective tax rate of 142 percent on monthly gross wages of between $700 and $1,200, and an even more incredible 278 percent on gross wages between $1,000 and $1,100 per month. Never before has there been such a paucity of opportunity for the law-abiding poor to better themselves. Disincentives have always been part of the welfare system. What has changed is the severity of those disincentives.

Under the Carter administration (1978), for example, if this same family of four had earned income from zero to $610 per month, it would have had more to spend. Thus, the loss of welfare benefits and the incurring of tax payments were less than the increases in wages from zero wages to approximately $610 a month (in 1983 dollars).

This is called the "incentive range" because individuals are better off when they earn more. However, it would be grossly inaccurate to convey the impression that incentives in this range are high. In 1978, the increase in spending power was only $148 as family earnings rose from zero to $610 per month. This corresponds to an average effective tax rate of 76 percent. In spite of the offensive nature of this confiscation, it still represents the best the poor have. In 1981 and 1984, this "incentive range" (in 1983 dollars) ranged up to $874 and $678, respectively (Table 7.2). Again, these "incentive ranges" for the years 1981 and 1984 do not live up to their billing. For 1981, the incentive range represents an effective tax rate of 79 percent and, for 1984, the effective tax rate is 74 percent.

In 1978, net spendable income declined $9 as gross wages rose to $1,220 from $610 per month. Thus, the after-tax wage increases were a little more than offset by the family's reduced eligibility for welfare benefits. Within this "disincentive range," the family's standard of living remained essentially unchanged as its earnings changed. The effective equivalent tax rate was, as a result, roughly 100 percent on any additional work effort. Beyond $1,220 per month, however, spendable income began, once again, to rise with higher earnings (Table 7.2).

TABLE 7.2. Comparison of the effect of taxes and "income" tests on family spendable income from wages and welfare benefits under the Carter and Reagan administrations

1978 (March 1983 $)		1981 (March 1983 $)		1983 (March 1983 $)	
Monthly gross wages	Net family spendable income	Monthly gross wages	Net family spendable income	Monthly gross wages	Net family spendable income
0	1,077	0	1,214	0	1,125
600	1,223	860	1,394	700	1,307
751	1,193*	968	1,391	800	1,300
1,200	1,214	1,291	1,281*	1,100	987*
1,350	1,248	1,398	1,302	1,300	1,078
1,500	1,287				

(1978: incentive range 0–600; disincentive range 751–1,200; incentive range 1,350–1,500)
(1981: incentive range 0–860; disincentive range 968–1,398)
(1983: incentive range 0–700; disincentive range 800–1,300)

*Low point in disincentive range.

Source: Department of Social Security, Los Angeles; County Welfare Office, Department of Social Services; Housing Authority of the City of Los Angeles.

By the fall of 1981, the top of the ''incentive range'' had increased to $874 per month. Because of spending reductions achieved under the Reagan administration's first budget, however, the disincentive zone became a chasm of declining living standards. In the course of increasing gross wages by $547 a month, the family's spendable income declined by $94, an effective tax rate of 117 percent. In 1984, the disincentive zone began at $1,000 a month. As gross wages increased to $1,600 per month, spendable earnings actually declined by $102—an effective tax rate of 117 percent in this income range (Table 7.2).

To understand the effect of such a system, imagine the dilemma facing a disadvantaged individual being paid $1,000 per month when he or she is offered a promotion with a 20 percent pay increase (cost to the employer) to $1,200 per month. The decision to accept the promotion will not only require the individual to take on more responsibility but also to accept a $217 per month reduction in spendable income. Unless the individual perceives the promotion as an investment in the future and, hence, is willing to forgo current consumption, he or she will turn the job down, perpetuating the low income that entraps the family.

DIMENSIONS OF THE POVERTY TRAP

The overall effect of these high effective tax rates on the poor and disadvantaged has been nothing short of tragic. During the 1970s, non-white and low-skilled workers fell further and further behind their white and high-skilled counterparts in the economic areas of participation in the labor force, unemployment, and earnings. At the same time, the rising crime rate of the inner city and further deterioration of the minority family unit created additional adversities for the disadvantaged sectors of our society.

The relative deterioration in the position of non-whites and the low-skilled results not from the exceptional economic performance of whites and the high-skilled, but has occurred in spite of poor white performance. While white performance has been discouraging, non-white performance has been even worse.

To those immersed in the political rhetoric of our times, such a contradiction must appear incredible. To an economist, however, these results are a fully predictable consequence. Dramatically increased economic disincentives and other legislated barriers have disenfranchised many non-whites from participation in U.S. economic prosperity.

Rising crime rates in the inner city are partially fueled by high unemployment rates and an antiquated penal system. The inner-city unemployed have little incentive to obtain a job, since any legitimate source of revenue would be accompanied by a reduction in welfare benefits and additional taxes. In the unlikely event that the criminal is apprehended and convicted, prison would merely take some of the time which, to him, is so abundant.

The quality of life in the inner city has been disrupted in several aspects by these extraordinarily high effective tax rates created by welfare-related legislation. Each aspect, in its own way, testifies to the power of incentives to influence human behavior.

Participation Rates

On one level, participation in the labor force by non-white males has fallen, both on an absolute basis and relative to whites. The percentage of the non-white male population looking for work or actually working was significantly lower in 1982 than it was 14 years before. White participation rates, by contrast, declined only slightly (Table 7.3). The proportional decline in participation rates for males is even greater for non-whites because the initial level of participation was lower.

At first glance, the decline in overall participation rates evident between 1968 and 1982 appears to be a continuation of a trend established between 1958 and 1968. However, an analysis of participation rates by age reveals that, for males between the ages of 25 and 55, participation rates during the 1958–1968 period remain essentially unchanged. Participation fell among the young and the elderly. One reason for the fall in teenage participation rates was the 60 percent increase in the minimum wage to $1.60 an hour that occurred between 1958 and 1968. The decline in participation rates among those 56 years and older is undoubtedly due, in part, to improvements in retirement plans during this period (Table 7.3).

An analysis of the experience of non-white females relative to white females yields much the same result. For both groups, participation rates rise but, on a relative basis, the participation rate of white females rose by a much greater amount (Table 7.3).

An individual may have diverse reasons for not participating in the labor force, but the economist focusing on incentives would surmise that rational individuals would not participate when the cost of participation exceeded the expected returns. As the costs of participating in the labor

TABLE 7.3.   Participation rates, by age and race

	White (%)			Non-White (%)		
Age	1958	1968	1982	1959	1968	1982
Male						
16–17	46.8	47.7	49.3	45.1	37.9	26.3
18–19	69.4	65.7	70.5	71.7	63.3	54.9
20–24	86.7	82.4	86.3	88.7	85.0	77.0
25–34	97.2	97.2	95.6	96.3	95.0	88.8
35–44	98.0	97.6	96.0	96.4	93.4	90.2
45–54	96.6	95.4	92.2	93.9	90.1	83.7
55–64	88.2	84.7	71.0	83.3	79.6	63.8
65 +	35.7	27.3	17.9	34.5	26.6	16.7
All ages combined	84.3	80.4	77.4	84.0	77.6	71.0
Female						
16–17	28.8	33.0	44.6	23.2	22.3	24.1
18–19	52.3	53.3	64.6	41.2	46.9	44.5
20–24	46.1	54.0	71.8	48.3	58.4	59.9
25–34	33.6	40.6	67.8	50.8	56.6	68.6
35–44	41.4	47.5	67.5	60.8	59.3	70.8
45–54	46.5	51.5	61.4	59.8	59.8	62.5
55–64	34.5	42.0	41.5	42.8	47.0	44.5
65 +	10.1	9.4	7.8	13.3	11.9	8.3
All ages combined	35.8	41.6	52.4	48.0	49.3	53.9

Source: U.S. Department of Labor. Bureau of Labor Statistics. *Employment and Earnings.* January 1983; *Employment and Training Report of the President.*

force rise and the benefits fall, participation should decline. As the probability of finding work and the gains from working decrease, participation should fall. When all these events occur at the same time, it should not be surprising that participation rates fall.

Employment Rates

One measure of the likelihood of finding work is the employment rate (100 percent minus the unemployment rate). This dimension of the poverty trap reveals the same trends as the participation rate, only to a more alarming extent. Table 7.4, which shows employment rates for males and females by age and race, clearly illustrates the trend since 1968.

TABLE 7.4. Participation rates, by age and race

Age	White (%)			Non-White (%)		
	1958	1968	1982	1959	1968	1982
Male						
16–17	85.1	87.7	75.8	72.9	73.4	53.1
18–19	83.5	91.8	80.0	73.3	81.0	57.3
20–24	88.3	95.4	85.7	80.5	91.7	70.8
25–34	94.4	98.3	91.1	85.3	96.2	81.9
35–44	95.6	98.6	93.8	88.6	97.1	87.8
45–54	95.2	98.5	94.7	89.7	97.5	91.5
55–64	94.8	98.3	94.9	89.9	96.4	90.5
65 +	95.0	97.6	96.8	91.0	96.0	90.7
All ages combined	93.9	97.4	91.2	86.2	94.4	81.8
Female						
16–17	84.4	86.1	78.8	74.6	66.1	58.9
18–19	89.0	89.0	82.4	70.0	73.6	54.7
20–24	92.6	94.1	89.1	81.1	87.8	73.2
25–34	93.4	96.1	92.0	88.9	91.6	83.6
35–44	94.4	96.9	93.6	90.8	95.0	89.9
45–54	95.1	97.7	94.5	95.0	96.8	91.7
55–64	95.7	97.9	95.0	93.8	97.2	93.6
65 +	96.5	97.2	96.9	94.4	96.0	95.4
All ages combined	93.8	95.7	91.7	88.2	91.7	83.6

Source: U.S. Department of Labor. Bureau of Labor Statistics. *Employment and Earnings.* January 1983; *Employment and Training Report of the President.*

In every age category, for those participating in the labor force, the probabilities of being among the employed for non-whites has decreased dramatically relative to whites (Table 7.4). This also is true for female employment rates when whites and non-whites are compared (Table 7.4). By contrast, during the 10-year period ending in 1968, employment rates for whites and non-whites, males and females alike, increased. Moreover, employment rates increased the most for black males.

As with labor force participation, there are many reasons a person may be unemployed. Unemployment takes place when firms cannot profitably hire workers at acceptable wages. Legislated contributors to unemployment can be direct, as with a minimum wage so high that no employer finds it worthwhile to hire the youth and low-skilled of the inner city. The minimum wage literally prohibits the employment of people who are, in strict economic terms, worth less than $3.35 per hour.

Those who have less productive ability because they are young, inexperienced, uneducated, or not fluent in English are particularly hard hit by this legislation. Despite the obvious beneficial intent of the minimum wage law, its effect on youth and low-skilled workers is so disastrous that an outside observer might well believe it was designed to create unemployment.

The extraordinarily high effective marginal tax rates facing welfare recipients also contribute directly to the relative loss in employment of non-whites. Other legislation contributing to unemployment is less obvious. Further regulatory burdens, higher taxes on employers, and a worsening capital shortage all contribute to a decline in the demand for workers. As these changes occurred in the past decade, the results have been additional unemployment and a disturbing fall in the purchasing power of the average worker's paycheck. This is illustrated by the third link in the poverty chain.

Real Earnings

Between 1968 and 1981, real earnings of black males employed year-round in most age groups have grown faster than real earnings of whites on a relative basis (Table 7.5). The same is true for non-white females. By contrast, between 1959 and 1968, the median income of white males and females rose relative to their non-white counterparts (Table 7.6).

On the surface, this is encouraging, but closer evaluation yields a more disturbing insight. Given the large increases in unemployment and decreases in participation rates among non-white males 20 years and older, large numbers of low-income blacks no longer are employed and earning income year-round. The increase in the median income of black males employed year-round apparently reflects the dropping of lower-income males and females from the calculation rather than an elevation in overall black welfare.

This interpretation of the data is supported by changes in the median family income. For both black and white families living in the central cities, median income in constant 1983 dollars declined between 1969 and 1981 (Table 7.7). For blacks, the decline was 71 percent greater than that for whites. The gap between black and white median family income in metropolitan areas outside the central city narrowed somewhat. On an overall basis, however, the disparity between the standards of living enjoyed by black and white families increased during the 12 years ending in 1981 (Table 7.7).

TABLE 7.5. Median income of males employed year-round, by age and race (1982 dollars)

Age	1959*	1968	1981	Increase (1959–1968)	Increase (1968–1981)
White					
20–24	8,958	16,100	13,504	7,142	− 2,596
25–34	16,687	22,420	20,807	5,733	− 1,613
35–44	18,810	25,120	25,528	6,310	408
45–54	17,631	23,822	26,597	6,191	2,775
55–64	15,236	21,696	25,175	6,460	3,479
All ages combined	14,362	22,326	22,476	7,964	150
Non-white					
20–24	5,739	12,432	11,104	6,693	− 1,328
25–34	9,640	15,864	16,261	6,224	397
35–44	10,647	15,778	17,280	5,131	1,502
45–54	9,312	16,206	16,093	6,894	− 113
55–64	7,448	13,775	16,521	6,327	2,746
All ages combined	7,643	14,899	15,903	7,226	1,004

*Median income is not available for employed year-round persons in 1959; instead the general category of persons was used in that year.

Source: Bureau of Census. *Current Population Reports, 1981,* series p-60, no. 137, Table 46; *1960 Census of the U.S., United States Summary,* 1964, vol. 1, part 1, Table 219.

To make matters worse, this increased disparity in living standards occurred at a time when the purchasing power of the average worker's income, adjusted for taxes, was declining. Real spendable earnings for a nonagricultural production (or nonsupervisory) worker with three dependents peaked in 1977 at $287.98 per week (1983 dollars). By 1981, real spendable earnings, as reported in the U.S. Department of Labor's *Employment and Earnings,* had declined to $227.08.

The Tragic Results

This fall in the purchasing power of the average worker's wages is tragic when compared to the almost constant advance in real wages that has occurred over the past century. The tragedy is felt most intensely by marginal workers who, by the very nature of their marginality, are the first to lose their jobs when the demand for workers falls. For marginal workers, the question is not whether their wages will keep up with in-

TABLE 7.6.   Median income of females employed year-round, by age and race (1982 dollars)

Age	1959*	1968	1981	Increase (1959–1968)	Increase (1968–1981)
White					
20–24	6,010	11,886	10,884	5,876	– 1,002
25–34	6,630	14,150	14,379	7,520	229
35–44	7,269	13,423	14,861	6,154	1,438
45–54	7,848	13,206	13,814	5,358	608
55–64	5,785	13,420	14,069	7,635	649
All ages combined	5,000	13,004	13,441	8,004	437
Non-White					
20–24	2,987	9,849	9,616	6,862	– 233
25–34	4,288	11,148	13,280	6,860	2,132
35–44	4,328	10,132	12,210	5,804	2,078
45–54	3,348	9,711	12,091	6,363	2,380
55–64	2,739	8,190	11,192	5,451	3,002
All ages combined	3,047	9,880	12,139	6,833	2,259

*Median income is not available for employed year-round persons in 1959; instead the general category of persons was used in that year.

Source: Bureau of the Census. *Current Population Reports, 1981,* series P-60, no. 137, Table 46; *1960 Census of the U.S., United States Summary,* 1964, vol. 1, part 1, Table 219.

flation, but whether they can remain productive, self-supporting members of society. The costs cannot be fully expressed in dollars. The personal degradation of continually seeking work and being told that their serv-

TABLE 7.7.   Median incomes of families (1982 dollars)

Category	White			Non-White		
	1969	1981	Increase	1969	1981	Increase
Inside central city	$26,440	$24,287	$ – 2,153	$17,264	$13,583	$ – 3,681
Metropolitan outside central city	29,509	30,588	– 688	18,209	18,804	595
All families	25,782	24,959	– 823	15,795	14,073	– 1,722

Note: Income of families in 1959 is not available by categories of inside central city and metropolitan outside central city. However, median income of white families in urban areas in 1959 (in 1982 dollars) is equal to $20,409 and for non-white families is $12,895. According to the 1960 census, places of 2,500 inhabitants or more are considered urban.

Source: Bureau of the Census. *Current Population Reports, 1981,* series P-60, no. 137.

ices are unwanted must also be taken into account. The fact that this type of degradation is focused on minority races can only add to the victims' feelings of resentment and social anomie.

An individual's decision not to participate in the labor force is an active statement of how that person sees his or her abilities relative to society's values. The individual might well say that the chances of finding a job are so low that it is not worth trying. Or it may be that the wages would be so low relative to welfare opportunities that it is not worthwhile to seek work. One way or another, nonparticipation is tantamount to having no hope of engaging in the productive activity that, for most people, is a central part of life.

The tragedy of unemployment is not fully reflected in the figures. The average unemployment rate misses the high and growing unemployment rates of non-white youth. For non-whites currently not in school within the 16–19 age group, for example, the participation rate is 40.6 percent. Of those participating, only 55 percent are employed. Taken together, that means more than 75 percent of this group are either looking for work and are unable to find it, or are not even bothering to look for work. These individuals are developing habits and a life style in which productive activity is absent. Moreover, they are missing the training and experience that past generations of non-whites have used to gain entry to the business world.

Family Deterioration

Disruption of the family unit is yet another aspect of the web of welfare disincentives that is a predictable outcome of our welfare benefit structure. Public assistance agencies allocate benefits generally on the basis of family units, and these benefits increase less than proportionately as family size increases. Two families of three members each generally will be eligible for more benefits than one family of six members when there is no outside income. This incentive leads to the breaking up of the family as income is earned. If the family of six earns income, its benefits fall at a faster rate than for two families of three or three families of two (Table 7.8).

The incentives to divide a family are even more striking when one considers that, in a family unit with two adults, one of the two must be working unless he is disabled or has been unsucccessful in his job search. In a family unit with only one adult, it is unnecessary that he or she work or search for a job as long as there are school-age children at home. By

TABLE 7.8. Maximum benefits under major welfare programs

Benefit	Family of 6	Two families of 3	Three families of 2
Food stamps	$360	$ 398	$ 417
AFDC	$771	$1,012	$1,224

Source: Department of Social Services, Los Angeles, California.

separating the family, simultaneously welfare benefits are increased and the need for one adult to work is eliminated.

Rewards for family division are most pressing when one member is fully employed. The income of one adult may sufficiently reduce benefits so that the family's spendable income suffers. By keeping himself separate from the rest of the family through lack of marriage or other legal connection, the employed father allows the mother to be eligible for the full array of entitlement programs. Thus eligibility requirements may make family desertion a parental duty, not an act of cowardice. It should not be surprising that more than half the black children under the age of 18 are not living with both parents and that nearly half of black births are illegitimate. Tables 7.8, 7.9, and 7.10 illustrate these family trends.

CONCLUSION

The financial incentive structure of the past 16 years has visited a tragedy on inner-city residents. Given current legislative initiatives, the inner-city poor may well find themselves even more isolated in the coming decade. In the 1960s, rapid, sustained economic growth created a climate of increased opportunities, higher standards of living, and the hope of a better life for the poor and disadvantaged. But the economic expansion the 1980s threatens to leave the inner-city family dependent on, and penned

TABLE 7.9. Female family householders, by race

	1960	1968	1981	Increase (1960–1968)	Increase (1968–1981)
Percentage of white families	8.1	8.9	11.9	0.8	3
Percentage of non-white families	20.9	27.7	41.7	6.8	14.0

Source: U.S. Bureau of the Census. *1960 Census of Population,* 1964, vol. 1, and *Current Population Reports,* 1981, series P-20, no. 371, and earlier issues.

TABLE 7.10. Rate of illegitimacy in births (percentage)

	1960	1968	1980	Increase (1960–1968)	Increase (1968–1980)
White	2.3	5.3	11.0	3	5.7
Non-white	21.6	31.2	48.5	9.6	17.3

Source: U.S. National Center for Health Statistics. *Monthly Vital Statistics Reports,* 1981, Washington, D.C.

within, the public assistance structure. Who among the poor will ask their families to take a 20 percent or 30 percent cut in their standard of living so that they can have the privilege of going to work? It would be a further tragedy for minorities to continue to fall behind while their white counterparts catch hold in an expanding economy.

A Positive Plan

What is needed is a reversal of those policies that have turned the safety net of a moral society into an immoral labyrinth that uses poverty itself to entrap the poor. Policy must be directed toward ensuring that the fruits of economic recovery can be harvested in the barrios and ghettos that comprise the inner city. A first and necessary step in that direction can be outlined in a five-point program:

1. Eliminate effective tax rates in excess of 100 percent through the relaxation of means, needs, and "income" tests.
2. Establish a corporate tax rate on operations inside the Enterprise Zone of a maximum of 10 percent.
3. Eliminate payroll taxes (both employer and employee) on the first $10,000 in annual earned income for individuals who live and work in the Enterprise Zone.
4. Eliminate or reduce the minimum wage for teenagers employed in the Enterprise Zone.
5. Require economic impact statements for all new and existing regulations and other forms of government strictures that apply to businesses and individuals in the Enterprise Zone, in order to identify regulations that would constrain economic activity and employment within the zones.

APPENDIX: CALCULATION OF THE INCURSION OF TAX LIABILITIES AND LOSS OF WELFARE BENEFITS AS EARNINGS INCREASE

The following tax and welfare disincentives apply to a family of four (a head of household and three dependent children) living in Les Angeles:

A. Tax Liabilities Incurred
   1. Employer taxes: 7.0 percent employer's share of Social Security plus 3.5 percent unemployment insurance contribution up to $7,000 in wages plus 1 percent contribution to mandatory workmen's compensation. Total: 11.5 percent of gross wages paid.
   2. Employee Social Security tax: 6.7 percent of gross wages.
   3. Employee disability insurance (SDI): 0.9 percent of gross wages.
   4. State and federal income taxes: increase progressively to 23 percent.

B. Welfare Benefits Lost
   1. *Aid to Families with Dependent Children (AFDC).* Payments terminate when income exceeds 150 percent of AFDC "standard of need." In the case of this family of four, the AFDC maximum aid payment is $625 and the 150 percent figure is $938. As wages are earned, the monthly payment of $625 is reduced progressively. For the first three months of employment, benefits are reduced about $67 per month as gross wages rise $100 per month. The fourth month, benefits are reduced dollar for dollar as additional income is earned above $75 per month. In other words, once an individual is above a minimum established by a formula, AFDC benefits fall by one dollar for every dollar earned. When computing AFDC benefits, it is assumed that half the working adult's wages are sheltered by expending the money on child care, which is deductible up to $160 per child per month. It also is assumed that Medicaid (full health insurance for the family of four) has a market value of $166 per month.

   2. *Rent subsidy.* The Los Angeles County Housing Authority will pay the difference between the tenant's portion of the rent (not more than 30 percent of the tenant's net income) and the actual rent. In our example, the family of four is eligible for a two-bedroom apartment with rent up to $538 per month including utilities. The tenant's share of the rent is calculated by taking all monthly "money income" (wages plus AFDC benefits) and subtracting a child care credit of $25 per child per month. The tenant's portion of the rent is 30 percent of the remaining monthly income. At zero income, with AFDC benefits of $625 per month, subtracting $75 in child care credits for three children, the family in our example would pay 30 percent of the remaining $550, or $165 per month. The rent subsidy would be $373, paid by the

. Housing Authority. The family becomes ineligible for rent subsidy when its income reaches $21,900.

3. *Medical.* For this family of four, as long as all income (including AFDC benefits) does not exceed $834 per month, Medical will pay the total monthly medical costs. When the family's income exceeds $834, each dollar of additional income must go to pay any medical costs that are incurred. For example, if the family's income was $1,000 (exceeding the "maintenance need" level by $166) and medical expenses during the month were $200, the entire $166 would go toward paying the medical costs.

4. *Food stamps.* This benefit is reduced in proportion to money income (wages plus AFDC benefits). For a family of four, food stamp payments range from $253 per month (with zero money income) to $10 per month (with $1,073 in gross income). Because of California's AFDC payments, at zero wages, this family qualifies for $92.20 per month in food stamp benefits.

Sources: State Department of Social Services, Los Angeles; County Welfare Office, Department of Social Services, West Los Angeles; Housing Authority of the County of Los Angeles, Applications and Eligibility Supervisor, Los Angeles; South West Family Aid, Department of Social Services, Los Angeles; California Franchise Tax Board, Los Angeles; Internal Revenue Service.

NOTES

1. This includes government unemployment insurance benefits, Aid to Families with Dependent Children, food stamps, Supplementary Security income, categorical and general public assistance, workman's compensation, and railroad retirement.

2. Based on the "Enterprise Zone Act of 1982," HR 6009, 97th Congress, 2d session (March 31, 1982).

REFERENCES

U.S. Department of Labor. *Employment and Earnings.* U.S. Government Printing Office, 1983.

8

The Productive Employment Program: A New Approach to Fighting Unemployment

Victor A. Canto, Charles W. Kadlec,
and Arthur B. Laffer

SUMMARY

It is time to try a new approach to reducing unemployment in the United States. The record clearly shows that existing programs aimed at reduced unemployment have failed to accomplish their goal. The problem resides in the fact that unemployment programs in their current form ignore the importance of individual incentives to employ workers and produce goods and services.

A new proposal, known as the Productive Employment Program (PEP), is outlined in this paper. PEP is designed to minimize the problem areas of conventional unemployment programs while increasing the number of employment opportunities for those out of work. Under this program, the unemployed person would be issued a voucher and would be given the option of collecting unemployment benefits directly if a job is not found, or indirectly by using the voucher to transfer the benefit to an employer. This transfer of benefits is called the production subsidy, and would not be taxable to the employer.

The Productive Employment Program is recommended for several reasons: it offers the immediate prospect of reducing the unemployment rate without requiring new taxes or government staff or increased spending; it is simple; and it encourages the unemployed to find a job as soon as possible.

A general equilibrium model was developed to analyze the potential effects of this program on employment and GNP. The results of this test indicate that PEP would create between 400,000 and 1.3 million jobs while contributing between 1.1 percent and 2.0 percent to real GNP.

October 24, 1984

THE PRODUCTIVE EMPLOYMENT PROGRAM

It is time to try a new approach to reducing unemployment in the United States. Over the past decade, unemployment has claimed a growing share of the United States' estimated output and squandered an even greater share of its potential.

In today's political milieu, it is popular to profess the need of rational people to understand that the economy will never return to the full employment so well known in the 1960s. Words like "structural deficit" are bandied about in learned circles while people resign themselves to the fact that full employment exists with more on the order of 6-plus percent than 4 percent unemployment. This implication of such perceptions, if they are to be believed, is profoundly depressing.

Fortunately, the renewed vigor of the economy casts considerable doubt on these purveyors of gloom. But, more to the point, the advent of supply-side economics provides a framework in which socially responsive policies, which are fundamentally fair, can be directed to alleviate the legacies of defeat arising from misguided demand-side policies.

The recent 10 percent unemployment rate is shockingly high, yet at the same time it is the culmination of a steady rise in unemployment evident since 1970. During the 1950s, unemployment averaged 0.5 percent, with a peak rate of 6.8 percent posted in 1958. Unemployment during the 1960s averaged a similar rate of 3.5 percent posted in 1969.

Since 1969, however, an increasing share of the labor force has found itself unemployed. During the first half of the 1970s, the unemployment rate averaged 5.4 percent; during the last half of the decade, 7.0 percent. And for the 1981–1982 period, the rate has averaged 8.1 percent (Fig. 8.1). This record speaks for itself. Existing programs aimed at reducing unemployment jobs bills, CETA programs, tax credits, training programs, and the like have failed to accomplish their goal.

The problem resides in well-intentioned efforts to protect individual members of our society from some of the harshest consequences of our market economy. Those who have lost their jobs are provided unemployment payments. But these and other transfer programs ignore the importance of incentives to individuals in the pursuit of their economic well-being. The role of the producer has been ignored.

To date, each of the programs to aid the unemployed have contained this fatal flaw. The creation of "jobs" was the stated goal. But the true purpose of a job (the creation of real income through the production of goods with a market value) was ignored. The dynamics of the job crea-

FIGURE 8.1. The unemployment rate, 1950–1982

Percent

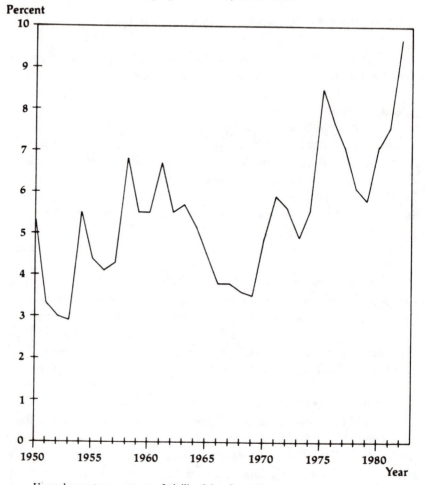

—— Unemployment as a percent of civilian labor force

Source: Economic Report of the President, Government Printing Office, Washington, D.C. 1983.

tion process in the private sector also were not considered in the design of most existing programs.

The Productive Employment Program (PEP) is designed to minimize each of these problem areas while increasing the number of employment opportunities for the unemployed. Central to the approach embodied in this program is the requirement that those companies benefiting from the subsidy generally keep their turnover rate from rising. This requirement assures that the jobs created by the Production Subsidy Program will not be "make work" jobs that disappear with the funding. Instead, the Productive Employment Program is designed to create productive employment opportunities that become self-sustaining, restoring to the individual the economic and social benefits of a meaningful job.

The New Program

The resources for this program already exist; no new taxes or bureacracy are required. PEP would take funds now spent on unemployment benefits and utilize them to subsidize the creation of jobs in the private sector. Under this program, the government in effect would buy from the private sector the creation of jobs without specifying the nature of the output. Simulation results indicate this program is capable of creating between 400,000 and 1.3 million jobs.

The resources available for such a program are substantial. During fiscal year 1982, $21.2 billion was paid by the federal and state governments in unemployment benefits alone. For FY 1983, unemployment compensation is expected to exceed $32 billion (Table 8.1). PEP utilizes this money as follows:

• The unemployed would be provided a voucher that entitles any employer hiring the individual to a subsidy equivalent to one-half the full amount of the worker's unemployment insurance payment. The individual would have the option of collecting the unemployment benefit directly if he or she remains unemployed, or indirectly by using the voucher to transfer the benefit to the employer. This transfer of benefits is the production subsidy.

• The voucher would entitle the employer to the subsidy for double the number of weeks remaining between the average duration of unemployment and the time the worker is actually employed.

—According to the Bureau of Labor Statistics' *Current Population Survey*, the average duration of unemployment in 1982 for those unemployed 26 weeks or less was approximately 8.5 weeks. Thus, the maximum subsidy period would be 17 weeks.

—For every week an individual collected unemployment benefits, the subsidy period would be reduced by two weeks.

• Under current law, unemployment benefits are not taxed. Similarly, the production subsidy payment would be nontaxable. The employer would

TABLE 8.1. Unemployment compensation program statistics

	1976	1977	1978	1979	1980	1981	1982 (rev. est.)	1983 (est.)	1984 (est.)
Total unemployment rate (%)	8.0	7.4	6.2	5.8	6.8	7.4	9.1	10.9	10.2
State unemployment compensation Claimants (mil. of individuals)	8.7	8.4	7.6	7.8	9.9	8.8	11.4	11.5	10.3
Regular benefit exhaustions (mil. of individuals)	4.1	2.9	2.2	2.0	2.7	3.2	3.7	4.1	3.7
Unemployment benefits paid ($ billions) State regular benefits	10.24	8.94	8.32	8.74	12.95	13.46	19.34	25.23	23.82
State extended benefits	1.41	0.95	0.51	0.12	0.56	1.06	0.93	2.20	1.20
Federal extended plus supplemental benefits ($ billions)	4.98	2.61	0.69	0.12	0.56	1.06	0.97	4.67	1.20
Total unemployment compensation ($ billions)	16.63	12.50	9.52	8.98	14.07	15.58	21.24	32.10	26.22

Source: Background Material and Data on Major Programs Within the Jurisdiction of the Committee on Ways and Means. Washington, D.C.: U.S. Government Printing Office, 1983.

deduct as an expense all wages paid to the subsidized worker without regard to the subsidy received and would not treat the subsidy as taxable income.

• If during participation in PEP the company's turnover rate rose by more than 3 percentage points, it would become disqualified from receiving additional vouchers from new hires for a period of six months.

> —Turnover rate is calculated by dividing the number of exits by the average number of employees for the period.
> —The base period would be either the previous quarter or the quarter a year earlier, at the company's election.
> —Disqualification will not reduce tax credit associated with existing PEP employees.
> —If the company becomes disqualified under PEP twice in two years, the disqualification period will be extended to one year from six months.
> —Companies with fewer than 100 workers would be exempt from the turnover test.

• No more than 10 percent of a company's work force could comprise subsidized workers (full-time equivalent basis).

• The Productive Employment subsidy could be used in payment of withholding taxes with the filing of a quarterly Employer's Federal Tax Return.

• An employer could not receive a voucher from a worker it has terminated or laid off for a year after the termination date. The provision is to prevent employers from abusing the system by firing and then rehiring workers.

• An employee could not receive a voucher within one year of a previous subsidy payment. This provision is to inhibit individuals from abusing the system by systematically being laid off and hired with a subsidy by a group of employers.

Theoretical Justification

The Productive Employment Program is recommended on several counts:

1. It utilizes the enormous resources that already exist within the private sector to employ individuals productively. Under the Productive Employment Program, the government in effect is purchasing jobs without specifying the nature of the output.

2. It allocates job-creating resources efficiently. Employers with the greatest opportunities to utilize the subsidy to expand output will do so. By contrast, public works expenditures, CETA, and other such jobs programs specify the output to be produced. Such an approach limits the type and location of jobs. Moreover, to the extent government-directed enterprise is less efficient than the private sector, fewer jobs and less output will be created per dollar of government expenditure.

3. The Productive Employment Program acts at the margin. Government-funded jobs programs essentially pay 100 percent of the cost of employing workers. By contrast, a subsidy to an employer has to cover only the deficit between the total cost of employing the worker and the expected incremental revenue. In essence, the production subsidy reduces the cost of hiring an additional worker, allowing the individual firm to expand its production, employment, and output into what had been unprofitable areas.

4. The Productive Employment Program does not require higher taxes. The program is funded by existing tax revenues. It better allocates existing government funds by providing unemployed workers a subsidy in their effort to gain employment, instead of providing them the same payment not to work. Moreover, reduction in other welfare payments associated with a decline in unemployment, such as food stamps and Aid to Families with Dependent Children, actually would reduce overall government expenditures.

5. The Productive Employment Program requires no new government staff. Individual workers become qualified under current laws governing eligibility for unemployment compensation. In addition, benefit calculations are identical to those used in today's unemployment compensation systems.

6. The program is simple; it requires only one form documenting the company's turnover rate and several items of general information to be filed each quarter with the company's Employer's Quarterly Federal Tax Return for income tax withholding and federal payroll taxes and with the Quarterly Contribution Return for state unemployment and disability insurance.

7. Employers receive the subsidy directly each quarter through reduced withholding tax payments. This approach improves cash flow and removes the subsidy from year-end "tax planning" associated with employment tax credits. Credits against corporate income taxes as embodied in the New Jobs Tax Credit have been relatively ineffective in creating jobs (Tannenwald 1982).

8. The program is self-policing. Employers cannot obtain the voucher unless the worker foregoes unemployment compensation and works for the employer.

9. The program does not interfere with an employer's incentives to make a PEP worker, like any other worker, as productive as possible.

10. The program encourages the unemployed to find employment as soon as possible. The decline in the available duration of the subsidy provides an added incentive to employer and worker alike to keep the unemployment period as short as possible.

11. The program is a realistic first step in trying a new approach to alleviate the nation's chronically high unemployment rate. In its first phase, PEP will not eliminate structural unemployment or create jobs for every individual now on welfare. It does offer the immediate prospect of reducing the unemployment rate without requiring new taxes or higher budget deficits.

12. The Productive Employment Program tests the concept of using existing trans-
    fer payments to subsidize job creation in the private sector. Successful implemen-
    tation of PEP would provide experience for the design of voucher programs for
    individuals now receiving Aid to Families with Dependent Children, Medicaid,
    and other welfare payments. Such a careful, step-by-step expansion of the pro-
    gram offers the prospect of eliminating much of the structural employment that
    now undermines the economy and budgetary position of the government alike.
13. The program complements the administration's proposed job tax credit for the
    long-term unemployed. Like PEP, this program would provide unemployed wor-
    kers with vouchers in lieu of their unemployment benefits. The vouchers under
    the administration's proposal would entitle an employer to a credit against in-
    come taxes for hiring the individual before April 1, 1984. But the administra-
    tion's program provides no relief for workers who have been unemployed less
    than 26 weeks.

UNEMPLOYMENT IN A HISTORICAL AND THEORETICAL CONTEXT

The Economics of Job Creation

The design of the Productive Employment Program begins with the observation that businesses do not expand their facilities or hire additional workers out of a sense of social obligation. Rather, they undertake such actions to earn a profit. From the perspective of the producer, workers can be hired only so long as the incremental revenue associated with their employment is greater than the total cost of their employment. In sim-plified form, this is illustrated by a standard break-even chart which shows the point at which revenues first exceed fixed plus variable costs. As long as increased expenses produce a greater increase in sales revenues, the firm will expand its work force. Throughout what accountants call the "relevant range," both variable costs and incremental revenues are as-sumed to increase in direct proportion to volume. As a result, both func-tions are drawn as straight lines (Fig. 8.2).

In a competitive market, price for an individual firm generally can be assumed to be constant. As a result, incremental revenues will con-tinue to increase in direct proportion to volume; the revenue line will re-main straight. But for the typical business, total costs are not a constant function of volume. Initially, marginal costs of adding a unit of output are very low relative to fixed costs. At first, the total cost curve is nearly flat. But as volume increases, marginal costs typically increase as well. This relationship is illustrated by allowing the total expense line to rise more steeply as volume increases. Once again, the break-even point is the intersection of the total cost and total expense curves (Fig. 8.3).

FIGURE 8.2. The break-even point as described by an accountant

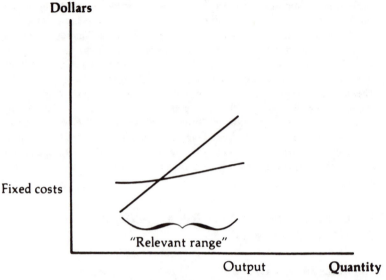

Total profits are equal to total revenues less total costs, or the distance between the two lines. This distance, or profits, reaches its maximum point when the slopes of the revenue and expense lines, respectively, are parallel. The greatest distance between the two lines exists at this point; it is where the rise in expenses equals incremental revenues (marginal cost equals marginal revenues). Any additional expansion in the firm's operations does not increase profits. To go further is to go backward: to hire another worker is to decrease profits and the viability of the business.

It is important to note that a business's total cost of employing an individual includes all payroll taxes and other tax payments associated with the individual's employment—in other words, gross wages paid. For the employer, the total cost is the basis of whether or not to hire an additional worker.

Workers, however, care little about the cost to the firm of employing them. Of far greater interest is wages received net of all taxes. Also of importance is the loss of government transfer payments such as unemployment insurance, food stamps, and the like, which are based on "means" or "needs" tests linked to income. In sum, workers are interested in increasing their incomes or living standards, and therefore respond to net wages received.

Income taxes, payroll taxes, and the imposition of "means" or "income" tests for the receipt of unemployment and other welfare benefits

FIGURE 8.3. The marginal unit

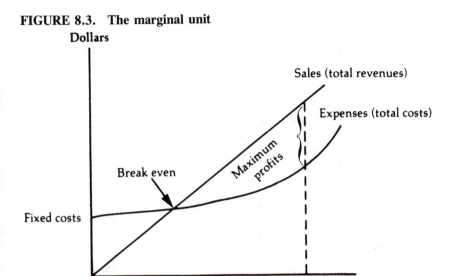

elevate the gross cost to the employer of hiring a new employee while reducing the benefits to the individual of returning to work. This spread between the gross wages paid and net wages received drives a wedge into labor markets, diminishing the opportunities for employment (Fig. 8.4).

Ironically, current programs designed to alleviate the hardship of unemployment tend to increase the difference between gross wages paid and net wages received, thereby aggravating the problem they are supposed to solve. A rise in unemployment produces increases in tax rates, both explicit and implicit. As unemployment insurance funds are depleted, for example, payroll tax rates are increased. Moreover, as the number of unemployed rises, expenditures on unemployment benefits and other welfare programs also rise. Such an increase in government spending implicitly increases the tax burden on those who remain productive.

Finally, on returning to work, an individual must forego unemployment benefits. This loss in transfer payments reduces the benefit of returning to work far more than is generally realized. Under the current unemployment system, payments typically approach 50 percent of a worker's gross wages. In California, for example, that state's unemployment development department reports that an individual with quarterly earnings of $2,600 (approximately $5 per hour) is eligible for weekly unemployment benefits of $92. On a quarterly basis, unemployment compensation would total $1,196, or 46 percent of gross wages.

FIGURE 8.4. How the wedge diminishes opportunities for employment

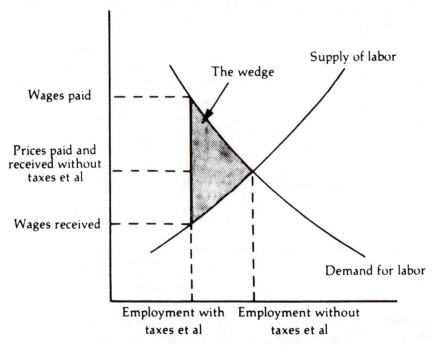

But such a comparison is mixing apples with oranges. Income and Social Security taxes must be paid on wages, whereas unemployment benefits are tax free for married individuals with incomes less than $18,000 (single taxpayers with incomes less than $12,000). To make the comparison correctly requires calculating wages on an after-tax basis.

Assuming the worker is single and takes the standard deduction, his marginal federal income tax rate is 17 percent. California's income tax rate is another 4 percent. And, Social Security taxes reduce the individual's income by another 6.7 percent. As a result, if the individual returns to work and earns $200 of additional wages ($5 x 40 hours), his or her after-tax income will be $145. The alternative, remaining unemployed, yields $92 in tax-free income. Thus, returning to work for $200 in gross wages increases spendable earnings by only $53 (145 − 92), an effective tax rate of 73.5 percent on the $200 of additional income.

As high as this tax rate is, it understates the true effective tax rate. Calculated correctly, gross wages would include payroll taxes paid by the employer (6.7 percent Social Security plus unemployment insurance tax rates as high as 6.2 percent). In addition, workers incur transportation and other associated costs with getting to and from work and being on the job. On this basis, the effective marginal tax rate exceeds 80 percent. Moreover, for individuals receiving other welfare benefits, including subsidized housing, medical care, and Aid to Families with Dependent Children, the loss of transfer payments can mean effective tax rates in excess of 100 percent (Laffer 1983).

However well intentioned, the current system taxes the employed while subsidizing the unemployed. In so doing, it reduces the rewards to work and increases the rewards for nonwork. Recognition of this fatal flaw in the current system is the key to the design of PEP. The concept is simply to redirect funds now spent on unemployment benefits toward the subsidization of productive employment. Such a program would narrow the spread between gross wages paid and net wages received. It is capable of reducing today's high unemployment (Fig. 8.5).

From the point of view of the employer, the production subsidy works because it reduces the costs of hiring an additional worker. Moreover, the subsidy is paid during the precise period when a new employee must be trained, when the employee is least productive. A reduction in the cost of hiring the unemployed will increase the demand for these workers.

From the point of view of the worker, the production subsidy works because it increases the rewards for returning to work. Unlike the current unemployment system, PEP payments would reduce the high effec-

FIGURE 8.5. How the productive employment program increases employment

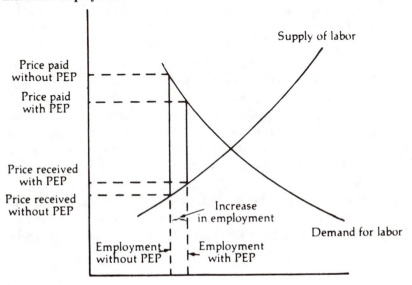

tive tax rate facing the unemployed worker. Instead of losing unemployment insurance payments the first day on the job, the unemployed worker could use these payments in acquiring employment. The availability of the subsidy increases the gross wages an employer can afford to pay the worker and thereby the benefits of returning to work.

PEP will work because it links the desire of employers to increase profits and of workers to elevate their standard of living, with the goal of a moral society to decrease the level of unemployment.

A general equilibrium model has been developed to analyze the potential effects of the Productive Employment Program on employment and GNP. The key parameters to the model were obtained from existing economic literature. The approach was to use a range of estimated values for each parameter, generating 10,000 stimulation outputs. The results of these tests indicate that PEP would create between 400,000 and 1.3 million jobs (full-time equivalents) for individuals with family incomes $10,000 and below. In addition, GNP would rise by between 1.1 percent and 2.0 percent (Davis 1983).

Fiscal Impact

The Productive Employment Program has been designed to leave total expenditures unchanged. Initially, total payments to the unemployed will be somewhat higher. All workers who become unemployed will be eligible for a minimum of 8.5 weeks of unemployment benefits without regard to the actual duration of their unemployment.

The distribution of unemployment duration, however, is heavily skewed toward the period of five weeks or less. Nearly 50 percent of those unemployed for 26 weeks or less find jobs within this period (Table 8.2). Providing this segment of the unemployed with a voucher worth up to 8.5 weeks of unemployment benefits roughly doubles the transfer payments associated with the incidence of their unemployment. A doubling of unemployment benefits paid those who would otherwise have been unemployed four weeks increases the average duration of unemployment payments (not actual unemployment) to 10.8 weeks from 8.6 weeks or 20 percent. That indicates an increase in unemployment expenditures of approximately $4 billion.

Several factors, however, will reduce this amount. First, PEP will tend to shorten the actual duration of unemployment. Some of those who would have been unemployed for longer than 8.5 weeks will find jobs more quickly, reducing unemployment payments.

TABLE 8.2. Distribution of unemployment by duration for those unemployed 26 weeks or less

Year	Duration			
	Less than 5 weeks (%)	5–14 weeks (%)	15–46 weeks (%)	Average duration (weeks)
1977	48.9	35.7	15.3	7.5
1978	51.6	34.6	13.8	7.4
1979	52.7	34.7	12.6	6.9
1980	48.3	36.2	15.5	7.5
1981	48.5	35.7	15.8	7.6
1982	43.7	37.2	19.1	8.4
Average (%)	49.0	35.7	15.3	7.6

Source: *Background Material and Data on Major Programs Within the Jurisdiction of the Committee on Ways and Means*. Washington, D.C.: U.S. Government Printing Office, 1983.

Second, by decreasing unemployment, PEP will reduce other welfare expenditures. Those who are unemployed soon become eligible for food stamps, Aid to families with Dependent Children, and the like. Indeed, for every percentage point increase in the unemployment rate, government expenditures rise automatically by $5 billion (including $2 billion in unemployment payments).

Third, by decreasing unemployment, and concurrently increasing overall economic activity, PEP will generate additional tax revenues. The revenue effects here are quite powerful. The Congressional Budget Office estimates that for every percentage point decrease in the unemployment rate, total federal government revenues rise by $20 billion. Both expenditures and revenue effects of lower unemployment rates increase in magnitude in the years ahead (Table 8.3).

TABLE 8.3. The budgetary impact of declines in the unemployment rate (billions of dollars)

For every percentage point decrease in the unemployment rate:	1983	1984	1985	1986	1987
Expenditures decline by	5	10	13	15	17
Revenues increase by	20	29	26	22	20
Total budgetary effect	25	39	39	37	37

Source: Congressional Budget Office, September 1982, *Economic and Budget Outlook*.

Thus, if PEP does nothing more than reduce the unemployment rate by 0.2 percent, it will narrow the deficit by $5 billion, more than enough to offset the $4 billion in additional unemployment payments.

ESTIMATION OF THE ECONOMIC RESPONSE OF PEP

There are several ways to obtain estimates of the effects of fiscal and monetary policy on the level of aggregate economic activity. The desirability of these estimates rests on the belief that the true structure of the economy is such that spending and/or tax rate changes affect economic activity.

An obvious way to incorporate any existing feedback effects would be to estimate a structural model that includes such effects. This model could be used to obtain forecasts of what economic activity, inflation, and tax revenues would have been in the absence of tax rate and/or spending changes. These forecasts could, in turn, be compared to actual levels of economic activity, inflation, and tax revenues. Alternatively, the model could be used to simulate the effects of various policy changes.

There are several difficulties with using a structural model of the economy. The sheer effort required to design and estimate a complete structural model is enormous. Furthermore, the resulting forecasts would be subject to certain sources of error in addition to the parameter estimation errors. Parameter estimation errors affect all attempts at statistical inference. An important source of error is misspecification of the true structural model, either through an incorrect choice of variables to be included in the model or through the imposition of incorrect identifying restricitions. Lucas (1976) points out that policy simulations based on the usual structural models (those consisting of decision rules such as consumption and investment functions) are inherently suspect because the parameters of the models are, in general, functions of policy variables and will change in response to shifts in those policy variables.

Sargent (1981) has shown that when agents form rational expectations about the future, there are rarely any zero restrictions to impose. If the structure can be identified at all, it can be identified only by imposing nonlinear restrictions on the covariance matrix.

An alternative approach is to develop a simple general equilibrium theoretical analysis, identify the key variables, and examine the model's sensitivity to parameter changes. Once this is established, individuals could specify what they consider to be reasonable parameter ranges in order to determine what type of response the model would predict. This is the approach used in the development of the model below.

One of the principal effects of PEP will be to reduce the cost of labor to employers while simultaneously increasing the take-home pay of the employees. The simulation will provide reasonable estimates of the economy's response to this program. Rather than estimate the key parameters in the model, the approach taken in this study is to survey the economics literature and to use as the parameters labor supply elasticities and effective marginal tax rates estimated by different economists.

The economics literature provides a wide range of estimated elasticities for each of the key parameters in the model. Different studies estimating labor supply response to net-of-tax wages provide different elasticity estimates based on the subgroup analyzed, for example, females versus males, or high- versus low-income individuals. These various subgroups make up for the overall labor force. Since PEP applies across all groups, the relevant parameter for this study is the aggregate response.

Rather than limit the inputs to the model to a single value for each parameter, however, a whole range of estimated values was utilized. Due to the multiplicity of parameters, 10,000 simulation outputs were obtained. The simulations that encompass the most likely estimates for the key parameters are reported in this study. (For a detailed description of the mathematical derivation of the model used in the simulations, see Chapter 6 of this book.)

SIMULATION RESULTS

This section analyzes the simulation results obtained by using the model developed in Chapter 6. All the simulation entailed a reduction in one effective, marginal tax rate on labor income. Three sets of parameters portraying low, medium, and high responsiveness to changes in incentives are reported respectively in Tables 8.4, 8.5 and 8.6.[1] This approach allows the model to capture the wide range of elasticities that can be found in the economic literature.

The first five columns of the tables denote the combination of exogenous variables used in the simulation. These include (1) the partial elasticity of substitution, (σ); (2) labor supply elasticity for high-skilled labor (E^s_{HS}) and (3) low-skilled labor, (E^s_{LW}) with respect to each of their after-tax salaries; and (4) and (5), the marginal tax rates on income from high-skilled and low-skilled labor $(t_H$ and t_L, respectively).

TABLE 8.4. Simulation results with low-elasticity parameters

	Parameters						Simulation results			
	Labor supply elasticity									
	Partial elasticity of substitution (σ)	High-skilled labor (E_{HS}^S)	Low-skilled labor (E_{LW}^S)	Tax on high-skilled labor (t_H)	Tax on low-skilled labor (t_L)	Before-tax wage rate (W)	Labor supply (L^S)	Output (Q)	Other revenue (OR)
Cell 1	0.25	0.15	0.30	0.35	0.50	0.2527	2214.16	2184.2	671.50
	0.25	0.15	0.30	0.35	0.55	0.2568	2156.03	2154.9	664.28
	0.25	0.15	0.30	0.35	0.60	0.2613	2092.85	2122.6	656.31
	0.25	0.15	0.30	0.35	0.65	0.2666	2023.47	2086.6	647.39
	0.25	0.15	0.30	0.35	0.70	0.2729	1946.22	2045.8	637.24
	0.25	0.15	0.30	0.35	0.75	0.2804	1858.65	1998.6	625.44
	0.25	0.15	0.30	0.35	0.80	0.2900	1756.83	1942.2	611.30
Cell 2	0.25	0.15	0.30	0.50	0.50	0.2462	2246.34	2173.1	829.52
	0.25	0.15	0.30	0.50	0.55	0.2501	2187.37	2144.0	820.61
	0.25	0.15	0.30	0.50	0.60	0.2546	2123.27	2111.9	810.76
	0.25	0.15	0.30	0.50	0.65	0.2597	2052.88	2076.0	799.74
	0.25	0.15	0.30	0.50	0.70	0.2658	1974.51	2035.4	787.20
	0.25	0.15	0.30	0.50	0.75	0.2732	1885.67	1988.4	772.63
	0.25	0.15	0.30	0.50	0.80	0.2825	1782.36	1932.4	755.16

Source: compiled by the author.

TABLE 8.5. Simulation results with medium-elasticity parameters

	Parameters					Simulation results			
	Partial elasticity of substitution (σ)	Labor supply elasticity		Tax on high-skilled labor (t_H)	Tax on low-skilled labor (t_L)	Before-tax wage rate (W)	Labor supply (L^S)	Output (Q)	Other revenue (OR)
		High-skilled labor (E^S_{HS})	Low-skilled labor (E^S_{LW})						
Cell 1	0.50	0.30	0.40	0.35	0.50	0.2732	2139.44	2262.3	701.34
	0.50	0.30	0.40	0.35	0.55	0.2805	2075.60	2245.2	698.58
	0.50	0.30	0.40	0.35	0.60	0.2889	2006.49	2226.3	695.50
	0.50	0.30	0.40	0.35	0.65	0.2987	1930.92	2205.0	692.02
	0.50	0.30	0.40	0.35	0.70	0.3104	1847.22	2180.7	688.04
	0.50	0.30	0.40	0.35	0.75	0.3249	1752.89	2152.3	683.35
	0.50	0.30	0.40	0.35	0.80	0.3435	1643.95	2118.1	677.65
Cell 2	0.50	0.30	0.40	0.50	0.50	0.2615	2191.52	2238.3	859.60
	0.50	0.30	0.40	0.50	0.55	0.2685	2126.13	2221.4	856.21
	0.50	0.30	0.40	0.50	0.60	0.2765	2055.34	2202.7	852.43
	0.50	0.30	0.40	0.50	0.65	0.2859	1977.93	2181.6	848.18
	0.50	0.30	0.40	0.50	0.70	0.2971	1892.18	2157.6	843.29
	0.50	0.30	0.40	0.50	0.75	0.3110	1795.55	2129.5	837.54
	0.50	0.30	0.40	0.50	0.80	0.3288	1683.98	2095.6	830.56

Source: compiled by the author.

TABLE 8.6. Simulation results with high-elasticity parameters

| | Parameters | | | | | Simulation results | | | |
| | | Labor supply elasticity | | | | | | | |
	Partial elasticity of substitution (σ)	High-skilled labor (E^S_{HS})	Low-skilled labor (E^S_{LW})	Tax on high-skilled labor (t_H)	Tax on low-skilled labor (t_L)	Before-tax wage rate (W)	Labor supply (L^S)	Output (Q)	Other revenue (OR)
Cell 1	1.00	0.50	0.75	0.35	0.50	0.3011	1933.38	2243.2	698.54
	1.00	0.50	0.75	0.35	0.55	0.3132	1852.37	2226.6	696.24
	1.00	0.50	0.75	0.35	0.60	0.3274	1765.82	2208.2	693.69
	1.00	0.50	0.75	0.35	0.65	0.3442	1672.58	2187.6	690.80
	1.00	0.50	0.75	0.35	0.70	0.3647	1571.05	2164.0	687.48
	1.00	0.50	0.75	0.35	0.75	0.3905	1458.89	2136.5	683.57
	1.00	0.50	0.75	0.35	0.80	0.4245	1332.46	2103.2	678.82
Cell 2	1.00	0.50	0.75	0.50	0.50	0.2820	2030.86	2229.4	858.97
	1.00	0.50	0.75	0.50	0.55	0.2933	1945.77	2213.0	856.15
	1.00	0.50	0.75	0.50	0.60	0.3066	1854.86	2194.7	853.01
	1.00	0.50	0.75	0.50	0.65	0.3223	1756.92	2174.2	849.45
	1.00	0.50	0.75	0.50	0.70	0.3415	1650.27	2150.8	845.37
	1.00	0.50	0.75	0.50	0.75	0.3657	1532.45	2123.4	840.57
	1.00	0.50	0.75	0.50	0.80	0.3976	1399.64	2090.3	834.73

Source: compiled by the author.

The remaining four columns summarize the simulation results. These columns report equilibrium values for: (1) an index for the before-tax wage rate for low-skilled labor (W); (2) an index for the overall supply of low-skilled labor (L^s); (3) the equilibrium level of output (Q); and (4) the amount of revenue collected from taxes on high-skilled labor income and capital income (OR).[2]

SIMULATION RESULTS WITH LOW-ELASTICITY PARAMETERS

The results reported in Table 8.4 are classified into two subgroups or cells. Within each cell the assumed value for four of the exogenous parameters is held constant while the value of the effective marginal tax rate on low-skilled labor is allowed to vary. Each cell highlights the effect of changes in tax rates on low-skilled labor (t_L) on output (Q) and on wages and employment of low-skilled workers (W and L^s, respectively). The move from one cell to another allows one additional parameter to change. For example, a comparison of the first and second cells allows for increases in the marginal tax rate on labor income for skilled workers (t_H) *to 50 percent from 35 percent.*

How Changes in the Marginal Tax Rates on Low-Skilled Labor Affect Employment and Output

The before-tax wage rate of low-skilled workers (W). Decreases in the effective marginal tax rate on labor income for low-skilled individuals results in a decrease in their before-tax wage rate. For example, in cell 1 (Table 8.4), as the marginal tax rate falls to 20 percent from 80 percent, the before-tax wage index declines to 0.2527 from 0.2900.[3] This decrease in the before-tax wage rate associated with a reduction in tax rates reduces the relative cost of hiring low-skilled labor. This effect will induce employers to use more of the now relatively less expensive low-skilled labor, and use less high-skilled labor and capital.

The after-tax wage rate of low-skilled workers. The model also captures the increase in after-tax wages associated with a decrease in tax rates. In each cell, the tax rate on low-skilled labor falls by a factor of four, but the before-tax wage rate falls by less than a factor of two. These two results combined indicate an increase in the after-tax wage rate. Higher after-tax wages imply increased incentives to work. Therefore, the effect of PEP is to decrease the before-tax wage rate (increase employers' incentives to hire these workers) and to increase the workers' take-home income (increase incentives to work). This simultaneous increase in the demand and supply of labor leads directly to an increase in employment of low-skilled labor (L^S). Notice that this effect occurs within each of the cells.

Employment of other factors. There are three effects which, when combined, determine how a change in tax rates on low-skilled workers affects the employment of high-skilled workers and capital. First, a decrease in the tax on low-skilled workers decreases the demand for the now relatively more costly high-skilled labor and capital. This is the substitution effect. Second, a decrease in tax rates implies more output and therefore more employment of all factors of production. This is the scale effect. Third, a decrease in the tax rate and consequent increase of low-skilled labor in the work force implies an increase in the efficiency (marginal product) of high-skilled labor and capital. This increase in efficiency is because low-skilled workers are in part complements to high-skilled labor and capital.

The overall employment of high-skilled labor and capital as well as the tax revenues generated by these factors may increase, decrease, and/or remain unchanged, depending on the relative strength of each of these three factors. If the substitution effect dominates, employment of high-skilled labor and capacity utilization will decrease. If the second or third effects dominate, either individually or collectively, then employment of high-skilled labor and capacity utilization will rise.

The results of the model indicate that the combination of the increase in employment of all factors and the improvement in efficiency of high-skilled labor and capital dominates the substitution effect. This result means a decrease in the tax on low-skilled labor increases total before-tax income of each and every factor of production.

OUTPUT

The model has been configured so that the magnitude of its output variable Q was of the same order of magnitude as the GNP expressed in 1972 dollars. The values of Q, which range from 1.9 trillion to 2.3 trillion, obviously overstate actual GNP, which in 1982 was nearly $1.5 trillion. The changes in output generated by the model, however, would roughly correspond in magnitude with expected changes in GNP.[4]

The results of the model demonstrate that a decrease in the effective tax rate on low-skilled labor will unambiguously increase the employment level of low-skilled labor, induce a substitution effect away from high-skilled labor and capital toward low-skilled labor; and increase the marginal product of the other factors of production. The combination of these effects increases the equilibrium level of output Q. This is apparent as one moves from high tax rates to low tax rates within each of the cells. Output rises as the tax rate on low-skilled labor falls.

Effect of Decreases in the Marginal Tax Rate on High-Skilled Income

A decrease in the marginal tax rate on high-skilled income will induce a substitution effect away from other factors of production. This results in a lower level of employment of low-skilled labor (L^S). This result is evident when comparing the first and second cells in each of the tables.

But there is also a second effect. A decrease in the marginal tax rate on high-income labor also is associated with an increase in the marginal product of low-skilled labor (before-tax wages W rise). The increase in the marginal product of low-skilled labor is less than the decrease in employment of low-skilled labor. The net result is that as the tax on high-skilled labor decreases, the total income of low-skilled labor rises. The effect on output is unambiguously positive.

SIMULATION RESULTS WITH MEDIUM- AND HIGH-ELASTICITY PARAMETERS

Next the effect of changes in labor tax rates on employment and output are examined using a higher partial elasticity of substitution for the factors of production, and higher elasticities for the supply of both high-skilled (E_{HS}^S) and low-skilled (E_{HS}^S) labor. Qualitatively, the simulation results using the medium- and high-elasticity parameters are the same as those obtained using the low-elasticity parameters. For example, as the tax rate on low-skilled labor decreases to 60 percent from 80 percent, employment, output, and revenues collected from high-skilled labor and capital all increase (Tables 8.5 and 8.6).

The magnitude of the effects, however, is different. The higher the elasticity parameters, the greater the increase in employment for a given reduction in tax rates on low-skilled labor. For example, when the tax rate on low-skilled labor falls to 60 percent from 80 percent, employment increases by 19.1 percent with the low-elasticity parameters (Table 8.4, cell 1: labor supply L^S rises to 2,092.85 from 1,756.83). For the medium-elasticity parameters the same tax rate reduction produces a 22.1 percent increase in employment (Table 8.5, cell 1). And for the high-elasticity parameters, this tax rate increase produces a 32.5 percent increase in employment (Table 8.6, cell 1).

In addition to this increase in responsiveness of factor supplies to changes in tax rates, the increase in the partial elasticity of substitution among the factors of production implies greater ease of substitution among low-skilled labor, high-skilled labor, and capital. At the extreme, for example, if capital and labor were perfect substitutes ($\sigma = \infty$) and labor supply elasticities were large, then a decrease in the tax rate on labor would lead to a large increase in employment of labor and an equivalent decrease in the employment of capital. The net effect would be to leave output unchanged. This result is an extreme example of employment diversion. With employment diversion, an increase in labor employment associated with lower tax rates on labor is offset in part by a decrease in the employment of capital.

The higher the elasticity parameters, the smaller the change in output for a given change in effective tax rates. With low-elasticity parameters, a decrease in the tax rate on low-skilled labor to 60 percent from 80 percent produces a 9.3 percent increase in total output at the same time employment is increasing by 19.1 percent (Table 8.4, cell 1: output, Q, rises to 2,122.6 from 1,942.2). As the elasticity parameters increase to medium and high levels, the increase in output associated with the same tax decrease declines to 5.1 percent (Table 8.5, cell 1) and 4.9 percent (Table 8.6, cell 1), respectively. By contrast, the employment effects increase to 22.1 percent (Table 8.5) and then to 32.5 percent (Table 8.6) respectively.

In sum, the higher the elasticity parameter, the larger will be the effect of a change in tax rates on labor employment and the larger will be the diversion of employment between capital and labor, resulting in ever smaller changes in total output.

Revenue Effects

A rate reduction in tax on low-skilled labor will have different effects on the revenue collected from each of the three factors of production. A reduction in tax rates on low-skilled labor implies higher before-tax income for high-skilled labor and capital. Thus, even with the tax rate on these factors unchanged, a tax reduction on low-skilled labor is associated with higher tax revenues from high-skilled labor and capital (*OR*). The lower the elasticity parameter, the greater will be the increase in other revenues. For example, a reduction in the tax rate on low-skilled labor to 60 percent from 80 percent is associated with a 7.4 percent increase in other revenues when the elasticity parameters are low (Table 8.4, cell 1: other revenue (*OR*) rises to 656.31 from 611.30). By contrast, when the elasticity parameters are high, other revenues increase by 2.1 percent (Table 8.6, cell 1).

In the normal range of the Laffer Curve, a reduction in legislated tax rates on low-skilled labor would be associated with a decline in revenue from this factor of production. Such a loss in revenue could more than offset the gain in other revenues. Under PEP, however, legislated tax rates are left unchanged. Effective tax rates associated with the granting of unemployment benefits are lowered instead. Thus, there are no offsetting revenue losses from income taxes. In fact, as previously unemployed people become employed, tax revenues would tend to increase. Thus, the increase in other revenue means that total tax revenues will rise with the introduction of the Productive Employment Program.

THE LIKELY IMPACT OF PEP

The results of the simulations clearly suggest that output and employment will unambiguously increase with a reduction of the marginal tax rate on low-skilled income (through PEP). The results also suggest that the likelihood of tax revenues collected from other factors will almost invariably increase. Whether or not overall revenues increase depends on how easy it is for currently employed people to qualify for PEP.

The stimulative effect of PEP depends on how successful it is in reducing the effective marginal tax rates faced by the currently unemployed. To illustrate, consider again the case of an unemployed single person living in California who had earned $200 a week or $2,600 during the previous quarter. If this individual returns to work, his or her take-home pay would be $145 a week. Health insurance benefits would add another $15 a week in effective take-home and before-tax pay. Employer Social Security contributions also increase wages paid by $13.40 a week. Thus, wages paid total $228.40, and wages received total $160.

Alternatively, the individual could remain unemployed and collect $92 a week in unemployment compensation. Returning to work for $228 a week in gross wages paid increases disposable income by $68 ($160 − 92). Thus, this person faces an effective marginal tax rate of 70 percent.

With PEP, unemployed individuals who find work can take to the employer one-half of their unemployment benefits for up to 17 weeks. In this example, the productive subsidy would total a maximum of $782. The individual's overall annual gross wages paid (inclusive of payroll taxes and insurance) totals approximately $12,000. Therefore, on an annual basis, PEP could reduce the effective marginal tax rate for low-skilled labor by approximately 6.5 percent ($782/$12,000).[5]

Based on this analysis, PEP would reduce the effective marginal tax rate to 63.5 percent from 70 percent. Simulation results based on a slightly more modest reduction in the effective marginal tax to 65 percent from 70 percent will be used to estimate the impact of PEP on GNP and employment.

The change in output resulting from implementation of PEP depends in part on the partial elasticity of substitution among the various factors of production. At low-elasticity parameters (Table 8.4), output increases 2.0 percent; at high-elasticity parameters, GNP increases 1.0 percent.

The effect of PEP on the increase in the total supply of labor to the market sector will depend on two variables: the increased supply of low-skilled labor and the relative importance of low-skilled labor in terms of the overall labor force (i.e., what fraction of total worker-hours supplied is due to the low-skilled labor force). The increase in labor supply can be determined within the context of the model. The model's result indicates that the effect of PEP on the supply of labor by low-skilled workers range from a low of 4.0 percent (Table 8.4) to a high of 6.5 percent (Table 8.6).

The fraction of total worker-hours supplied by low-skilled labor is somewhat more difficult to establish, so an operational measure of low skill is needed. The approach taken is to use income as a proxy for skill. The distribution of income by families is then used to estimate the percentage of the labor force that is low-skilled labor (Table 8.7). This measure of the distribution of income does not provide any information on whether the families had one or more earners and/or how many hours were worked during the year by each member of the family. Nevertheless, by any reasonable measure, families (with two adult members) with an annual income of under $10,000 can be classifed as low-skilled. In this case, 20 percent of the families are classified as such. In fact, an argument can be made that those earning $15,000 or less may qualify as low-skilled (36 percent of the families).

TABLE 8.7.   Distribution of income

Money income by family	Income level (in 1979 dollars)
7.0	under 5,000
20.6	under 10,000
36.2	under 15,000
51.2	under 20,000
65.6	under 25,000
84.8	under 30,000
95.1	under 50,000

Source: Bureau of the Census. 1981. *Statistical Abstract of the United States, 1981*, p. 435. Table 725, "Money Income of Families—Percent Distribution by Income Level, by Race of Householder in Current and Constant (1979) Dollars: 1950 to 1979."

At these low-income levels, the families qualify for welfare benefits. Given the disincentives implicit in these programs, it is highly unlikely that all family members will be employed full time. This suggests then that the distribution of income will substantially underestimate the over-all supply of labor of low-skilled workers. Once again, a range of estimates is used to simulate the effects of the PEP program. A low estimate of 10 percent and a high estimate of 20 percent are used for the low-skilled workers' share of the fraction of total labor services.

The possible ranges for the estimates of the effect of the PEP on employment (full-time equivalent basis) can be calculated by multiplying the range of possible values for the increase in the supply of low-skilled labor times their share of the overall labor force. The calculations indicate a possible range of a low 0.40 percent to a high of 1.30 percent. Civilian employment now totals 99.1 million people. Thus, PEP is likely to increase the number of employed by between nearly 400,000 and 1.3 million workers (Table 8.8).

Targeted versus Across-the-Board Benefits

The estimation of the impact of PEP makes two simplifying assumptions: all low-skill workers are treated as identical workers; and all individual producers are also treated as identical firms. These assumptions led to the result that it was impossible within the model to target the PEP benefits to particular groups of workers such as the currently unemployed

TABLE 8.8. Estimated effect of PEP on output and employment

Increase in GNP (%)	Increase in employment of low-skilled labor (%)	Low-skilled labor's share of work force (%)	Increase in overall employment (% of civilian workers)	Increase in employment (full-time equivalent basis)
2.0	4.0	10	.40	396,000
2.0	4.0	20	.80	793,000
1.1	4.5	10	.45	446,000
1.1	4.5	20	.90	892,000
1.1	6.5	10	.65	644,000
1.1	6.5	20	1.30	1,288,000

Source: compiled by the author.

(PEP I) or those currently on welfare (PEP II). Similarly, the assumptions about the identical producers precluded identifying the marginal economy for each individual firm (i.e., the 90–100 percent production capacity). In short, the basic model could not be refined to incorporate all of the details of PEP. To the extent that these details were not incorporated, it is fairly apparent that the implementation of PEP under the simplifying assumptions above will overestimate the costs of the program, the reason being that our calculations will give the benefits to all of the low-skill workers as opposed to all of the currently unemployed.

This line of reasoning suggests that if PEP could be targeted without any additional administrative or other costs by redirecting the efforts of existing agencies (i.e., welfare and unemployment), then the net benefits of the program will be even larger than suggested by this study.

To verify and fine-tune these results, Dubin and Rivers (1984) developed a model using a methodology totally different from ours. Although slightly larger, their estimation of the impact and net benefit of PEP I was remarkably close to that of our model.

However, neither of the two models seriously investigated the potential cost of policing and enforcing a target program, given the incidence of fraud and other abuses of the welfare system reported with some regularity in the news media. If benefits are provided to all low-skilled workers, benefits will be given to people who would not qualify under the targeted programs. Although the benefit outlays would be larger than under the targeted programs, the enforcement and policing cost would be significantly lower. Which of the two alternatives—across the board or targeted—is less expensive cannot be determined a priori. It would require the construction of a more complex strategy that would include the cost of monitoring and enforcing a targeted program.

Conclusion

Over the years, unemployment, as unattractive as it is, has become far less onerous. With all of the federal and state programs aimed at alleviating poverty, unemployment has become a survivable condition, and one known by increasing numbers. Simultaneously, employment—with all the attendant taxes and regulations—has become relatively less attractive than it was in the past. These two factors working in concert have led many to the prognosis that the U.S. economy must inevitably be shackled with persistently high unemployment.

Such a conclusion is utterly wrong. There is no reason why a moral society that adequately provides for those in need cannot also attain economic prosperity. In fact, the most immoral act of all by government is to engage in policies that effectively destroy the production base on which all benefits ultimately rest.

As it stands, society pays twice for its unemployed—once in the form of lost output and again in the form of taxes used to fund transfer payments. Under the Productive Employment Program, expenditures at least initially would remain unchanged. But total output, and therefore real incomes, would be increased. Society would benefit through lower tax payments and increased supplies of goods and services. And those now unemployed would benefit by obtaining productive jobs with a future.

NOTES

1. Throughout the table we assume that capital share of output, $(1-\sigma_1-\sigma_2)$, and low-skilled income share of output, σ_1, are both equal to 25 percent. Similarly, we assume that the marginal tax rate on income from capital is 50 percent, and that the overall factor supply elasticity from the home or underground sector to the market sector, t, is 0.25.

2. To the extent that the tax system is progressive, the average tax rates will fall below the marginal tax rate, hence the revenue estimates reported will significantly overstate the revenue collections.

3. It should be noted that alternating cells have the same value for W. The relationship between W and the various parameters in the model (Equation 6.25, Chapter 6) depends in part on the factor's share of income and the partial elasticity of substitution. In this part of the analysis, each of these parameters was given a single value. The tax rate on capital is also assumed to be constant. The only parameter remaining that influences the before-tax wage rate is the marginal tax rate on the two types of labor. Within a cell, the tax rate on high-skilled labor remains constant; between cells, it alternates between 35 percent and 50 percent.

4. In a simple case, labor supply can be described with two parameters, the elasticity (slope using a logarithmic scale) and the wage rate at which people enter the market (intercept). The structure of the model does not allow for changes in the entry wage rates. As a consequence, the total supply of labor will relate directly to the factor supply elasticity.

5. These calculations assume that the low-skilled find employment on January 1. In the other extreme, for a worker who finds a job the last 17 weeks of the calendar year, the reduction in labor cost would be 25 percent on a calendar-year basis.

REFERENCES

Congressional Budget Office. 1982. *Economic and Budget Outlook* (September).

Davis, Allen V. C. 1983. "A Productive Employment Program Utilizing the Marginal Economy." A. B. Laffer Associates Rolling Hills Estates, CA. (June).

Dubin, Jeffrey A., and R. Douglas Rivers. 1984. "Stochastic Simulation of Labor Demand under Wage Subsidation." California Institute of Technology (October).

Laffer, Arthur B. 1983. "The Tightening Grip of the Poverty Trap." *Policy Analysis* 41, Cato Institute, Washington, D.C. (August): 1–22.

Lucas, R. 1976. "Econometric Policy Evaluation: A Critique." In *Phillips Curve and Labor Markets,* edited by K. Brunner and A. Meltzer. North Holland, pp. 19–46.

Sargent, T. 1981. "Interpreting Economic Time Series." *Journal of Political Economy* 89:213–248.

Tannenwald, Robert. 1982. "Are Wage and Training Subsidies Cost-Effective? Some Evidence from the New Jobs Tax Credit." *New England Economic Review* (September–October): 26.

U.S. Department of Labor, Bureau of Labor Statistics. *Current Population Survey.* Table 8B, "Duration of Unemployment by Single Weeks."

9

The State Competitive Environment

Victor A. Canto, Charles W. Kadlec, and Arthur B. Laffer

SUMMARY

Fiscal policy is a singularly important variable in the determination of a state's competitiveness and, hence, in its relative growth rate. In some respects, the 50 states are analogous to corporations. Tax rates can be thought of as the price a state charges an individual or corporation for locating production within its borders. Just as with companies, pricing policies are not the only element in success, but they are important.

On average, 50 percent of the variation in a state's economic performance is associated with changes in the overall U.S. economy and, therefore, lies outside the purview of state policies. Of the remaining 50 percent that is affected by state policies, approximately two-thirds of a state's performance is associated with changes in the average tax rates relative to the national average. The remaining one-sixth can be attributed to various other economic factors such as changes in a state's natural endowments, regulatory policies, and business climate.

The conclusion: A state's tax policies are not the only thing that influences economic development. A preponderance of evidence, however, indicates that investors and corporate planners can improve their performance by being aware of current and proposed changes in state and local tax policies as they make investment and location decisions. Companies with production facilities in a state where the relative tax rates are declining, for example, can, in general, expect to reap higher after-tax rates of return than will those companies with facilities located in states with rising relative tax rates. The duration and magnitude of such gains or losses are tied inextricably to the mobility of the company's competitors, its workers, and the sensitivity of consumers to the price of its goods. Mobility of capital and labor is influenced by several factors. One of the most important factors is the time horizon involved; mobility increases with the passage of time. In the shortest of runs, factories will not be constructed in response to a tax reduction. But there will be an increased utilization of facilities and perhaps even of labor in the form of overtime. As time horizons lengthen, there will be an actual movement of individuals and plants to the state and a retention of plants and jobs that might otherwise have left the state. This migration will continue until after-tax returns for the mobile factors within the state are equalized with after-tax returns for their counterparts elsewhere in the economy.

In general, a change in tax rates will have the effect of changing:

• The quantity and pre-tax price of factors that can move easily between states while leaving their after-tax returns unchanged.

• The after-tax returns and the pre-tax price of factors that cannot leave the state with their quantity unchanged.

From 1967 to 1977, the strength of the relationship between relative growth rates and relative tax burdens is particularly apparent. This was a time of widely divergent state tax policies and a mushrooming of federally funded programs. Most of these programs took the form of matching grants, which induced states to generate new funds by raising taxes in order to participate in the federal largesse. The average state and local tax burden rose by 16 percent during this period.

Virtually every state that lowered its relative tax burden during this period experienced better-than-average growth in personal income. These states (which included Arizona, Florida, Colorado, and Texas) also experienced above-average gains in total employment and private-sector employment.

From 1977 to 1982, the same relationship between changes in relative tax burdens and relative growth rates is evident, although it is not as strong. During this time, the steady growth in federal grants-in-aid peaked, then began a gradual decline that extended through 1982. This reduction in federal aid was accompanied by a sharp decline in state and local tax burdens. The 1981–1982 recession, however, did lead to a spate of tax increases at state and local levels. The combination of increased taxes and the strong national economic recovery in 1983 increased the aggregate state and local government surplus by $20 billion. The strength and duration of the expansion indicates that these surpluses will continue to increase, bringing heightened pressures to reduce state and local tax burdens.

Tracking the changes in relative tax burdens among states is key to understanding the competitive environment. States that lower their relative tax burden can be expected to become more competitive, creating opportunities for the realization of better-than-average growth or higher-than-average after-tax returns. States that raise their relative tax burden can be expected to become less competitive, with companies located within their borders suffering below-average sales performance and after-tax returns.

As a result of changes in tax policy through the current fiscal year, states that can be expected to increase their competitive position are Massachusetts, Arizona, Nebraska, Missouri, and South Dakota. States that also deserve monitoring include California, Delaware, New Jersey, Virginia, New York, Rhode Island, and Oregon. States that can be expected to lose competitiveness are New Mexico, West Virginia, Montana, Ohio, Iowa, and the District of Columbia. Special situations that deserve monitoring include Florida and Texas.

August 8, 1984

In the coming decade, every state in the country will be striving for its share of economic growth—some with enviable success, others with disappointing results. As states seek to attract and hold industries and workers within their borders, the winners and the losers will be separated by their ability to "read" the competitive environment and then influence events in such a way as to enhance their own state's appeal.

The forces at play in this environment touch on all the elements of competition. Climate, waterways and seaports, the location of airport facilities, and price of energy all have differential effects on economic development among states. Other factors, such as the shift to low-sulfur coal and/or the discovery of vast new quantities of oil, have helped such states as Wyoming and Texas to post outsized gains in personal income and employment in recent years.

But fiscal policy is the most important factor common to all states, since it strongly influences competitiveness and, hence, relative economic growth rates. Within fiscal policy, the change in a state's tax burden relative to the nation is most important. The tax burden, arrived at by dividing total tax revenue by total personal income, is a widely accepted measure used to compare tax policies across states. As such, the tax burden indicates the effective average tax rate of a particular state.

The responsiveness of the relative growth rates to changes in this tax variable plus two expenditure variables was estimated for each of the 48 contiguous states. This empirical research yielded three fundamental results (Canto and Webb 1983):

1. The impact of a change in the tax burden relative to the U.S. average was negative and significant in 22 states.[1] The chance of such a result occurring at random is approximately 1 in 6 billion. This result gives strong statistical support to the assertion that an increase in a state's relative tax burden subtracts from its economic growth. On average, for every one percent rise in a state's relative tax burden its rate of growth declines by approximately 0.5 percent in the year of the relative tax increase.

2. The impact of a change in real per capita government purchases relative to the U.S. average was significant in four of the 48 states. There is approximately a one in eight chance of this result being random. In three states, an increase in per capita government expenditures was associated with higher relative growth. This result indicates that state and local government expenditures in goods and services have little impact on a state's economic performance.

3. The impact of a change in real per capita transfer payments relative to the U.S. average was statistically significant in only two of the 48 states. This result could be due to random results. In addition, the coefficient in each of these two states was negative, indicating that to the extent increases in per capita transfer payments make a difference, they are associated with slower economic growth.

This last result a first seems surprising. Transfer payments financed by state taxes do not increase aggregate income. For every dollar received by a transfer payment recipient, a dollar is paid by a taxpayer; thus, the income effects of transfer payments cancel, leaving only the negative effects (substitution effects) of taxation on economic activity. As a result, an increase in a state's transfer payments relative to the U.S. average would be expected to be associated with a relative decline in economic growth (Canto and Webb 1983).

But if the transfer payments are financed by the federal government, there are no negative effects of taxation unique to the state, leaving only the income effect. In this case, an increase in a state's transfer payments would result in an increase in its relative growth rate.

In actuality, 54 percent of the states' public welfare expenditures are funded by the federal government. As a result, the negative effects of a state-financed system are canceled by the positive effects of the federally funded welfare payments, leaving no net impact on states' relative growth rates.

Just as important, this research demonstrated the relative importance of fiscal policy to a state's economic growth rate.

- On average, approximately 50 percent of the variation in a state's performance is associated with changes in the U.S. economy and is, therefore, outside the purview of state economic policies (Fig.9.1). Changes in the U.S. economy have a proportionate effect on each state's performance, leaving unchanged each state's relative performance. The 1981–

FIGURE 9.1. The relative importance of state and local fiscal policy to a state's economic growth

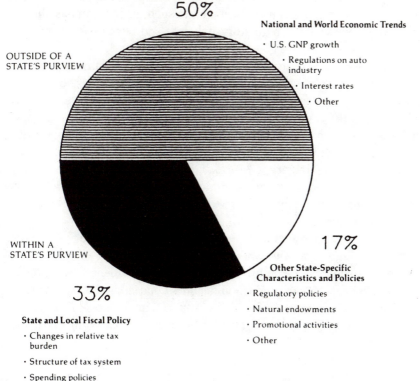

50%

OUTSIDE OF A
STATE'S PURVIEW

National and World Economic Trends

· U.S. GNP growth

· Regulations on auto industry

· Interest rates

· Other

WITHIN A
STATE'S PURVIEW

17%

Other State-Specific Characteristics and Policies

· Regulatory policies

· Natural endowments

· Promotional activities

· Other

33%

State and Local Fiscal Policy

· Changes in relative tax burden

· Structure of tax system

· Spending policies

1982 recession, for example, lowered growth in all states, while the recovery has buoyed output and employment across the nation.

Specific events outside a state's purview also can have a disproportionate effect on its growth rate. For example, employment and production in the domestic steel industry have decreased due to a combination of factors, including U.S. tax and regulatory policies, a shift in the cost advantage to foreign producers, foreign subsidies, and excess worldwide steel capacity (Canto, Eastin, and Laffer 1982). In states where the steel industry is a major source of manufacturing jobs, such as Pennsylvania, Maryland, Ohio, and Indiana, the economies of these states suffered.

• Changes in effective average state tax rates relative to the rest of the United States are a major determinant of a state's relative and absolute performance. On average, approximately one-third of a state's overall performance (two-thirds of the area affected by state policies) is associated with changes in the state and local tax burden relative to the mean for all states (Fig. 9.1).

• The remaining one-sixth of a state's competitiveness and relative economic performance can be attributed to such other factors as changes in natural endowments, regulatory policies, and business climate.

The importance of the responsiveness of a state's relative growth rate to changes in tax rates goes well beyond the changes in each state's relative position. First, an analysis of the states' responsiveness to changes in their relative tax rates provides insight into the the importance of fiscal policy to the health of a national economy. In essence, each state is being treated as a country with an open economy. Just as states compete with each other for the location of factories, offices, and jobs with the U.S. economy, the United States must compete with countries around the world for the location of economic activity. Moreover, since monetary policy is the same for all of the states, the effect of fiscal policy is isolated.

Second, for investors and corporate planners, knowledge of a company's exposure to a state where taxes are either rising or falling relative to the nation can be an important input in investment or location decisions. Companies with production facilities concentrated in a state where relative tax rates are declining, for example, can, in general, expect to reap higher after-tax rates of return than those companies in states with rising tax burdens.

The extent of the duration and magnitude of such gains or losses is tied inextricably to the mobility of each company's competitors, workers, and the sensitivity of its customers to the price of its goods (see the Appendix at the end of the chapter).

GROWTH AND THE RELATIVE TAX BURDEN

The period 1967–1977 is particularly useful in illustrating the sensitivity of states' relative growth rates to changes in their relative tax burdens. Beginning in 1967, states embarked on widely divergent tax policies. This variation in the changes in relative tax burden permits a clear comparison of various tax policies with relative growth rates among the states. Moreover, the 10-year span allows the cumulative effects of divergent tax policies to become evident.

Problems do exist with the cross-state comparison, because states respond differently to a given change in the relative tax burden. Anecdotally, this can be explained by the experiences of two states. Tax revenues in Alaska and Wyoming have grown very rapidly due to the imposition of severance taxes on newly discovered oil and coal, respectively. Although such taxes are reflected in the overall tax burden, they, in effect, act as a tax on an immobile factor. Moreover, in both cases, these tax increases were associated with low marginal tax rates on personal and corporate income; tax rates on mobile factors declined. As a result, both states enjoyed exceptional growth in spite of an upwardly spiraling tax burden. Because of these considerations, Alaska and Wyoming have not been included in this analysis.

For the remaining 47 states and the District of Columbia, the strength of the relationship between growth rates and changes in relative tax burdens is readily apparent in the 1967–1977 period. Virtually every state that significantly increased its relative tax burden experienced below-average growth during this period. Moreover, 27 of the 34 states that reduced their relative tax burden experienced above-average growth (Fig. 9.2).

High-growth states such as Arizona, Florida, Colorado, and Texas (all Sunbelt states) were among those that reduced their tax burdens most during this period. Such other southern states as Virginia and North Carolina, which enjoyed a reputation for attracting business during this decade, also reduced their tax burdens relative to the nation. Conversely, Massachusetts and New York (located in the Snowbelt) raised their relative tax rates more than any of the other states in our sample.

A similar strong negative relationship is evident between changing relative tax burdens and employment growth for the 1967–1977 period. In the vast majority of cases, states that lowered their relative tax burden experienced above-average growth in overall employment (Fig. 9.3A) and in private-sector employment (Fig. 9.3B).

A state's tax policies are not the only thing that matters when it comes

FIGURE 9.2.   Economic growth and changes in relative tax burden, 1967–1977

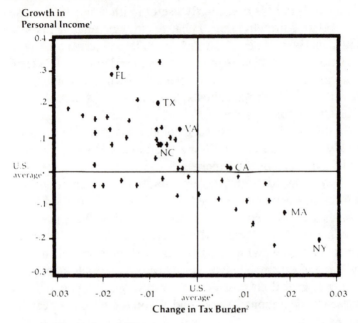

*excluding Alaska and Wyoming
1) Change in (log of real personal income by state relative to log of the U.S. average.*)
2) Change in (tax revenue per $1,000 of personal income by state relative to U.S. average.*)
Source: Survey of Current Business. U.S. Department of Commerce, Bureau of Economic Analysis. Government Printing Office, Washington, D.C.; *Governmental Finances.* U.S. Department of Commerce, Bureau of the Census. Government Printing Office, Washington, D.C.

to economic development. But the preponderance of evidence indicates that investors and corporate planners can improve their performance by incorporating changes in state and local tax policies into their investment and location decision making.

Changes in State and Local Fiscal Policies

A new pattern of state and local government fiscal policies has evolved during the past five years. For the 10 years ending in 1977, federal grants in aid to state and local governments rose fourfold, to $62.8 billion in 1977 from $15.5 billion in 1967 (Fig. 9.4A). This surge in federal aid was accompanied by an almost equally large increase in state and local spending. In this 10-year period, revenues from the federal government rose to 22 percent from 17 percent of total state and local general revenues (Fig. 9.4B).

FIGURE 9.3. Employment growth and changes in relative tax burden, 1967–1977

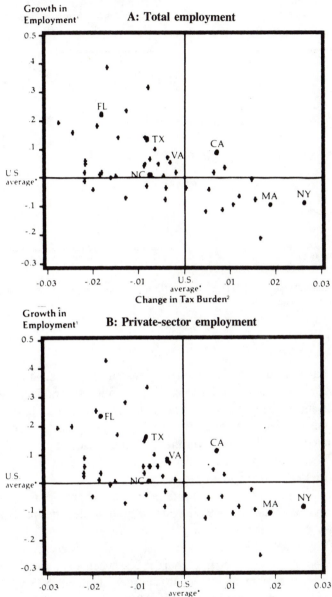

*excluding Alaska and Wyoming

1) Change in (log of real personal income by state relative to log of the U.S. average.*)

2) Change in (tax revenue per $1,000 of personal income by state relative to U.S. average.*)

Source: Survey of Current Business. U.S. Department of Commerce, Bureau of Economic Analysis. Government Printing Office, Washington, D.C.; *Governmental Finances.* U.S. Department of Commerce, Bureau of the Census. Government Printing Office, Washington, D.C.

FIGURE 9.4. The federal role in funding state and local expenditures

A: Federal government transfers
to state and local governments

B: Percentage of total state and local
expenditures funded by federal government

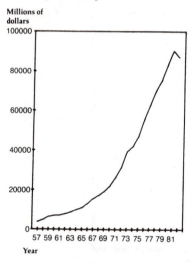

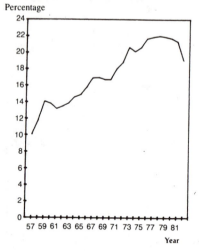

Source: *Governmental Finances*. U.S. Department of Commerce, Bureau of the Census. Government Printing Office, Washington, D.C.

Most federal programs took the form of matching grants, inducing states to generate new funds in order to participate in the federal largesse. The fear that an increase in the tax burden would drive businesses to other states was diminished sharply because the programs were national in scope and largely funded by the federal government. Not coincidentally, the national aggregate state and local tax burden rose to $114 per $1,000 of personal income in 1977 from $98 in 1967.

The steady advance in federal grants in aid as a share of state and local general revenue peaked in 1978, began a gradual decline in 1979, and fell nearly 2 percentage points in 1982, the last year for which data are available (Fig. 9.4B). This reduction in federal aid was accompanied by a sharp decline in state and local tax burden. Between 1977 and 1981, the national aggregate state and local tax burden declined $13.92 to $100.75 per $1,000 of personal income (Fig. 9.5). Even in 1982, when actual revenue transferred to state and local governments declined by $4 billion (the first decline in federal assistance since before 1957), the state and local tax burden increased only slightly.

**FIGURE 9.5. The tax burden of all state and
local governments, 1957–1983**

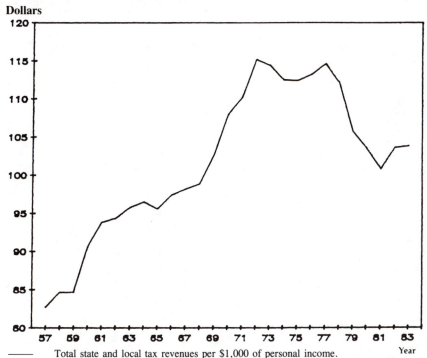

Dollars

Total state and local tax revenues per $1,000 of personal income.

Source: Survey of Current Business. U.S. Department of Commerce, Bureau of Economic Analysis. Government Printing Office, Washington D.C.; *Governmental Finances.* U.S. Department of Commerce, Bureau of the Census. Government Printing Office, Washington, D.C.

The 1982 recession, however, did lead to a spate of tax increases at state and local levels. Between 1981 and 1983, nearly two-thirds of the states raised their income, sales, or motor-fuel taxes. The biggest increases came in Ohio, Michigan, Washington, Indiana, and Florida (Table 9.1). During this period, eight states (New York, Arkansas, Virginia, Georgia, Illinois, Wyoming, Texas, and Alaska) did not raise any of those three taxes. Nine states cut taxes; Vermont and California led the tax cutters with reductions of 10 percent and 6 percent, respectively.

Increases in these broad-based taxes, combined with the strong economic recovery experienced in 1983, increased the aggregate state and local government surplus by $20 billion, to $51.4 billion in 1983 from $31.3 billion in 1982. This increased surplus is equally dramatic when social insurance and pension fund contributions are included as state ex-

TABLE 9.1. State tax increases for a typical family of four

State	1983 state taxes	2-year change	Percentage change
Ohio	$2,696	+ $1,111	70
Washington	782	+ 241	45
Indiana	1,986	+ 530	36
Michigan	3,253	+ 787	32
North Dakota	1,225	+ 285	30
Florida	507	+ 106	26
Nevada	548	+ 94	21
West Virginia	2,437	+ 368	18
New Mexico	1,558	+ 230	17
Minnesota	4,384	+ 602	16
New Hampshire	118	+ 13	12
Wisconsin	4,080	+ 437	12
Iowa	2,939	+ 280	11
Mississippi	2,101	+ 215	11
Nebraska	1,938	+ 183	10
Pennsylvania	1,661	+ 155	10
Kansas	1,804	+ 154	9
Missouri	2,122	+ 156	8
Oregon	3,792	+ 287	8
Colorado	2,080	+ 135	7
Utah	2,568	+ 161	7
Louisiana	740	+ 43	6
Idaho	3,356	+ 148	5
Connecticut	656	+ 19	3
New Jersey	1,682	+ 54	3
Alabama	1,570	+ 36	2
Kentucky	2,458	+ 38	2
Tennessee	573	+ 10	2
Maine	2,829	+ 18	1
Maryland	2,507	+ 31	1
North Carolina	3,041	+ 39	1
Delaware	3,713	+ 11	0.3
South Carolina	3,177	+ 9	0.3
Alaska	87	0	0
Arkansas	2,713	0	0
Georgia	2,454	0	0
Illinois	1,538	0	0
New York	3,274	0	0
Texas	346	0	0
Virginia	2,538	0	0
Wyoming	459	0	0
Oklahoma	2,426	− 2	0.1
Arizona	1,885	− 26	− 1
Massachusetts	2,934	− 33	− 1
Hawaii	3,810	− 100	− 3

TABLE 9.1. *(Continued)*

State	1983 state taxes	2-year change	Percentage change
Montana	2,464	− 74	− 3
Rhode Island	2,128	− 117	− 5
South Dakota	618	− 31	− 5
California	2,282	− 157	− 6
Vermont	2,248	− 263	− 10

Source: Steven Gold. "State Tax Increases of 1983: Prelude to Another Tax Revolt?" Legislative Finance Paper #40, National Conference of State Legislatures. 1983.

penditures. Even as social insurance expenditures in 1983 rose $3 billion to $36.1 billion, the actual operating surplus for state and local governments increased to $15.3 billion in 1983 from a deficit of $1.9 billion in 1982 (Fig. 9.6). It should be noted that on a National Income and Prod-

FIGURE 9.6. State and local governments annual surplus or deficit, including funding of social insurance

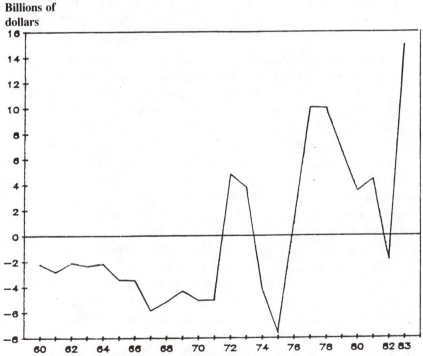

Billions of dollars

——— State and local governments receipts less expenditures (including social insurance funds). *Source: National Income and Product Accounts.* U.S. Department of Commerce, Bureau of Economic Analysis. Government Printing Office, Washington, D.C.

uct Accounts basis, money used to fund social insurance and pension funds against future claims is not considered an expenditure and therefore reduces state and local deficits or augments this surplus.

The combination of the new surplus and the declining federal role in state and local government fiscal policy decisions points to a wave of competition among states to establish tax climates conducive to economic growth.

For the 1983–1984 fiscal year, 14 states refused to raise any of their tax rates. Moreover, many of the tax increases passed last year are legislated to expire during 1984. In Michigan, for example, the state's personal income tax rate has been reduced to 6.1 percent from 6.35 percent. This tax rate is scheduled to fall to 5.35 percent on September 1, 1984. Under current law, as the state's fiscal position improves, the rates will decline further, perhaps to 5.1 percent during 1985. The following year, Michigan's personal income tax rate is scheduled to revert to the 4.6 percent rate that applied in 1981. Temporary sales tax increases are also due to lapse in Arizona, Colorado, Idaho, and Utah during 1984, while several other states have promised decreases when the states' revenues reach a certain level.

The Changing Competitive Environment

During the 1977–1982 period, the same negative relationship between changes in relative tax burden and economic growth that existed in the 1967–1977 period is evident, although the relationship is not nearly so strong (Fig. 9.7A). Only six of the 14 states that reduced their relative tax burden experienced above-average growth. Of the 34 states that raised their relative tax burden, 21 experienced below-average growth.

One reason for this weaker overall association is the growing importance of severance taxes on oil, coal, and other mineral deposits in several states. Severance taxes by definition are imposed on relatively immobile factors. As long as the tax is less than the difference between the selling price and the marginal cost of extraction, output will remain unchanged. For the revenue, taxes have a small impact on economic activity.

Oklahoma and New Mexico, in particular, were among the top three states in increased relative tax burden. Yet, during this period, they both posted well-above-average growth rates. When state severance taxes are subtracted from all of the states' tax burdens, however, these two states register much smaller increases in their respective tax burdens (Fig. 9.7B). In addition, this adjustment reveals that North Dakota had posted the largest reduction in its relative tax burden based on non-severance taxes, a result consistent with the well-above-average growth it posted in the 1977–1982 period.

FIGURE 9.7. Economic growth and change in relative tax burden 1977–1982

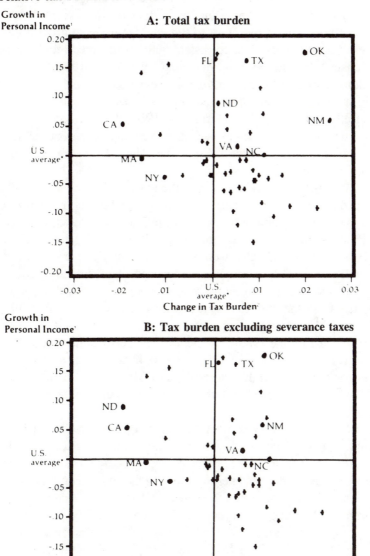

*excluding Alaska and Wyoming

1) Change in (log of real personal income by state relative to log of the U.S. average.*)

2) Change in (tax revenue per $1,000 of personal income by state relative to U.S. average.*)

Source: Survey of Current Business. U.S. Department of Commerce, Bureau of Economic Analysis. Government Printing Office, Washington, D.C.; *Governmental Finances.* U.S. Department of Commerce, Bureau of the Census. Government Printing Office, Washington, D.C.

A closer look at states that reduced their relative tax burden but grew at below-average rates during this period also is revealing. Five of these states experienced only a slight reduction in their relative tax burden. Of these states, three were quite close to the average national growth rate. Thus, these states' results were consistent with documented relationships between changing relative tax burdens and relative growth rates.

In addition, two of the remaining states experiencing below-average growth in spite of a substantial reduction in their relative tax burden were Massachusetts and New York. During the 1967–1977 period, the relative tax burden in these two states had risen more than in any of the other contiguous states or the District of Columbia. They also had been among the slowest-growing states.

In the 1977–1982 period, however, the increase in both states' relative tax burdens was reversed (Fig. 9.8). In Massachusetts, property tax rates and the overall tax burden began a significant decline with the passage of Proposition 2½ in November 1980. The capital gains tax, auto excise tax, and other taxes also were reduced during this period (Kadlec and Laffer 1981). Overall, Massachusetts reduced its tax burden by $15.30 relative to the national average, a reduction second in size only to California's. It rose from the 40th fastest-growing state during the 1967–1977 period to the 20th fastest-growing state in our sample for the 1977–1982 period. Moreover, for the 1980–1982 period, real personal income in Massachusetts grew at a 1.47 percent annual rate, 0.42 percentage points above the national average, the 16th fastest rate. For Massachusetts, the significant reduction in its relative tax burden has been associated with above-average growth.

In New York, the story is much the same. Between 1978 and 1982, the maximum state tax rate in wages and other "earned" income was lowered to 10 percent from 15.375 percent. Beginning in 1978, New York City's property tax burden also began to fall. In the subsequent four years, the effective real estate tax rate fell by nearly 40 percent (Adams 1981).

Overall, the relative tax burden in New York declined $10.18, the fifth largest reduction among the states analyzed. Its personal income growth rate increased to 35th from 48th (Fig. 9.8). Moreover, for the 1980–1982 period, New York's real personal income grew at a 1.35 percent annual rate, 0.50 percentage points above the national average. New York, too, had become an above-average growth state.

Symmetrically, the relative performance of North Carolina and Virginia deteriorated during the 1977–1982 period. Both states increased their tax burdens relative to the nation: North Carolina's growth rate declined

**FIGURE 9.8. Economic growth and changes in
relative tax burdens 1967–1977 versus 1977–1982**

Growth in
personal income
(annual rate)[1]

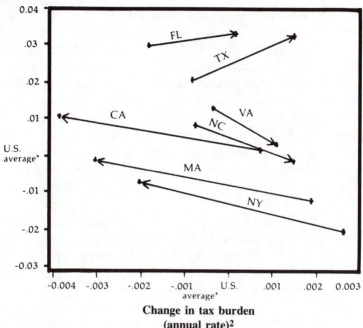

**Change in tax burden
(annual rate)[2]**

- 1967–77
- 1977–82

*excluding Alaska and Wyoming.

1) Change in (log of real personal income by state relative to log of the U.S. average.*)
2) Change in (tax revenue per $1,000 of personal income by state relative to U.S. average.*)
Source: Survey of Current Business. U.S. Department of Commerce, Bureau of Economic Analysis. Government Printing Office, Washington, D.C.; *Governmental Finances.* U.S. Department of Commerce, Bureau of the Census. Government Printing Office, Washington, D.C.

to just below the national average while Virginia's declined to near the national average.

The results in Florida and Texas, however, ran counter to the general trend. Both Florida and Texas increased their relative growth rates even as they increased their relative tax burdens (Fig. 9.8). These results can be attributed, at least in part, to the structure of their states' tax systems. The revenue increase in Texas, for example, was attributable in part to revenue gains from its severance tax on oil and gas. And Florida, which has no personal income tax, has consistently pursued a low-tax-rate, broad-tax-base strategy. In addition, until the recent controversy over its imposition of a unitary corporate income tax, Florida had had a consistent record of providing a low-tax environment.

The states that have been most successful in translating reductions in relative tax burdens into above-average growth have been committed to such a policy over the long term. In the case of California and Massachusetts, commitment came in the form of referenda that amended each state's constitution. Tax rates were reduced. Just as important, limits were placed on future increases in tax rates. This same commitment to lower tax rates was evident in New York. The reduction in personal income tax rates was undertaken as part of an overall strategy to improve New York's competitiveness. Similarly, until recently, Florida, which is perhaps the most successful state at reaping the benefits of reductions in its relative tax rate, has championed its low-tax-rate environment. Moreover, this policy has enjoyed strong and wide-based support among Florida's residents.

Other states where falling relative tax burdens have been associated with above-average growth (such as New Hampshire and California) also have been marked by a strong political constituency that opposes significant tax hikes. As a result, the declines in these states' relative tax burdens are likely to continue into the future.

A well-articulated policy in favor of stable, lower tax rates is an important element of a state's ability to grow at above-average rates. With all else the same, a reduction in a state's relative tax burden would be expected to increase its relative growth rate. But if a reduction in the tax burden is likely to be reversed, then its impact will be reduced. Individuals choose to live or invest in a given state not only because of its current tax environment, but also because of the promise of lower taxes in the future.

Competitive Update

Last year, state and local governments curtailed the big push toward higher taxes.[2] Nonetheless, according to the Federation of Tax Administrators, 36 of the 50 states did raise one or more tax rates for the 1983–1984 fiscal year. No state was reported to have reduced tax rates (Table 9.2). The data for the 1983–1984 fiscal year are for state governments only and do not reflect local government tax changes, including changes in local property taxes.

TABLE 9.2. State tax increases in 1983

State	None	Sales	Income Indiv.	Income Corp.	Motor Fuels	Tobacco	Alcoh. Bev.	Misc.
Alabama								X
Arizona		X						
Arkansas						X	X	
California		Xa						
Colorado		X				X		
Connecticut			X	X	X	X	X	
Delaware	X							
Florida						X		X
Georgia	X							
Hawaii	X							
Idaho		X		X	X			
Illinois		X	X	X	X			
Indiana	X							
Iowa		X						
Kansas						X	X	X
Kentucky	X							
Louisiana			X					
Maine				X	X	X		
Maryland	X							
Massachusetts						X	X	
Michigan			X					
Minnesota			X		X			
Mississippi		X						
Missouri	X	Xb						
Montana						X	X	
Nebraska		X	X	X	X			
Nevada						X	X	
New Hampshire				X		X	X	
New Jersey						X		
New Mexico		X	X	X	X		X	
New York						X	X	
North Carolina								X
North Dakota		X	X	X	X	X		
Ohio			X	X	X			
Oklahoma								X
Oregon					X			
Pennsylvania			X		X			
Rhode Island			X	X	X			
South Carolina							X	
South Dakota	X							
Tennessee	X							

TABLE 9.2. *(Continued)*

| | | | Income | | Motor | | Alcoh. | |
| | | | Indiv. | Corp. | | | | |
State	None	Sales	Indiv.	Corp.	Fuels	Tobacco	Bev.	Misc.
Texas	X							
Utah		X		X			X	
Vermont			X		X	X		
Virginia	X							
Washington		X			X			
West Virginia			X	X	X			
Wisconsin			X	X	X			
Wyoming	X							
District of Columbia					X			

This is preliminary compilation, based on legislation reported through September 1983.

aThe increase is contingent on state receipts remaining below a certain level.

bThe increase must be approved by the electorate.

Source: Tax Administrators News, Federation of Tax Administrators: "State Tax Increases of 1983: Prelude to Another Tax Revolt?" National Conference of State Legislatures.

Since the tax revenues that are actually flowing from these tax increases won't be known for at least a year, the significance of the state tax changes is approximated by comparing the revenue estimate associated with the tax change to the prior year's tax revenues. In the 36 states where taxes were raised, increases ranged from 0.2 percent in South Carolina to 23.6 percent in North Dakota, with an average increase of 7.23 percent. Increases tended to be the largest in the Great Lakes and Plains states. Half the 14 states that did not increase taxes in 1982 are Middle-Atlantic and southeastern states.

Regionally, the increases looked like this:

• The New England states all raised taxes. Increases ranged from 1.3 percent of 1982 revenues in Rhode Island to 10.4 percent in Connecticut.

• Of the five Middle-Atlantic states, only New York and Pennsylvania increased taxes (5.1 percent and 7.0 percent, respectively). Delaware, Maryland, and New Jersey voted no increases.

• With the exception of Indiana, which did not raise taxes, the Great Lakes states' increases ranged from 6.2 percent in Ohio to 15.8 percent in Michigan.

• In the Plains states, only Missouri and South Dakota did not raise taxes. In addition to North Dakota's 23.6 percent increase, tax increases in other Plains states ranged from 2.2 percent to 14.0 percent.

• In the Southeast, increases were in single-digit figures, with the exception of Arkansas, where a 15.5 percent increase will take effect in 1985. Four states (Georgia, Kentucky, Tennessee, and Virginia) did not raise taxes. Increases in the remaining seven states ranged from 0.2 to 9.6 percent.

• In the Southwest, only Texas did not increase taxes. The other three states ranged from 1.0 percent in Oklahoma to 8.4 percent in Arizona.

• Two Rocky Mountain states (Idaho and Colorado) got substantial increases, 17.4 and 15.2 respectively. Wyoming did not raise tax rates; Utah and Montana taxes went up 5.3 percent and 7.1 percent respectively.

• Alaska and Hawaii did not raise taxes. Other Far West states had moderate increases ranging from 0.4 percent in California to 4.2 percent in Nevada (Gold 1983).

THE CHANGING COMPETITIVE ENVIRONMENT

From a competitive point of view, it is important to identify changes in relative tax burdens among states. States that are lowering their relative tax burdens can be expected to increase their competitiveness. On the other hand, those that are increasing their relative tax burdens represent fertile markets for competing states.

States Gaining Competitiveness

Each state can expect increasing competition from those states that are reducing their taxes relative to that state or where large tax rate reductions have recently taken place. An examination of the change in each state's tax burden relative to the national average for the 1977–1982 period, the 1980–1982 period, and the legislated tax changes during 1983 (for fiscal year 1984) (Table 9.3) point to Massachusetts, Arizona, Nebraska, Missouri, and South Dakota as the states most likely to be increasing their competitiveness.

Other states that deserve close monitoring include:

• *California.* Posted the largest reduction in its tax burden in the 1977–1982 period, due in large measure to the 1978 passage of Proposition 13, which reduced property taxes by two-thirds, and to the repeal of the state's inventory tax. In 1982, the state's inheritance tax was also repealed through the initiative process. The state is expected to run a surplus of between $950 million and $1.4 billion for the 1984–1985 fiscal year, suggesting further tax rate reductions.

TABLE 9.3. Changes in states' relative tax burdens

1977–82			1980–82			FY 1984 Tax increases		
Rank	State[a]	Change[b]	Rank	State[a]	Change[b]	Rank	State[a]	Change[c]
1	Ca.	− 19.37	1	Ariz.	− 14.65	1	Del.	.0
2	Mass.	− 15.32	2	Mass.	− 12.13	2	Ga.	.0
3	Ariz.	− 15.25	3	Neb.	− 8.27	3	Hi.	.0
4	Vt.	− 11.24	4	Hi.	− 6.93	4	Ind.	.0
5	N.Y.	− 10.20	5	Colo.	− 6.49	5	Ky.	.0
6	Colo.	− 9.33	6	Ark.	− 5.12	6	Md.	.0
7	Neb.	− 6.31	7	Mo.	− 4.77	7	Mo.	.0
8	Conn.	− 2.20	8	Ill.	− 4.73	8	S.D.	.0
9	Md.	− 2.03	9	Kans.	− 3.77	9	Tenn.	.0
10	N.J.	− 1.84	10	S.D.	− 3.53	10	Texas	.0
11	S.D.	− 1.24	11	Md.	− 3.35	11	Va.	.0
12	Kans.	− 1.06	12	Del.	− 2.89	12	N.J.	neg.
13	Minn.	− 0.52	13	Ca.	− 2.44	13	S.C.	0.2
14	Wisc.	− 0.18	14	Pa.	− 2.29	14	Ca.	0.4
15	Fla.	0.80	15	Minn.	− 2.21	15	Okl.	1.0
16	Tenn.	0.94	16	Utah	− 1.77	16	R.I.	1.3
17	Nev.	1.17	17	Miss.	− 1.37	17	N.C.	1.7
18	N.D.	1.31	18	Ky.	− 1.32	18	Ala.	1.9
19	Mo.	2.57	19	N.J.	− 1.21	19	Ore.	2.1
20	Idaho	2.93	20	Va.	− 0.83	20	Neb.	2.2
21	N.H.	3.16	21	N.Y.	− 0.80	21	Miss.	2.3
22	Wash.	3.26	22	N.C.	− 0.76	22	Vt.	2.6
23	Miss.	3.95	23	Fla.	− 0.68	23	Mass.	3.0
24	Pa.	4.02	24	Idaho	0.52	24	Wash.	3.5
25	Ill.	4.49	25	S.C.	− 0.37			

[a]excluding Alaska and Wyoming; including the District of Columbia.

[b]Change in tax burden relative to mean in dollars per $1,000 of personal income.
The relationship between growth in private sector employment and changes in relative tax burden is stronger.

[c]Fiscal year 1984 tax increases as a percentage of state tax revenue in calendar year 1982.

Source: Governmental Finances, U.S. Department of Commerce; "State Tax Increases of 1983: Prelude to Another Tax Revolt?" National Conference of State Legislatures.

• *Delaware.* Placed eleventh with its reduction in relative tax burden for the 1980–1982 period and had no legislated tax increases last year. In addition, Delaware has developed an aggressive strategy to attract out-of-state banking facilities. The state's tax policy should be monitored for additional changes aimed at attracting other forms of financial businesses such as insurance companies. In addition, the state government enacted a personal income tax rate reduction effective January 1, 1985. The top rate of 13.5 percent, which was effective at a taxable income of $40,000, has been reduced to 10.7 percent effective at a taxable income of $30,000. All other tax rates were reduced by 10 percent. (The current marginal tax rate for taxable income of $30,000 is 12.2 percent.)

• *New York.* Posted a significant decrease in its tax burden in the 1977–1982 period and continued its marginal personal income tax rate reductions in 1981 and 1982. The state increased its taxes an estimated 5.1 percent last year by raising levies on tobacco and alcoholic beverages. Even so, the expected increase in total tax revenues was below the national average. Finally, New York City continues to run a budget surplus. New York State has arrested its downward slide and has all the attributes and history of a very strong competitor.

• *Rhode Island.* The "Greenhouse Compact," a ballot measure that would have created a $250 million program to foster existing and new businesses was defeated by a 4:1 margin earlier this year. Although the intention of the Greenhouse Compact was to increase economic growth, the program would have raised taxes immediately by $70.5 million, with higher taxes on personal income, payroll tax, and the loss of tax deductions to business. Nonetheless, the support of the state's business and government leadership for the initiative is symptomatic of a search for a new economic policy. The legacy of the defeat of the Greenhouse Compact could be a pro-growth agenda based on economic incentives. Such an agenda could propel Rhode Island into a very competitive position.

• *Oregon.* For the fourth time, Oregon voters will have the opportunity to vote to reduce property taxes to 1.5 percent of 1981 assessed value or rate in existence on July 1, 1983, whichever is lower. If passed, property taxes will be cut an average of nearly 30 percent. In addition, the initiative would require any future tax increase or the imposition of a new tax (either at the state or local level) to be approved by a majority of the voters, or 25 percent of the registered voters, whichever is more.

States Losing Competitiveness

In general, every state that has raised its tax burden substantially more than the national average will find it more difficult to retain existing facilities and increasingly difficult to attract new businesses. Corporations with a significant amount of their business in these states can be expected to fare poorly relative to companies with activities concentrated in states that are reducing their relative tax burden. The relative growth effects would be expected to be the most pronounced in neighboring states with widely divergent tax policies. The shift of business from Minnesota to South Dakota is a ready example of this phenomenon.

An examination of the change in the relative tax burden for the 1977–1982 period, the 1980–1982 period, and the legislated tax changes during 1983 (for fiscal year 1984) (Table 9.4) points to New Mexico, Washington D.C., West Virginia, Montana, Ohio, and Iowa as the states most likely to be losing competitiveness.

Special situations include:

• *Florida.* The state's reputation as a low-tax state suffered a blow in 1982 when the sales tax was increased to 5 percent from 4 percent. More important, Florida's imposition of a unitary tax, which taxes businesses on the basis of their worldwide profits, has reduced the desirability of locating operations in Florida for companies with highly profitable overseas operations. International Business Machine (IBM), for example, announced in February its decision to sell nearly 2,000 acres of land in the northern part of the state, due to the introduction of the Unitary Tax. The land had been acquired in 1980 as a potential manufacturing site (Askari 1984).

At the local level, taxes also are rising in order to fund new transfer programs. In December 1983, Dade County, which includes Miami, began levying a 0.45 percent surtax on all sales involving commercial and multifamily rental real estate. Revenues from the tax will be used to provide mortgages for "low and moderate" income families ("Mortage Aid" 1984).

Widespread criticism of the unitary tax by Florida's business community suggests that it may be repealed. In addition, the popularity of tax cutting in Florida was demonstrated by the easy qualification of Proposition One for the November ballot. The Florida Supreme Court, however, struck the proposition from the ballot because it dealt with more than one issue, which is forbidden under the state's initiative provisions. Proposition One sought to reduce tax revenue for fiscal year 1985–1986 to the level of revenues collected in fiscal year 1980–1981, an estimated 22.6 percent tax cut. In addition, this measure would have limited subsequent tax revenue growth to no more than two-thirds of the percentage change in the consumer price index (CPI). As a result, the tax burden would have declined with any expansion in the state's economic output.

• *Texas.* The possibilities of further declines in the price of oil will slow directly the growth in Texas and other energy-producing states. In

TABLE 9.4. Changes in states' relative tax burdens

	1977–82			1980–82			FY 1984 Tax increases	
Rank	State[a]	Change[b]	Rank	State[a]	Change[b]	Rank	State[a]	Change[c]
1	N.M.	25.30	1	D.C.	13.31	1	N.D.	23.6
2	D.C.	22.55	2	Okl.	11.60	2	Idaho	17.4
3	Okl.	20.01	3	N.M.	8.03	3	Mich.	15.8
4	W.V.	16.72	4	Nev.	6.52	4	Ark.	15.5
5	Mont.	14.96	5	Mont.	6.35	5	Colo.	15.2
6	Ohio	13.20	6	La.	5.50	6	Ill.	15.2
7	Maine	12.01	7	Ohio	5.18	7	Kans.	14.0
8	S.C.	11.14	8	Mich.	5.12	8	Wisc.	10.7
9	Utah	11.00	9	W.V.	5.12	9	Conn.	10.4
10	Iowa	10.71	10	N.D.	4.69	10	Iowa	10.4
11	La.	10.49	11	R.I.	4.55	11	W.V.	9.6
12	Ala.	10.14	12	Ind.	4.02	12	N.H.	9.2
13	Ore.	9.29	13	Texas	3.98	13	Ariz.	8.4
14	R.I.	8.90	14	Ore.	3.42	14	N.M.	7.8
15	Mich.	8.81	15	Wisc.	2.37	15	Mont.	7.1
16	Ark.	8.71	16	Conn.	2.23	16	Pa.	7.0
17	Ga.	8.29	17	Wash.	2.01	17	Ohio	6.2
18	Texas	7.44	18	N.H.	1.55	18	Fla.	5.4
19	N.C.	7.37	19	Iowa	1.33	19	Utah	5.3
20	Ky.	6.95	20	Vt.	0.44	20	Maine	5.1
21	Hi.	6.01	21	Maine	0.43	21	N.Y.	5.1
22	Del.	5.76	22	Ga.	0.33	22	Minn.	5.0
23	Ind.	5.45	23	Ala.	0.28	23	La.	4.5
24	Va.	5.38	24	Tenn.	0.00	24	Nev.	4.2

[a]excluding Alaska and Wyoming; including the District of Columbia.

[b]Change in tax burden relative to the mean in dollars per $1,000 of personal income. The relationship between growth in private sector employment and changes in relative tax burden is stronger.

[c]Fiscal year 1984 tax increases as a percentage of state tax revenue in calendar year 1982.

Source: Governmental Finances. U.S. Department of Commerce, Bureau of the Census. Government Printing Office, Washington, D.C.; Steven Gold. "State Tax Increases of 1983: Prelude to Another Tax Revolt?" Legislative Finance Paper #40, National Conference of State Legislatures. 1983.

addition, the concomitant decline in severance tax revenues will increase the pressure on these governments to raise other taxes.

In Texas, such tax increasing pressures already are evident. The state government in June passed a tax package that will increase revenues by an estimated $1.2 billion, or approximately 8 percent of existing state and local tax revenues. Effective October 2, the state's sales tax will rise to 4.125 percent from 4 percent. Most local incorporated governments impose a one percent sales tax, bringing the total rate to 5.125 percent. The sales tax base also will be broadened to include tangible repairs and other work done on personal property. This category includes everything from the installation of cable TV to drycleaning.

In addition, effective August 1, the state's gasoline tax was doubled to 10 cents per gallon, while the per gallon tax on diesel fuel will be increased to 10 cents from 6.5 cents. Effective January 1, 1985, the corporate franchise tax was increased to $5.20 per $1,000 of capitalization from $1 per $1,000 of capitilization. Finally, cigarette taxes were increased by 1 cent per pack, while alcohol taxes were raised by 20 percent. Plans call for the additional revenues to be used to fund increased educational and highway expenditures.

In both Florida and Texas, the key is whether these latest tax increases are symptomatic of a change in the direction of fiscal policy. If these tax hikes are but the first in a series of steps that will raise each of these states' tax burdens, then their relative growth rates can be expected to slow. This result will be even more pronounced if the current high tax states in the industrial North (such as as Michigan, Illinois, and Ohio) reverse policies and begin to sharply reduce their respective tax rates. In such a case, the supposed competitive advantage of the Sunbelt states may prove as ephemeral as a sunny day.

APPENDIX: THEORETICAL DISCUSSION

In theory, changes in a state's or a nation's tax rates relative to the average for all states or all other nations will alter its competitiveness and, therefore, its relative growth rate during the period of adjustment to higher or lower tax rates. For example, a reduction in tax rates reduces the cost of doing business in a state. This, in turn, increases the demand for the now less expensive goods and services produced within the state (Fig. 9.9). The higher demand for the state's goods and services will result in an increased demand for capital and labor services within the state.

If all else remains the same, a reduction in tax rates also increases the return to capital and work effort, leading to an increase in the supply of capital and work within the state (Fig. 9.9). Higher returns to labor and capital also will induce a migration of mobile factors into the state. Initially, this migration may take the form of a shift in production to existing facilities or perhaps even an increased utilization of existing labor

FIGURE 9.9. How a tax rate reduction increases economic activity

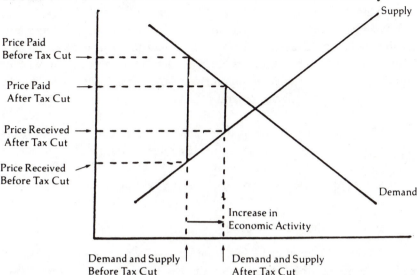

in the form of overtime. As time horizons lengthen, however, migration will incorporate the actual movement of individuals and plants to the state and the retention of plants and jobs that might otherwise have left the state. This migration will continue until after-tax returns for the mobile factors within the state are equalized with after-tax returns for their counterparts elsewhere in the economy.

A reduction in state tax rates creates new opportunities for the employment of existing capital and labor. The lower tax rate also results in migration of capital and labor into the state. In short, a tax rate reduction relative to other states increases a state's competitiveness. Its production base expands relative to the rest of the economy until returns to mobile factors once again are equalized within the national economy. At that point, the state's growth rate will once again approximate the national rate.

Changes in tax rates have the greatest impact on the supply of capital and labor most sensitive to a change in price. Alternatively stated, the more mobile a factor of production is, and/or the greater the ease with which the factor may switch to the underground economy, the more sensitive it will be to changes in returns. For example, capital in the form of a new steel mill is highly immobile. Its operating level initially will be affected relatively little by a change in a state's tax rates. By contrast, consider the case of a highly mobile worker, one who is prepared to relocate in order to improve his or her standard of living. This worker's availability to the work force within a state will be extremely sensitive to a change in state tax rates.

Whether the price of a commodity or factor of production is equilibrated across states on a before-tax or after-tax basis depends on each item's mobility. The price of mobile factors of production will be equilibrated across states on an after-tax basis. This means that changes in tax rates will have two general effects:

• They will change the quantity and pre-tax price of mobile factors within the state and leave their after-tax rates of return unchanged.

• They will change the rate of return of factors of production that cannot leave the state and leave the quantity within the state unchanged.

Determinants of Factor Mobility

Mobility of capital and labor is influenced by several factors. For example, the longer the time horizon, the easier it is to amortize transportation costs; therefore, capital and labor increase their mobility with the passage of time. In the shortest of all runs, factories will not be constructed or open their doors in response to a tax reduction. In the medium run, however, opportunities for expansion will arise, and the state will begin to increase its share of the U.S. market.[3]

Similarly, workers will not relocate solely in response to a change in tax rates. With lower tax rates, however, companies can afford to increase their competitiveness by offering prospective employees higher take-home pay even as the total, pre-tax cost to the employer goes down. In the medium run, such an improvement in a state's ability to attract both employers and employees will result in an expansion of its labor force and employment. In the longest of all runs, everything becomes mobile, including fixed plant and equipment.

All this suggests that the more mobile the factors of production in a state, the more sensitive that state's economic performance is to other states' changes in tax policies. That is, if a neighboring state lowers its effective tax rates, workers will tend to migrate out of the surrounding states into that state. Business will be more inclined to build new facilities in the now lower-taxed neighbor and so forth. Similarly, if a state raises its effective tax rates, capital and labor will tend to migrate out of that state into neighboring states (Sjaastad 1967).

Other variables also influence the responsiveness of factors of production to changes in factor reward. For example, the more alternatives readily available to the taxable or "above-ground" economy, the more responsive the economy will be to changes in tax rates. The lower the tax rates, the less attractive non-taxpaying "underground" activities, will be relative to the market or taxable economy.[4]

The Level of Taxation

The existence of trade and factor mobility implies that the level of taxation should not be correlated with a state's relative economic growth rate. Once the combination of migration and lower after-tax returns has restored competitive, after-tax returns to mobile labor and capital, economic growth in the state once again would be expected to approximate the national growth rate. In fact, findings from some of the original empirical research on the effects of state taxation (Due 1961), and from the most recent polls by business-location specialists, support the conclusion that the level of taxation is of little consequence as a determinant of a state's relative economic growth.

This result may, at first, seem counterintuitive. In the most extreme form, it suggests that a high-tax state on average will grow as fast as a low-tax state and that if a high-tax state reduces its tax rate relative to the low-tax state, its growth will accelerate relative to the still-lower-tax state. To see this result, liken the level of taxes among the states to price differentials among similar, but not identical, products. For example, Cadillacs have a higher price than Chevrolets. But, in general, the growth in sales for the two cars is highly correlated in any given year.

Imagine, however, that holding all else the same, the price of Cadillacs was reduced relative to that of Chevrolets. Even though the price of a Cadillac was still higher than a Chevy, Cadillac sales would be expected to grow relative to Chevrolet sales.

In general, the same is true for states. High-tax states are populated by companies and individuals that can or must accommodate the higher tax burden. Their incomes would be expected to grow along with the national average. But when a high-tax state lowers its taxes, it increases its competitiveness in retaining and attracting new business and new jobs. Conversely, a tax increase relative to the average, even by a low-tax state, decreases its competitiveness. Its relative growth rate declines.

NOTES

1. A negative coefficient indicates an inverse relationship between the two variables. The relationship is considered significant because using standard statistical techniques, there is less than a 5 percent chance that the association between the movements in these two variables is random.

2. This section draws heavily on research reported in the monthly newsletter of the Federation of Tax Administrators and a legislative finance paper by Steven Gold, director of State/Local Finance Project of the National Conference of State Legislatures.

3. For a discussion of the problems of imperfect mobility, see M. Mussa, "Dynamic Adjustment in the Heckscher–Ohlin–Samuelson Model." *Journal of Political Economy* 86 (1978): 775–792.

4. There is extensive literature on this issue. See Canto, Joines, and Laffer, 1983, *Foundations of Supply-Side Economics;* Arthur B. Laffer, 1981, "Supply-Side Economics," *Financial Analysts Journal* (September–October); A. B. Laffer, 1981, "Government Exactions and Revenue Deficiencies," *Cato Journal* 1, no. 1 (Spring): 1–21; Victor A. Canto and D. H. Joines, 1983, "Tax Rates, Market Production and Welfare," *Economic Inquiry* 21, no. 33 (July): 431–438.

REFERENCES

Adams, James R. 1981. "New York Moves to the Supply-Side." A. B. Laffer Associates Rolling Hills Estates, CA. (April).

Askari, Emilia. 1984. "IBM Blames Unitary Tax for Sale of Land." *Miami Herald* (February, 3, p. 5c).

Canto, Victor A., and Robert I. Webb. 1983. "Persistent Growth Rate Differentials Among States In a National Economy with Factor Mobility." In *Foundations of Supply-Side Economics.* New York: Academic Press, pp. 226–254.

Canto, Victor A., Richard V. Eastin, and Arthur B. Laffer. 1982. "Failure of Protectionism: A Study of the Steel Industry." *Columbia Journal of World Business* 17, no. 4 (Winter): 43–57.

Due, John T. 1961. "Studies of State–Local Tax Influences on Locations of Industry." *National Tax Journal* 14, no. 2: 163–173.

Federation of Tax Administrators. 1983. "State Tax Legislation in 1983 Includes Many Rate Increases." *Tax Administrators' News* vol. 47 (Washington D.C.) (October): 1.

Gold, Steven, 1983. "State Tax Increases of 1983: Prelude to Another Tax Revolt?" National Conference of State Legislatures, Denver, Colorado, p. 14.

Kadlec, Charles W., and Arthur B. Laffer. 1981. "An Analysis of Fiscal Policy and Economic Growth in Massachusetts." A. B. Laffer Associates Rolling Hills Estates, CA. (April).

Laffer, Arthur B. 1984. "The Tightening Grip of the Poverty Trap." *Policy Analysis* 4 (Cato Institute) (August) p. 1–22. (See also Chapter 7 of this book.)

"Mortgage Aid... A Comeback for Hotel Condos... Lottery." 1984. *The Wall Street Journal* real estate column (March 14), p. 31.

Sjaastad, L. 1967. "The Costs and Returns of Human Migration." *Journal of Political Economy* 70 (October): 80–93.

Index

219

About the Authors

Victor A. Canto received a B.Sc. from MIT and his M.A. and Ph.D. in economics from the University of Chicago. He has been an Assistant Professor and an Associate Professor at the University of Southern California as well as Visiting Professor at the Universidad Central Del Este, Dominican Republic.

In addition to his academic position, Dr. Canto has been economics advisor to the Finance Minister of the Dominican Republic, economist for the economics studies division of the Dominican Republic Central Bank, as well as a consultant to Puerto Rico's Treasury and Government Financial Council.

Dr. Canto's other books include *Foundations of Supply Side Economics, Apuntaciones Sobre Inflacion y Economica en Republica Dominicana,* and *The Determinants and Consequences of Trade Restrictions in the U.S. Economy.* His publications have appeared in *Economic Inquiry,* the *Southern Economic Journal, Public Finance,* and the *Journal of Macroeconomics,* among others.

Charles W. Kadlec is executive vice-president and director of research at A.B. Laffer Associates. Mr. Kadlec obtained his MBA with honors at the University of Chicago. His area of interest was international trade and finance. Prior to that time, he was a member of the *Business Week* editorial staff. Before joining A.B. Laffer Associates, Mr. Kadlec worked in the international division of Crocker Bank in San Francisco, and was a general partner of W.C. Wainwright & Co., economics, Boston.

He has authored or co-authored several articles in the *Wall Street Journal* and the *New York Times*, and co-authors the monthly *Economy in Perspective* for A.B. Laffer Associates. He has also done extensive research on the effect of state and local fiscal policies on economic growth, co-authoring studies on fiscal policy in Delaware and Massachusetts, and consulting for the Maryland Growth Coalition Project.

Arthur B. Laffer is a Distinguished University Professor at Pepperdine University. Previously, he was the Charles B. Thornton Professor of Business Economics at the University of Southern California, and he was Associate Professor of Business Economics at the University of Chicago. Dr. Laffer received a B.A. in economics from Yale University in 1963, prior to which he also attended the University of Munich, Germany. He received an MBA (1965) and a Ph.D. in economics (1972) from Stanford University.

Dr. Laffer currently is a member of the Economic Policy Advisory Board to the President of the United States. He is also a member of the *Los Angeles Times* Board of Economists, and a member of the Policy Committee and Board of Directors of the American Council for Capital Formation (Washington, D.C.). He has received two Graham and Dodd Awards from the Financial Analyst Federation for outstanding feature articles published in the *Financial Analyst Journal*.

Dr. Laffer is also founder and chairman of A.B. Laffer Associates, an economic research and financial consulting firm. He has been a consultant to the Secretaries of Treasury and Defense. He served as an economist for the Office of Management and Budget since October 1984. Dr. Laffer was also a Research Associate at the Brookings Institution, on leave from the University of Chicago.

Dr. Laffer's other books include: *Foundations of Supply Side Economics, International Economics in an Integrated World, Future American Energy Policy, The Economics of the Tax Revolt: A Reader, Private Short Term Capital Flows,* and *The Phenomenon of Worldwide Inflation.* His publications have appeared in *The American Economic Review, Journal of Political Economy, Journal of Business,* and the *Journal of Money, Credit and Banking,* among others.